CURT FLOOD IN THE MEDIA

Abraham Iqbal Khan

Curt Flood in the Media

BASEBALL, RACE, AND THE DEMISE OF THE ACTIVIST-ATHLETE

University Press of Mississippi / *Jackson*

www.upress.state.ms.us

The University Press of Mississippi is a member of
the Association of American University Presses.

First printing 2012

∞

Library of Congress Cataloging-in-Publication Data

Khan, Abraham Iqbal.
  Curt Flood in the media : baseball, race, and the demise
of the activist-athlete / Abraham Iqbal Khan.
      p. cm. — (Race, rhetoric, and media series)
  Includes bibliographical references and index.
  ISBN 978-1-61703-138-0 (cloth : alk. paper) — ISBN 978-1-
61703-139-7 (ebook) 1. Flood, Curt, 1938–1997. 2. Flood, Curt,
1938–1997—Trials, litigation, etc. 3. African American baseball
players—Biography. 4. Baseball—Law and legislation—United
States. 5. Discrimination in sports—United States. 6. Free
agents (Sports)—United States. I. Title.
  GV885.F45K43 2012
  796.357092—dc23
  [B]   2011024032

British Library Cataloging-in-Publication Data available

For my mom and dad

CONTENTS

ix . . . . . Acknowledgments

3 . . . . 1. Curt Flood and the Demise of the Activist-Athlete

26 . . . . . . 2. Curt Flood's Public Case

55 . . . . . . 3. Jackie Robinson and the Rhetoric of the Black Press

87 . . . . . . 4. The Disappearance of Curt Flood's Blackness

116 . . . . . 5. Race, Slavery, and the Revolt of the Black Athlete

156 . . . . . 6. Race and Memory in Sport's Public Sphere

185 . . . . . Notes

197 . . . . . Bibliography

205 . . . . Index

ACKNOWLEDGMENTS

This book owes its largest debt to the people I encountered at the University of Minnesota, where as a student in the Department of Communication Studies I was fortunate to be surrounded by extraordinary colleagues and mentors. First and foremost, sincere thanks go to Kirt Wilson, whose encouragement and immeasurable patience were instrumental not only in producing this book but also in modeling for me what it means to be a scholar. When I write, he is always in the front row of my imaginary audience. I also owe appreciation to the other members of my doctoral committee: Edward Schiappa taught me to know what a clear, developed argument looks like—and how to make one; Ron Greene taught me to be on alert for slippery assumptions and continually to search for the way that things in the world fit together; Malinda Alaine Lindquist provided me with the intellectual resources necessary to say insightful things about the politics of race. Mary Vavrus's interest in my project and concern for its completion went well beyond the call of duty. The essential ideas for this project were born in the presence of Keletso Atkins. And Karlyn Kohrs Campbell—as she surely knows—sits right next to Kirt in my imaginary front row.

Bringing this book to completion required assistance and support from individuals at other institutions as well. During my time at Georgia State University, Carol Winkler and David Cheshier did their best to supply me with any scholar's most precious commodity: time. David was always ready for a talk about the book (or the world) and to me personifies academic professionalism. Michael Bruner became a trusted friend and colleague by reading chapter drafts, providing detailed feedback, and chatting about theory when he certainly had other things to do. The faculty of the Department of Communication at Villanova University graciously welcomed me as one of their own, and my students there (especially Jessica Lu, Nick Romeu, and Lillian Campbell) were terrific sources of conversation about African American history and politics.

In 2001, when I was a student at Florida State University, I met Davis Houck, without whom this book simply would not exist. His advice, support, and friendship have been crucial to every phase of the project and of my professional development. Davis's influence touches nearly everything I have accomplished over the last decade, and I don't think I'll ever be able to thank him enough. Scott Varda has been an indispensable friend and colleague as well. He read drafts, played devil's advocate, listened to my histrionic rants, had a few of his own, and did it all with unfathomable energy. I am also grateful for the counsel of Mike Butterworth, whom I consider a colleague in arms in the study of sport. And I am indebted to James Brey, the best baseball fan I know and the person who in 1999 first shared the Curt Flood story with me. At the University Press of Mississippi, thanks are owed to Walter Biggins for his interest and patience and Ellen Goldlust-Gingrich for the tremendous care she took with the manuscript.

Above all, I owe thanks to the family and friends who made all of the time and energy I put into this project worthwhile. My grandmother, Irene House, embodies a love of reading. My four parents, Parvez Khan, Suzanne Cook, Dennis Cook, and Mussarat Khan, are responsible for my intellect and aspirations. More than any person in my life, my mom has modeled perseverance and attention to detail. My four brothers, Adam Khan, Arbob Khan, Omar Khan, and Samir Khan, allow me to feel like I am part of a tribe. The Poker Board (consisting of Cy Kiani, Andy Nishioka, Paul Skiermont, Jonathan Reeve, and Jay Finch) provides an annual dose of togetherness and mental nourishment. They listened to me ramble on about my project, debated the finer points with incisive wit, and rooted for me year after year. Cy and Andy have been brothers to me for so long that they should think of this book as partly their own. Mariela Rodriguez generously shared her distinguished intellect, prodigious sophistication, and warm and ready laugh. Sanjay Agrawala lent a critical ear on many occasions, often late into the night. Kara Wilder was a trusted friend and stimulating conversant and saw me through crucial moments of my personal life over the course of this project.

In addition to Miles Davis (my biggest fan), special thanks are owed to Danielle Hegedus, who may have sacrificed more time and emotional energy than any other person as I wrote this book. She was an endless well of encouragement who coped patiently and gracefully with my anxieties and doubts. Danielle remains an insightful critic, peerless advocate, and committed cheerleader. Nobody roots for me more passionately, and I am grateful for her affection and support.

Mom and Denny deserve additional recognition for believing in me even when I gave them few reasons to have faith, and unconditional appreciation goes to my brother, Adam, whose creativity and good humor serve as a constant source of inspiration. Thanks also to my dad—-I can only hope that his sensitivity to injustice, his capacity for respect, his ability to put himself in another person's shoes, and his generosity are reflected both in my ideas and in my character.

CURT FLOOD IN THE MEDIA

1

Curt Flood and the
Demise of the Activist-Athlete

The contrasting images featured in the 1990 U.S. Senate race in North Carolina could not have been more pronounced. The Republican candidate was incumbent Jesse Helms, whose racist and reactionary politics had helped him secure reelection since 1972. His chief opponent was Democrat Harvey Gantt, the first African American admitted to Clemson University and former mayor of Charlotte. Legend holds that Gantt's associates appealed to Wilmington native and University of North Carolina alum Michael Jordan, then arguably the most famous person in the world, to offer the Democratic challenger a small measure of support in an election that was certain to be close. Jordan's now-infamous response? "Republicans buy sneakers, too."[1] Whether discouraged by a greedy conscience or dissuaded by Nike, whose sneakers he sold, His Airness avoided the political stage. Helms was once again reelected, and Jordan ascended into a transnational commercial brand.[2]

In November 2002, a *New York Times* editorial implored defending champion Tiger Woods to boycott the Masters golf tournament, held each April at Augusta National Golf Club, a cloister of the power elite that refuses to admit women as members. "A tournament without Mr. Woods," the *Times* insisted, "would send a powerful message that discrimination isn't good for the golfing business."[3] Five years earlier, Woods's professional career had been inaugurated by a Nike commercial that declared, "There are still golf courses in the United States that I cannot play because of the color of my skin. I'm told that I'm not ready for you. Are you ready for me? Hello world!"[4] In response to the *Times*'s appeal to that hopeful salutation, Tiger's political voice became paper-thin: "It would be nice to see everyone have an equal chance to participate, but there is nothing you can do about it."[5] That year, Woods finished nine strokes off the lead, and "discrimination" failed to hurt business much at all. Augusta National has still not added a woman to its membership, but Woods was recently declared the world's first billion-dollar athlete.[6]

On the strength of examples such as these, reports of the "demise of the black athlete" abound.[7] Depending on who is asked, the emergence of the black "activist-athlete" can be traced to 1936, when Jesse Owens repudiated white eugenic fantasies right before Hitler's eyes; or 1947, when Jackie Robinson endured a summer of racist insults in Major League ballparks; or 1967, when Muhammad Ali refused to go to Vietnam. Regardless of where the origin is placed, the black activist-athlete is frequently embodied in John Carlos and Tommie Smith, the American sprinters who raised their black-gloved fists in iconic unity at the Mexico City Olympics in 1968. Symbolically speaking, Smith and Carlos were escorted to the podium by Harry Edwards, a Cornell-educated sociologist from California who had attempted to lead an international boycott of the Olympics by black athletes. Known as the Olympic Project for Human Rights, Edwards's endeavor failed to create the mass absence it desired, but its spirit of protest produced one of the most recognizable images in the history of sport. Believing that the Olympic moment had set something powerful in motion, Edwards wrote in 1969 that "the black athlete has left the facade of locker room equality and justice to take his long vacant place as a primary participant in the black revolution."[8]

More than three decades later, Edwards offered an account of the vivid contrast that distinguishes Jordan and Woods from Carlos and Smith: "Black athletes have become sufficiently integrated into the sports system. They have a stake in . . . the business matrix of sports. Thirty years ago that was not the case. We are talking about different times."[9] His observation loads terms to describe the shift—*black athletes have become integrated*—and extends a taunting invitation to root for these developments. After all, this is how sport's progress narrative typically takes shape: From Owens to Robinson to Ali to Jordan, things keep getting better; at least we are moving in the right direction. However, Edwards adds a revelatory juxtaposition between past and present. "The outcome of the actions of Muhammad Ali, Tommie Smith, John Carlos, Jim Brown, Curt Flood, Bill Russell, Spencer Haywood and others who paved the way is Dennis Rodman, Deion Sanders, and so forth," recites Edwards, whose pantheon of the selfless has been displaced by the disconnected and selfish: "There are a whole bunch of athletes whose focus is on ME, and I am so militantly about me, that there are no rules I need to recognize. Whatever serves to promote me is legitimate. So you have guys who are not demonstrating and raising a fist at a podium in deference to a greater cause, but doing anything to draw attention to themselves as individuals."[10] As a historical narrative, this statement is compelling in its tragic simplicity: Once integrated successfully into the business matrix, black athletes acquired the self-commodifying instincts the business matrix always demands.

Black modernity, Houston Baker suggests, "is figured in the textural and textual interweavings of nostalgia and critical memory." On the one hand, as a kind of homesickness, "nostalgia is a purposive construction of a past filled with golden virtues, golden men and sterling events" that "writes the revolution as a well-passed aberration [and] actively substitutes allegory for history." On the other hand, says Baker, "critical memory judges severely, censures righteously, renders hard ethical evaluations of the past that it never defines as well-passed."[11] So goes the modern sensibility of Edwards, whose golden virtues, golden men, and sterling events have been displaced by narcissists and publicity stunts. Mourning the loss of a black civic ethos, a mode of political activity made possible and rendered visible by the public address of black athletes, Edwards bemoans a potential energy incrementally eclipsed every time a black athlete deposits a paycheck. Instead of refusing racial identifications to sell sneakers, like Jordan, or inventing racial categories into which a collective political will could never possibly fit, like Woods (who once called himself "Cablinasian"),[12] blackness was the crucial signature—the symbolic nucleus—of a forgotten mode of political engagement. All at once, Edwards delivers a righteous censure of the contemporary black athlete and purposively constructs an ideal past that crystallized improbably on the medal podium in the summer of 1968. Since then, the meaning of the black athlete has been sold to Nike, this story seems to go, and the activist-athlete is simply a figure frozen and flattened in a famous photograph, a well-passed aberration given over to history.

Carlos and Smith certainly seemed to embrace a civic ethos that once gripped the social and political imaginary of black America. Remembrances of them work today as an auspicious cure for an apparent bout of amnesia. Those stricken include, most significantly, the black athletes of today, who, according to Edwards, "don't care about whose shoulders they stand on. They have no idea about who set the table at which they are feasting. And the worse part about it is not that they are ignorant of this history, but that they are militantly ignorant."[13] Edwards is certainly not alone in his lamentation. In 2006, *New York Times* sports columnist William Rhoden published a social history, *Forty Million Dollar Slaves: The Rise, Fall, and Redemption of the Black Athlete*, that criticized the politically crippling investments that black athletes have made in corporate America. And in 2008, *Newsday* columnist Shaun Powell published a series of essays bound thematically by the selfish forgetfulness of contemporary black athletes. The image on the cover of Powell's *Souled Out? How Blacks are Winning and Losing in Sports* puts today's black athlete at odds with history. Instead of two black fists raised in iconic unity, the fists on Powell's book are at cross purposes, headed in opposite directions, one gloved in black, the other tattooed, bejeweled, and clutching a wad of cash.

Perhaps the most impassioned admonition to appear in the last few years comes from filmmaker Spike Lee, who in 2005 wrote the introduction to a reprint of Jackie Robinson's 1964 integrationist treatise, *Baseball Has Done It*. Capturing the spirit of its theme and deriving a lesson from its purported failure, Lee traces over the familiar golden lineage of black athletes from whom the current stars ought to take their cue:

> Today's African-American athletes owe everything to Jackie Robinson, and to others like him, such as Jesse Owens, such as Joe Louis, such as Curt Flood, who sacrificed his career, sacrificed his life, in challenging the reserve clause in baseball. If it weren't for people like Curt Flood, and Jackie, and Jesse, and Joe, the athletes of today wouldn't be making the kind of money they're making. Unfortunately, the only thing that matters to today's players is getting paid. They're not educated about the past, so their level of consciousness is not high. They know nothing of the many African-American athletes who put their careers on the line to fight for future generations, men like John Carlos, Tommie Smith, Mohammed Ali, Jackie, Jim Brown, Kareem Abdul Jabbar, Bill Russell. We can't forget these people, can't forget their stories—they are great American stories.[14]

Those who watched professional basketball in the early 1990s may detect an uneasy irony in Spike's commentary. His alter ego, Mars Blackmon, appeared in a popular series of Nike commercials with Michael Jordan, selling sneakers. Mars obviously got paid.

Be that as it may, Lee claims privileged access to an instructive past. He, like Edwards, places contemporary black athletes on the shoulders of giants—and Dodgers and Cardinals. The chafing noise sounded by Lee's final point, however, reveals the limits of his allegory. From one angle, he enacts a rhetoric of recognition that claims representational space for the black athletes who took risks and made sacrifices to widen the repertoire of identities included in the American image. From another angle, however,

Lee's injunction to remember records a narrative of national identity in which the civic ethos of these black champions has been consumed by the progress entailed in their sacrifices. The difference and the tension turn the question of the *we* who must not forget. Taken as a didactic history aimed at the black athletes of today, Lee's observation urges a form of civic engagement borne from black experience. On this view, the obtuse failure to know history is a sellout's willful amnesia. But if Lee's *we* is all of us, a plural collective romanticized longingly in the "American story," then the amnesia is widespread, not confined to the lost consciousness of a forgotten few but structured into a sputtering national narrative that continues to conceal its injustices. If the social significance of sport is its ability to measure progress, then trying to tell the "American story" through the consciousness of black athletes becomes perilous work—it seems that they inaugurated an era of social progress that we are supposed to measure as no progress at all. Herein lies the paradoxical limit of the allegory: the long-lost revolutionary subject is both the victim and the agent of a flawed national character.

In 1969, Edwards declared in unequivocal terms that the revolt of the black athlete was the "newest phase of the black liberation movement in America." Edwards put black athletes at the center of history, insisting that "America's response to what the black athlete is saying and doing will undoubtedly not only determine the future course and direction of American athletics, but also will affect all social relations between blacks and whites in this country."[15] Given his current disappointment, maybe this strident prediction was simply an ephemeral rallying cry that vaporized once its moment passed. Or maybe Edwards was just wrong—the revolution never materialized. But set against Lee's invocation of these "great American stories," it is important to emphasize that Edwards had envisioned a dialectical history: America's *response* to the black athlete was what would matter most. He imagined black athletes to be a collective voice of opposition angling in from the margin, "speaking out not only on their own behalf, but on behalf of their downtrodden race."[16] As righteous public advocates, Carlos, Smith, Ali, Jim Brown, and others at the forefront of the black athletic revolt were spokespersons for the black masses, or what Baker calls the "black majority." These golden men, these representatives of the downtrodden, presciently transgressed the "exclusively middle-class beautification of history designed to erase the revolution, pray blessings upon the heads of white people and give a rousing cheer for free enterprise individualism."[17]

Contemporary accusations of deliberate ignorance urge critical reflection on the historical details of the black athlete as a revolutionary subject. One wonders if that familiar pantheon of lost heroes has not somewhere

been corrupted from within. Jordan, to be sure, is free enterprise individualism incarnate, and Woods fist-pumping his way around Augusta National
often looks like a middle-class beautification. So it is easy and perhaps even
worthwhile to idealize Jackie Robinson and Muhammad Ali and John Carlos and Tommie Smith and cobble them together into a bygone civic ethos,
the memory of which might recuperate sport's civic spirit. But viewed as
individuals engaged in concrete, historically specific negotiations over
the meaning of national identity, the stitching that holds our lost heroes
together begins to fray. The dialectic motion of the black athletic call and
American response produced fissures sealed by compromise, illuminated
omissions redressed by inclusions, and mounted challenges managed by
accommodations. If a revolution did materialize, it was hardly defined by
the spirit of permanent protest.

Manning Marable's historical analysis of black political culture
describes liberalism as "a strategy of political action that calls for the
deconstruction of institutional racism through liberal reforms within the
government and the assimilation of blacks as individuals within all levels
of the labor force, culture, and society." Conceding that the motivational
"thesis" of liberal integrationism was "largely true during the era of Jim
Crow segregation," he argues that this political strategy has produced a
dilemma for formulations of black political action in the post–civil rights
era.[18] Personified most starkly by Clarence Thomas, the dilemma involves
a disjunction between "reactionary ideology" on the one hand and the
promise of symbolic representation on the other. As the "guiding star" of
"inclusionism," "symbolic representation" presents the hope that "black representatives within the system of power will use their leverage to carry out
policies benefiting the entire African-American polulation."[19] According to
Marable, the shifting social conditions of black leadership have arrested
the development of a reliably transformative political vision. His worry? "A
new type of African-American leadership emerged inside the public and
private sectors; this leadership lives outside the black community and has
little personal contact with other African Americans." Symbolic representation consequently has become a grave political risk, since it "no longer
works with bureaucrats and politicians who, like Clarence Thomas, feel no
sense of allegiance to the Black freedom struggle."[20]

It would be unfair to both men to liken Michael Jordan to Clarence
Thomas, but if the story of the activist-athlete's demise is understood in this
historical context, the train of thought offered by today's Harry Edwards
enters the station of historical insight. In its most incisive iteration, the

demise of the activist-athlete is a story about the social entailments of racial integration in sport and their cumulative influence on the experiences and memories of black athletes. Edwards says that today's black athletes are "very different. Their identity is different—they live in a rich, largely white world, a world where black individuality is tolerated so long as it is without reference to the black community. If you asked them about the history of the black athlete, many couldn't tell you much."[21] By locating the loss of the activist-athlete within the changing sociology of black participation in public life, in the way that black athletes have been encouraged to measure the progress of themselves and others, Edwards gestures toward but does not fully elucidate the broader historical narrative into which the demise fits: The political dynamic that he hoped would emerge from a revolutionary dialectic materialized as the triumph of American liberalism.

This is a grand summary, uncomplicated by the problems of fact and detail. In 2006, FoxSports.com columnist Dayn Perry evaluated the status of the activist-athlete in surprisingly animated terms: "It's a belated blessing that the strains of racism in our society have been reduced, but it's lamentable that professional athletes have been co-opted by the inwardly rotten corporatists in the enduring American class struggle. That's why we miss Curt Flood, Tommie Smith, John Carlos, Muhammad Ali, Jim Brown, Bill Lee, Dick Allen and those like them more than we probably realize."[22] *Co-optation*, always a provocative term, directs our attention to a cunning antagonist who lines its pockets by duping our heroes. And unlike Edwards and Lee, Perry offers a genealogy that contains a key nuance, and in this genealogy, an otherwise marginally significant baseball player, Curt Flood, acquires profound importance. In rehearsing the pantheon, Perry pauses on Flood to say, "In an odd way, Flood's cause bears some of the blame. That's because his challenge to baseball's economic structure laid the groundwork for the lushly moneyed professional athletes we have in our midst today. Flood, in being such a prominent and vital activist athlete, actually heralded the sad death of the activist-athlete."[23] Though I would disagree that the increasing wealth of black athletes provides a sufficient account of their co-optation, Perry points to an idea necessary to any critical memory of the activist-athlete. Problematizing the present through the loss of a shared consciousness risks obscuring instructive differences between the figures that appear on the lists of immortals, those black athletes of uncanny courage and conscience. To paraphrase Stuart Hall, the representational space occupied by our golden lineage offers few political guarantees.[24]

. . .

Against the backdrop of a dominant cultural narrative with symbolic invest-ments in nostalgic memories of black activist- athletes, this book conducts a historical investigation of the public discourse and political culture sur-rounding Curt Flood, a black professional baseball player for the St. Louis Cardinals throughout the 1960s. Flood was a notable ballplayer in his era; in 1968, *Sports Illustrated* labeled him the "best center fielder in baseball."[25] He started in center field for the Cardinals for almost a decade, including the World Series–winning teams of 1964 and 1967. His career batting aver-age was .293 (respectable but unremarkable), and he neither hit many home runs nor stole many bases. If Flood's baseball achievements stand out for any reason, it is that he was a superior defensive player with great speed, talents that helped to forge a 223-game errorless streak—impressive at any position but a staggering feat for a center fielder.[26]

In October 1969, after having lived and played for ten years in St. Louis, Flood was traded to the Philadelphia Phillies. At the time, all Major League Baseball players were subject to a contract condition called the reserve clause, which in essence bound a player to work in perpetuity for his original team unless that team traded him for another player or sold him for cash, in which case he worked under the same reserve conditions for the next team. Today, baseball players and athletes in other professional leagues, including the National Football League, National Basketball Asso-ciation, and National Hockey League, enjoy the benefit of some form of free agency. Though the terms of free agency vary from league to league and often from one contract to the next, each of these leagues (which are the largest in North America) operates a labor market that permits play-ers the opportunity to negotiate their salaries, the duration of their con-tracts, and sometimes even their power to veto potential trades. But when Flood was traded to the Phillies, a mediocre team with a dysfunctional organization and a reputation for having insufferable fans, baseball owners simply did not offer contracts without the reserve clause. Literally every Major League Baseball (MLB) contract specified that the team "reserved" the exclusive right to sign the player for the subsequent year. Every year a player signed a contract, he agreed to play for the same team the following year or not to play at all. Baseball owners publicly claimed that this arrange-ment was necessary to protect an equitable economic order, since with-out it, the wealthiest owners could purchase the best players at the highest prices and undermine league competition. Flood and others countered that

this economic order relied on a collusive labor practice that unlawfully limited wages, unfairly curtailed careers, and bore a striking resemblance to
slavery. With the support of the Major League Baseball Players Association,
the nascent labor organization, Flood sued MLB in federal court.

Refusing his assignment to Philadelphia as a matter of self-professed
principle, Flood argued that baseball had violated both U.S. antitrust laws
and the Thirteenth Amendment's prohibition of involuntary servitude.
In a defiant letter to Commissioner Bowie Kuhn asking for his contractual release, Flood wrote, "After twelve years in the major leagues, I do not
feel that I am a piece of property to be bought and sold irrespective of my
wishes." Most significantly, however, Flood appeared on national television
with the notorious Howard Cosell and in a dramatic close-up described
himself as a "well-paid slave," an explosive accusation thrust into public
circulation under vexing conditions for talking about race and class in
the United States. Flood's characterization of baseball in terms that referenced the nation's foundational moral error violated the social agreement
that had provided the game with its public significance since at least 1947,
Jackie Robinson's first year with the Brooklyn Dodgers. Sometimes called
a "microcosm," other times called a "crucible," baseball's status as an index
of racial progress rested on its ability to publicly announce the accumulating liberalization of its labor practices.[27] And Flood said that baseball was
slavery. He lost his federal case in the spring of 1970 and lost again on a
Supreme Court appeal in the summer of 1972, a decision that many people
perceived as torturing even the most flexible principles of American juris-
prudence.[28] He had been an all-star center fielder and had won two World
Series and played in a third, but after a year away from the game and sev-
enteen games during which he batted .200 with the dreadful Washington
Senators in 1971, Flood fled to Spain, broke and beaten, and never played
pro baseball again.

His story has been presented in a variety of lights. The subject of a
handful of recent books and scholarly essays, Flood is seen variously as
free agency's "pioneer," a courageous martyr, a lonely rebel, and in at least
one case, a self-destructive alcoholic.[29] Historians and biographers agree on
at least one fact, though: To even have a chance in his fight against baseball owners, the support of the Players Association was no less than necessary. He needed the association's money to pay his legal expenses, and
he needed its symbolic capital to put public pressure on baseball's team
owners. Flood presented his case to twenty-four players (each representing
a Major League team) during the association's winter meetings in Puerto

Rico in December 1969. After Flood explained the details of his lawsuit, Los Angeles Dodgers team representative Tom Haller asked a pivotal question: "With today's social situation, is being black a motivation?"[30] Flood responded by "telling the meeting that organized baseball's policies and practices affected all players equally and that my color was therefore beside the point." However, he subsequently added, "It occurred to me later that the answer, while valid, had by no means exhausted the subject."[31] Perhaps that was for the best, since Haller, who had asked the question, remarked later, "I didn't want it to be just a black thing. . . . I wanted it to be a baseball thing."[32]

These two moments had profound consequences. Taken together, the meeting in Puerto Rico with the players and the television appearance with Cosell illuminate the quandary that frustrated Flood's efforts to craft an effective political rhetoric. His best argument, the one that condensed all the others into a vividly recognizable injustice—*the slavery argument*—was also his most incendiary; it would easily translate his case into the "racial thing" from which his white colleagues were sure to symbolically flee, taking their money with them. Flood faced the task of fashioning a constructive position out of this tension. Should his blackness matter, and if so, in what way and to whom?

Marable's history of black political culture identifies three "strategic visions" that have organized the black freedom struggle in the United States since the Civil War: inclusion (also called integration), black nationalism, and transformation. "Inclusionists have operated philosophically and ideologically as 'liberals,'" writes Marable, attempting to "influence public opinion and mass behavior on issues of race by changing public policies, education, and cultural activity." Black nationalists, by contrast, "distrusted the capacity of whites as a group to overcome the debilitating effects of white privilege, and questioned the inclusionists' simpleminded faith in the power of legal reforms."[33] (Transformative visions with transformative results, Marable worries, have yet to find mass expression.) In the late 1960s and early 1970s, inclusionism set the terms according to which interracial coalitions could be established and "progress" collectively announced. Following a logic similar to what critical race theorists call "convergence theory," institutional reform in baseball and elsewhere would "succeed only where it converge[d] with white interests."[34] Were Flood a good liberal, a reasonable inclusionist, he would take care to demonstrate the universality of his challenge to baseball and the various ways in which white players would benefit from any precedent he might set. But calling baseball a slaveholding institution and himself a slave most certainly did not make him sound like a good liberal. It made him sound like a black nationalist. As the "well-paid slave" comment made its way through the sports press, including the nation's largest newspapers, it was a promiscuous expression whose overtones of anger and distrust put Flood's ability to influence public opinion at risk.

On even the most superficial level, Flood's choice was a curious one: Calling himself a "well-paid slave" was provocative, perhaps even confrontational, especially to those in the national sports press who had grown accustomed to writing baseball into idyllic narratives of racial progress. Though such an expression was sure to capture the wide attention he needed to succeed in his challenge, it also appeared to be a figure of speech destined to invite derision. At the emotional nadir of his challenge, Flood himself wondered about his "decision to have it out in public with the owners of organized baseball."[35] And quite a public dispute it was. In the theater of public life, Flood was a fascinating character. Whether viewed as a protagonist or antagonist, his persona achieved a gripping, if fleeting, stage presence. The lawsuit itself was a surprisingly expensive, high-profile affair. One benefit of Players Association support was having legal expenses paid to Arthur Goldberg, who in the previous fifteen years had brokered the merger of the AFL-CIO, represented the United Steelworkers, served as President John F. Kennedy's secretary of labor, and replaced Felix Frankfurter on the U.S. Supreme Court. Goldberg's services did not come cheaply, but in securing them Flood proved his sincerity and legitimized his case as something worthy of sustained public attention. For a time, he was captivating news. His effort, of course, made for good stories, and it still does, even if they currently lack the dramatic realities of Flood's life and baseball career.

Some version of the race question continues to baffle Flood historians; some fit him into the evolution of baseball's labor laws and overlook race politics altogether. Others individualize Flood's "sensitive consciousness" in sentimental remembrances of the "spirit of the 1960s." And still others claim that Flood failed in his challenge because of a white racist backlash. Those who make the backlash argument are right to point to the owners' paternalism and to the fact that some writers asked a version of the old racist question, "What more do you people want?" Be that as it may, these historians and biographers mistake one fundamental fact with astonishing regularity: Flood was not the victim of a uniformly hostile press. He was supported consistently by writers in the *New York Times* and the *Sporting*

News and by the most influential opinion columnists in virtually every black newspaper in the United States. Along these lines, this book offers an important correction to our historical understanding of Curt Flood: Those who supported him did so in ways that were often at odds with each other. Flood's greatest challenge was not that his critics outnumbered his advocates but that he opened himself up to competing forms of advocacy. The hopeful universality of his cause notwithstanding, Flood's best argument, the slavery argument, existed in elaborate form in the public spaces occupied most conspicuously by Harry Edwards, the author of *Revolt of the Black Athlete.*

Kwame Anthony Appiah asserts that "if there is a liberal form of life, it was always characterized not only by institutions but also by a rhetoric, a body of ideas and arguments."[36] His anecdotal take on the American revolution is that "life, liberty, and the pursuit of happiness" were not simply songs to be sung, but that the colonists who advanced persuasive ideas on such topics were people who attempted to build democratic institutions reflective of their ideas. Appiah makes the important point that insightful criticism attends to the disparities between politics as they are written and politics as they are done. "It's possible," he says, "that an emphasis on practices rather than principles can be helpful in showing just how heterogeneous those principles can be."[37] Black American soldiers returning to the Jim Crow South after fighting Nazis in World War II certainly attested to the power of this kind of insight. But it is premised on a common distinction that I would challenge, namely that rhetoric—our body of ideas and arguments—is separable from practice, as if what we "really" think can simply be read off of what we do. Insightful rhetorical criticism, from my perspective, attends to the reverse of this as well, to the ways that our institutions and the political practices they make possible are not only shaped by ideas and arguments but are also constituted in part by the rhetoric through which those ideas are rendered. The "liberal form of life," in this sense, is partially lived in and through saying the things that a "liberal" would say. These speech genres are not foreign to American democracy. Appiah generally has them right: "life, liberty, and the pursuit of happiness." It is surely possible to live life, demand freedom, and pursue happiness by talking in profoundly nonliberal ways, but if one's politics are defined explicitly through this kind of talk, one *behaves* as if one lives a liberal form of life; such talk this helps make up the fabric of liberal practice. Hence the dilemma of Curt Flood, who was unsure if his blackness should matter or in what way and to whom it would matter. On the one hand, his case was not a "black thing," it was a simple matter of life, liberty, and the pursuit of happiness—or so he told the group of white men assembled in Puerto Rico. "Slavery," on the other hand? Well, that sure *sounded* like a black thing.

As many readers are likely to detect, the theoretical assumptions and terminology I advance in this book are generally derived from a body of public sphere scholarship that exists in rhetorical studies and in other fields concerned with the meaning and agency of public address. Obviously, we cannot know what Flood was thinking when he claimed to be a "well-paid slave," nor can we be sure (despite his persistent appeals to "principle") that he even knew exactly what motivated him. So this book does not attempt to discover what the case "really meant" to Flood, nor does it attempt to read-judicate his case as containing "valid arguments" that were somehow mis-understood in their own time. Instead, this project attempts to track, from a broad perspective, the paths through public discourse that Flood's rhetoric traveled. As a work of historical criticism, I consider the discourses Flood brought into being by examining the rhetorical performances through which his cause was advocated. I do not mean to imply that what Flood wanted or intended is completely beside the point. After all, Flood's case came to matter in public life because he wanted to become a free agent, and it is fair to assume that the things he said were intended to bring about that result. I do mean to suggest, however, that regardless of what he may have intended and despite the care he took to shape the manner in which his case would be interpreted, his advocates engaged in divergent rhetorical practices that were brought to bear on the uses to which his racial identity was put. At stake, then, in my corrective reading is this book's most sig-nificant insight about Flood: Between 1970 and 1972, Flood found himself positioned fatally on the fault line between liberal and radical modes of black political speech.

Reading Flood's case in this way requires attention to what Michael Warner calls "the poetic function of public discourse." A particular "lan-guage ideology," Warner says, encourages us to think of public speech as a form of rational debate and of "the public" as an arena in which a clash of ideas allows the force of reason to emerge from the vicissitudes of con-versation.[38] Scholarly theories of the public sphere have typically operated within the confines of this ideology, especially theories that are guided by a consideration of Jurgen Habermas's *Structural Transformation of the Public Sphere*. Baker summarizes Habermas's idealized model as "an associational life of male property-owners gathered to exchange rational arguments and critical opinions shaped and mirrored by novels and the press."[39] From a variety of angles, critics have attended to the troubling aspects of this formulation, which problematically reifies the difference between public and private spheres of political action and which seems to be premised on social exclusions; not everyone is a bourgeois male property owner, so public subjectivity is not universally available. From my perspective, these are fair criticisms worth noticing and revisiting, but even they are often constrained by thinking of discourse as "propositionally summarizable."[40] In other words, critiques of the public sphere that highlight the exclusion of women, blacks, or the poor (for example) are often advanced in the hope that the argumentative discourses of these groups might enter effectively into a neutral public space—that is, in the hope that their "propositions" receive fair hearings. But this language ideology overlooks consequential formal and stylistic aspects of public address in assuming that all of the salient features of discourse are contained in the arguments themselves and are independent of the manner in which those arguments are uttered. "Other aspects of discourse, including affect and expressivity," Warner says, "are not thought to be fungible in the same way." Public discourse, along these lines, consists in identifiable affective modes and expressive forms that are concealed when it is ideologized as rational-critical debate. As Warner puts it, "the perception of public discourse as conversation obscures the important poetic functions of both language and corporeal expressivity in giving a particular shape to publics."[41]

Consider, for example, the proliferation of lists of black activist-athletes that began to emerge in iconic form in the 1960s. The names sometimes change, but the recitations generally include Jackie Robinson, Muhammad Ali, John Carlos and Tommie Smith, occasionally Jim Brown and Arthur Ashe, and—these days—Curt Flood. Following other critics of Habermas in noticing that "black Americans . . . have traditionally been excluded from these domains of modernity," Baker allows that "nothing might seem less realistic, attractive, or believable than the notion of a black public sphere."[42] Nevertheless, the idea of the black public sphere seems to be exactly what holds together the figures in the pantheon of black activist-athletes. As highly visible symbolic actors, as ideal black political participants, perhaps what gives these figures their contemporary significance is the nostalgic memory of their virtuous public activity. What they seem to have in common, and the reason they are linked together, is their willingness to speak, to decry injustice despite the risks, and to embody in the category they create what it means to speak truth to power. There can be no question that all of these athletes holds a claim in the larger context of the black freedom struggle, but the language ideology that always urges more conversation hides differences between the manner in which these athletes offered their ideas and arguments. Within the black public sphere, blackness itself offered forms of affect and expressivity rejected by some and embraced by others. Here is where Marable's "strategic visions" matter most: inclusionists attempted to mute the negative social effects of blackness by insisting on the irrelevance of race, and black nationalists engaged in rhetorical practices fundamentally defined by the racial identity and racialized experiences of its speakers.

Inclusionism, above all, placed U.S. society on an evolutionary trajectory that measured progress by the breaking of institutional barriers. It was oriented toward a time in which race would be an individual difference that made no social or political difference. "By assimilating the culture of whites and by minimizing the cultural originality and creativity of African Americans," Marable says, inclusionism might provide "the basis for a 'universalist' dialogue transcending the ancient barriers of color."[43] This rhetorical practice supports the language ideology of the public sphere: To participate in a "universalist dialogue," public address demands a way of speaking that disjoins speakers from the particular facts of their identities; to speak in public is to project oneself to others as anyone. From a Habermasian perspective, this is where the public sphere's promise lies; the force of reason emerges when speakers distance themselves from the biases entailed in the particularities of their bodies and social locations. But, says Warner, "The rhetorical strategy of personal abstraction is both the utopian moment of the public sphere and a major source of domination, for the ability to abstract oneself in public discussion has always been an unequally available resource. Individuals have to have specific rhetorics of disincorporation; they are not simply rendered bodiless by exercising reason. And it is only possible to operate a discourse based on the claim to self-abstracting disinterestedness in a culture where such unmarked self-abstraction is a differential resource."[44] This point is crucial: It is not simply that those who are excluded from social and political life cannot have their arguments heard, it is also that speaking in public discussion itself demands strategies of self-abstraction that are readily available to some but are difficult for others to access. Put differently, since their public discourses were not marked by blackness, participation in a "universalist dialog" involved a form of self-abstraction that was standard rhetorical practice for speakers in the *New York Times* and the *Sporting News*. For speakers in the black press, those widely circulating newspapers and magazines owned by black citizens and in which black citizens did the speaking, participation in public discussion meant a kind of self-abstraction that entailed a disavowal of the meaning, significance, and influence of blackness, precisely the particularity that signified these speakers' exclusion.

. . .

In his 1970 book, *The Way It Is*, Flood (and coauthor Richard Carter) attempted to marshal the racial ambiguity of "well-paid slavery." Generically speaking, the book resists categorization: It is part autobiography, part memoir, part apologia, and part polemic. The book was released between Flood's loss in federal court and his appeal hearing, and he delivers his experiences with racism and segregation as a Minor Leaguer in the Deep South to formulate a view of baseball with which his white baseball colleagues could, he hoped, identify. In chapter 2 of this volume, I present a close reading of *The Way It Is* that finds Flood wanting the public and other players to see and hear a truth that was always hidden from view: Baseball was a dehumanizing institution that concealed its moral errors in disingenuous appeals to the public interest. "The Good of the Game!" cried the owners; "the reserve clause is necessary to protect the Good of the Game." In response, Flood insisted that baseball's public space was like a cinema screen running the owners' propaganda flicks. Perhaps in an attempt to direct his discourse through paths that led around the national sports press, Flood wrote *The Way It Is*. I examine his book as a strategic document that attempts to negotiate the racial trouble his case seemed to generate.

Flood believed that team owners and sports reporters collaborated in curating baseball's mythic status, which consigned players to public vilification as greedy and ungrateful whenever they asserted their labor interests—as happened to Flood. Baseball owners said and many reporters wrote that if the reserve clause were abolished, baseball would be thrown into "chaos" and would "simply cease to exist." With scathing sarcasm and a cynic's wit, Flood's book attempted to show that baseball owners were sanctimonious liars and that baseball players were simply compelled, as slaves, to enact their own subordination in self-abnegating refrains about the "Good of the Game." But Flood struggled to exchange the owners' dystopian projection for a more helpful one. His strategy was to offer a form of double-consciousness derived from black experience but deprived of racial identity. The "slave" that Flood urged others to embody might recognize the abstract conditions of slavery without having necessarily lived life in ways that felt like slavery. Flood's slave in this sense was potentially raceless, its subordination following from an abstract relation of bondage but dislocated from the concrete social experiences that had allowed Flood to recognize racist dehumanization for what it was.

Flood's definitive biographer is Brad Snyder, whose *A Well-Paid Slave* is an exhaustively researched personal and legal history. Snyder claims, as do most others who look closely at Flood's case, that "Flood's most consistent supporter was the black press."[45] And Charles Korr, whose history of baseball's labor relations identifies contemporaneous reaction to Flood as racist and vitriolic, admits, "The black press treated Flood quite differently."[46] According to many accounts, black newspapers were crucial to setting baseball's progress narrative in motion, most notably through Jackie Robinson. "The crusade by the Negro press" on Robinson's behalf, write Gene Roberts and Hank Klibanoff in a recent Pulitzer Prize–winner, "was providing the precise dynamic that [Gunnar] Myrdal felt most essential for improvement of blacks' lives: creating publicity."[47]

Chapter 3 views the black press as a primary context of Flood advocacy fundamentally shaped by Robinson in the 1940s. Black newspapers had become accustomed to fighting the inclusionist fight in baseball, and the sport arguably represented the social arena in which black newspapers possessed greatest influence. By the time of Flood's case, the Robinson model situated black reporters' talk about sport in a disincorporated mode of address. Through a rhetoric of self-abstraction, black newspapers simply denied the importance of Flood's blackness in advocating careful labor reforms in pro baseball. For reporters and columnists in papers such as the *Chicago Defender* and *Baltimore Afro-American*, reference to Flood's blackness worked gratuitously, as something that was there but always said to be beside the point. Newspapers' reflexive discourses—those moments in which they actively imagined their purpose in the early 1970s—revealed an aspiring ephemerality, a hope that the black press would soon disappear, a rhetorical orientation toward a utopian era when the black press would be the archaic site for a superfluous political identity stitched into a universal public sphere. By considering the proposition that the black press constituted a "counterpublic," chapter 3 concludes with an examination of the disincorporated rhetoric through which speakers in the black press advocated Flood's case.

Chapter 4 takes a closer look at the rhetorical consonances between black press support for Flood and the national sports media's advocacy of his case. This chapter examines the support Flood received in the *New York Times* and the *Sporting News*, the era's two most nationally significant newspapers to report on sports. Problems of race and class—both of which were incipient in the image of Flood's "well-paid slave"—came to be subsumed and occluded by an ill-defined sense of universal principle. Shortly before Flood sued baseball, the national press had stirred a general consternation regarding the growing financial architecture of sport. The story went that baseball and football had become big business, athletes' salaries were beginning to dwarf the salaries of ordinary people, and owners had become sophisticated in their use of media instruments. Flood's case fit seamlessly within these narratives, so advocating his cause entailed a productive reiteration of the things the *Times* and the *Sporting News* had been saying about baseball already: It was time to grow up and recognize that sport was a lucrative economic enterprise for everyone. In this era, sport gained recognition as an element of the business matrix.

Most important, black newspapers, following their inclusionist rhetorical logic, mirrored these moves according to a three-step process. First, they noted that Flood's racial experiences had made him a "sensitive" person and then confined the significance of race to Flood's individual consciousness, removing race from the repertoire of arguments occupying the realm of sincere public deliberation. Race mattered to Flood for good reason, they said, but it had no bearing on the principle for which he stood. Second, they compared baseball to other forms of labor, such as plumbers and auto workers, collapsing a sequence of racial and class distinctions into a free labor market wishfully characteristic of the "American way." Third, black newspapers mediated Flood's claim about slavery into a purely metaphorical expression that might urge baseball owners to reform the reserve clause. Again following from Robinson, baseball had become a prized cultural showcase for integration's successes, and the frank possibility that a successful challenge to the reserve clause would mean the "end of baseball as we knew it" brought with it an entire liberal vocabulary of balanced adjustments and fair compromises. Black and white interests were converging, and along with the significance of Flood's blackness went any productive potential the "well-paid slave" may have held to narrate the race and class inequities in sport or society at large.

At the same time, Edwards recognized not only that rhetorics of disincorporation were unequally available but also that when advanced into political discourse, universal abstractions withheld from public expression those particular experiences in integration that were humiliating and degrading to black athletes. In 1969, Edwards wrote *Revolt of the Black Athlete*, which tried to both contextualize and formalize a recent history of black athletic protest. Though Edwards understood well that the revolt was best communicated in the gestures of Carlos and Smith, he called Ali the "patron saint" of the emerging movement. Whether or not the movement really "emerged" is a complicated question, but the black athlete in *Revolt* was a radicalized persona whose lived experiences in sport's integrated social spaces, both on campuses and in pro clubhouses, failed to achieve that which was imagined in liberalism's quixotic appeals to universality. Black athletes, according to Edwards, were "for the first time reacting in a human and masculine fashion to the disparities between the heady artificial world of newspaper clippings, photographers, and screaming spectators and the real world of degradation, humiliation, and horror that confronts the overwhelming majority of Afro-Americans."[48] In contrast to the black press—indeed, in explicit contradistinction to the black press—Edwards formalized a black political rhetoric that depended fundamentally on the calculated assertion of racial identity for its persuasive force. Chapter 5 analyzes Edwards's implicit critique of the black public sphere and attends to the ways that slavery provided insightful points of criticism that *Revolt*'s racialized mode of address delivered through Flood.

The problem, of course, was that the revolt of the black athlete stood much farther from practicable politics than Edwards would have liked or than Flood would have needed. Aligning with radicals would not help Flood's suit against Major League Baseball. Such a strategy would certainly not impress the likes of Haller—*Are you doing this because you're black?* Thus, Flood's dilemma seems to be a chronic condition in the contemporary public square: the race-effacing move was the smarter move, the realistic move, and the one with the better odds. But that argument was not the truth as Flood had claimed to live it in *The Way It Is*. Flood stood at the enduring gap between experience and expression that characterizes liberal race politics. By 1970, the figure of the black athlete had begun to occupy a widening zone of the cultural landscape. The protean racial constitution—black and not black—of Flood's slave metaphor bespoke the difference between the modes of public address in black newspapers and in Edwards's *Revolt*. It was the difference between the effacement of blackness and its principled assertion, between the black athlete who would help to tell the progressive story of sport's evolving meritocracy and the black athlete who would deliver his criticisms in the name of his blackness.

An awareness of this gap between experience and expression helps in diagnosing the nostalgic excess that frustrates the search for critical memory in the present. Chapter 6 fits Flood into the sport's current public memory and explains the variety of ways in which he is trapped within the contradictions of black activist-athletes' purported demise. Here, I argue that the relationship of co-optation that doomed Flood in the early 1970s manifests now in an anxiety that struggles to discover and reanimate the black activist-athlete as a subject of public address and agent of history. Where are our black activist-athletes now? They may or may not be around, and despite the hegemonic effacement of race crystallized for many in Tiger Woods and Michael Jordan, black athletes unquestionably cannot be condemned as a class. But the call to conscience as it is issued today often takes such anxious form, asking athletes to speak out for *something* in exasperation over their inability speak truth to power, that one wonders whether liberalism has put itself in this position and whether what passes as critical memory too often merely speaks its own psychosis through the subject position that has worked historically to sustain its political logic. As far as the black athlete is concerned, it seems, liberalism is left only to devour its young.

. . .

With respect to the present, Curt Flood prompts attention to a pair of inter-related ironies. First, in noticing that Flood may have produced a progeny of wealth by pioneering free agency in professional sport, he is implicated in producing the damaging allure of athletics for the latest generation of black youth. Without exception and to only slightly varying degrees, base-ball historians and Flood biographers credit him with having forged the path to free agency in sports, even though he never benefited from his efforts. (In fact, Flood's courage is often said to reside in the fact that the pursuit destroyed him; he never personally gained from the wealth his sac-rifices conferred.) This sociological argument about the shifting aspirations of black youth was made over a decade ago by John Hoberman in *Darwin's Athletes: How Sport Has Damaged Black America and Preserved the Myth of Race*. Now this argument has its most articulate proponent in Edwards, himself a founder of the "sociology of sport." Edwards is cautious about sport's effects as an aspiration for young black men, who are "not moving at all ... being left behind, and increasingly, in the 21st Century, living an early 20th Century existence."[49] Perry identified the second irony, insisting that Flood the activist heralded the "sad death" of athletic activism. So despite our memories of Flood's better conscience, which presumably trumps the cynicism of our age, he corrupts our canon of "golden men" from within in two ways: Flood helped to manufacture the false dreams that reproduce inequity and despair, and Flood helped cultivate the financial climate that robs our athletes of their incentive to speak with courage. The binding questions are these: What are we to make of Curt Flood in our present? Where does his story fit? How should we regard him?

Attempts to answer these questions produce a familiar constellation of responses: canonical lists that start with Carlos and Smith and end with brooding lamentations over the malfeasances of our exorbitantly wealthy athletes. One thing about constellations, though, is that the stars are open to purposive configuration, depending on where the astrologist chooses to point his or her gaze. In this sense, my perception of stars such as Flood, Carlos, and Smith as figures (in the sense that they are both persons and tropes) is guided by a nagging instinct that sport's progress narrative, at least with regard to the question of race, has finally found the boundary it cannot transgress, the barrier it cannot break, in the incapacity to lend expression to the kind of experiences that make activism worthwhile and rewarding.

If the story of progress that the familiar lineage of activist-athletes helps to tell is becoming counterproductive, then it would seem that the demands of our speaking situation are no longer met by political rhetorics dependent on symbolic representation. Marable argues that as a political rationality, symbolic representation urged "select numbers of well-educated, affluent, and/or powerful blacks into positions of authority,"[50] which perhaps explains sport's most pronounced contribution to social life in the United States. My suspicion, as Robinson's place in this story clarifies, arises from the fact that symbolic representation invited and often enforced a dubious type of political performance that foreclosed challenges to the central assumptions of American social life in the interest of dramatizing the mutual benefits of racial integration. Symbolic representatives were those who could "speak for" racial minorities in ways that qualified those representatives for inclusion into a commons conditioned by precisely the interests that had engineered their exclusion. Symbolic representation enacted a rhetoric of recognition for which those unmarked identities, as Michael Warner might put it, had already set the terms. That, after all, is how Robinson fits into Lee's "great *American* stories."

But in the late 1960s and early 1970s, when Flood's case was being made, Edwards aimed a challenge directly at the prevailing terms of symbolic representation. He countered the performance of blackness for whites with the performance of blackness for blacks. Edwards's rhetoric came complete with the accusation that black liberals were "Uncle Toms." One can debate the persuasive effects of such labels, but the crucial point is that he worked to disclose the dehumanizing experiences of black athletes *in integration*. As Edwards attempted to reclaim "black dignity," he insisted on a mode of black speech that was openly hostile to integration's most sacred symbols. Broadly construed, Edwards resisted the logic of tokenism through which symbolic representation often did its work. Wondering about Robinson's cozy relationship with Nelson Rockefeller in 1968, Edwards asked if black athletes were making "a truly significant contribution to black progress or merely prostitut[ing] their athletic ability for the sake of other aims."[51] The difference between Robinson and Edwards demonstrates the need to take notice of the forms of political expression that abetted liberalism's triumph in the 1970s and beyond. As Herman Gray explains, "The discourse of integration was deeply rooted in the logic of assimilation, which, in the aftermath of the civil rights movement, was codified into a social project of colorblindness, a legal project of equal opportunity, and a moral project of individualism and self-responsibility."[52] From Edwards's point of view, and perhaps on the view of the *black* version of Flood's well-paid slave, assimilation and color-blindness were dangerous tricks that held together the power relations against which these figures militated.

"Out of critique and modulation, alteration and adjustment," Baker says, "the analytical instrument of the public sphere suggests revised notions of how human interactive modes—other than reason alone—bear on publicity."[53] Baker's point is that the idea of a "black public sphere" is not without warrant, especially if "it can make its way through the interruptions and fissures of an idealized notion of universal man without class, racial, and gender distinctions."[54] I engage that possibility by viewing baseball in the black public sphere through the modes of address that cast the universality of reason into doubt. To say that Flood's case was or was not a "racial thing" is to resort to a form of historiography that attempts to pin him to an argument and fix his coordinates in deliberative space. To recognize that it *both* was *and* was not a "racial thing" is to understand that Flood's influence on and position within the black public sphere reflected the internal complexity of the political culture in which he found himself. Flood's "well-paid slave" was not simply a metaphorical veneer that brought attention to a better form of reason that lay somewhere beneath; it was instead a tropological force that, for better or for worse, activated the kind of racial imagery that some black advocates dismissed as meaningless and that other black advocates embraced with poetic passion. The central task of this book is to trace the figurative resonances of Flood's racial identity occasioned by his rhetorical performances and those of his advocates. It is certainly critical to remember the various ways in which Flood was "demonized and denounced,"[55] but noticing all that, however true, leads us no closer to understanding the interruptions and fissures he disclosed in the notion of the universal man. Nor does it necessarily explain his significance to the present. Perhaps if we dwell closely on what it meant to root for him, we might also come to understand something insightful about the "textural and textual interweavings"` through which the black activist-athlete seems to have met his so-called demise.

Consider, finally, the most common way in which Flood is remembered. None of Flood's playing contemporaries testified at his trial in the summer of 1970, but the most golden of all luminaries did. An aged Jackie Robinson hobbled into the courtroom and shook Flood's hand, announcing that he couldn't let Flood "be out here all alone." Thus, as race finds its way into Flood's story, as it does in the closing words of Snyder's biography, summaries like these flow easily from a storyteller's pen: "Robinson and Flood took professional athletes on an incredible journey—from racial desegregation to well-paid slavery to being free and extremely well paid. Robinson started the revolution by putting on a uniform. Flood finished it by taking his uniform off. Robinson fought for racial justice. Flood fought the less-sympathetic fight for economic justice. They never stopped fighting for freedom."[56] In contemporary discussion, this kind of insight has become a banality: a revolution initiated by Robinson and consummated in Flood's pioneering pursuit of free agency. Race and class disjoined, freedom struggle defined. Everybody got paid. Flood reveals at least this much: In our revolutionary figures, we see the political errors masked carefully by the optimism of compromise; we see liberalism's insidious conservatism, which leaves only our amnesiac athletes to blame. Instead of demanding more from the framework of our political culture, we take our shots at Michael and Tiger for their refusal to be Jackie and Curt, when perhaps who they are is exactly who liberalism hoped they would be.

2

Curt Flood's Public Case

When the Cardinals traded Curt Flood to the Phillies in 1969, he was disgusted not just by the trade itself but by his treatment that day. Flood received an unceremonious telephone call from Cardinals office assistant Jim Toomey, a "middle-echelon coffee drinker," just before dawn on a chilly October morning. "If I had been a foot-shuffling porter," he recalled, "they might have at least given me a pocket watch." After that, said Flood, "one miserable telephone call released the poison of self-pity. The hard-boiled realist who answered the telephone was a weeping child when he set the receiver down. The lightning had struck. The dream lay shattered. It was a bad scene." The moment provided Flood with an epiphany that came to influence the appearance of his case in public discourse for the following forty years. "Player trades are commonplace," said Flood, "The unusual aspect of this one was that I refused to accept it. It violated the logic and integrity of my existence." And thus he initiated pursuit of a line of reasoning that echoed his defiant letter to Bowie Kuhn and that might illuminate the dehumanizing entailments of being a Major League Baseball (MLB) player: "I was not a consignment of goods. I was a man, the rightful proprietor of my own person and my own talents."[1]

In February 1970, four months after receiving that phone call, Flood and Richard Carter spent several weeks at a St. Louis Holiday Inn intending to write a book but spent most of their time enjoying more frivolous pursuits.[2] Despite the distractions, those thirty boozy days produced *The Way It Is*, which from just about any angle is saturated with the kind of cutting sarcasm that seems to have emerged from a person lost in a deep malaise. Flood's biographers tend to read his emotional disposition by interpreting this tenor as bitterness and resentment. Whether or not that is a fair assessment, I consider Flood's experiential and affective rhetoric not for what it says about Flood's state of mind but instead for how the forms of experience and affect that he introduced into public argument helped him address the quandary presented by his blackness. In that sense, I regard *The Way It Is* as a strategic document that helped Flood make his way between the whims of the Players Association and the racial imagery of the well-paid slave. Tom Haller would not be the only person to ask if Flood's challenge was a "black thing." "Let a black person utter the word slavery, and the room instantly empties," says Houston Baker, noting that "many white Americans move emotional and logical mountains to dissociate themselves from slavery."[3] To at least that extent, Flood's self-description as a well-paid slave staged an awkward encounter between the well-meaning liberalism of his white colleagues and the embodied racial justice discourses that had preceded him.

The Way It Is relied for its rhetorical energy on a fundamental, persistent ambiguity regarding those racial justice discourses. Even while weaving allegorical connections to race throughout the text, Flood refused to be explicit. The narrative revealed the concrete meaning of blackness as feature of lived experience, but it also dwelled closely on the abstract economic principles violated in baseball's reserve clause. On the one hand, these themes worked symbiotically as Flood attempted to lend expression to the idea of "well-paid slavery." On the other hand, these themes worked parasitically as Flood struggled to make his politics practical. Are you doing this because you're black? The answer to that question was often left to speculative inference. After presenting a life history nuanced by detailed memories of racial experiences, Flood offered a tellingly ambiguous capstone to The Way It Is: "Frederick Douglass was a Maryland slave who taught himself to read. 'If there is no struggle,' he once said, 'there is no progress. Those who profess to favor freedom, and yet deprecate agitation, are men who want crops without plowing the ground. . . . Power concedes nothing without a demand. It never did and it never will.' To see the Curt Flood case in that light is to see its entire meaning."[4] Uttered in strident and dramatic tones, the comparison to Douglass condensed an array of implied meanings that without explicit elaboration constituted his case's "entire meaning." Douglass, after all, was not simply an agitator—he was a black slave turned free abolitionist, just as Flood had imagined himself. Centered neither on the matter of Douglass's blackness nor on the way that the history of racial injustice may have motivated him but instead on freedom in the abstract, Flood stood vaguely between a racialized allusion and a universal expression, between an opaque invocation of race and its deferring gesture toward the abstracted nature of freedom struggles.

Unlike "the Maryland slave who taught himself to read," Flood's constituency—the fellow slaves he claimed to represent—was not defined by its racial identity. If he spoke for anyone, Flood spoke for a constituency bound by a shared economic labor relation that needed to be divorced from the problems of race and class. Most ballplayers, especially the Players Association reps, were white, and many of them were quite wealthy. To address the public otherwise was to risk alienating white players who might benefit from his lawsuit and whose support was necessary to the case's immediate success. But if Flood situated himself entirely outside of a racial idiom (or if the significance of race was denied too insistently), he risked sacrificing the powerful discursive forms that characterized the identity politics of the late 1960s and early 1970s. His blackness could help him, but he would need carefully to manage its influence.

The Way It Is is saturated with an undercurrent of anxiety over the basic public perception of the reserve clause challenge. Much of Flood's consternation centered on the sports press, the writers and columnists who both brokered and ensured baseball's romantic parcel of the cultural landscape. Flood believed that this image would remain inviolate without active, unrelenting intervention in the face of public mockery and vilification: "To challenge the sanctity of organized baseball was to question one of the primary myths of American culture. To persist in the heresy required profound conviction, with endurance to match. I knew in advance that litigation might take years. I had become thirty-two in January 1970, and could not expect my athletic skills to survive prolonged disuse. The proprietors and publicists of baseball could be depended on to remind me of this at every turn, meanwhile reviling me in print as a destroyer, an ingrate, a fanatic, a dupe."[5] Baseball journalists, acting as agents of the owners would, Flood feared, do their damage by perpetuating an ideology designed to demonize and expunge the game's heretical expressions.

Flood engaged in three basic rhetorical moves in *The Way It Is*. First, he destabilized baseball's pastoral and romantic image with irony and sarcasm. "Customary though it may be to write about that institutionalized pastime as though it existed apart from the general environment, my story does not lend itself to such treatment," he insisted, allowing him to both insert justice claims into the discourses of sport and rebut the owners' obtuse appeal to the public interest. "The facts are that nobody who plays professional baseball or owns its teams or reports its goings-on to the public is exempt from what takes place beyond the stadium walls." Second, Flood enacted a speaking position derived from black experience—what W. E. B. Du Bois once called "double-consciousness"—that Flood hoped his baseball colleagues could assume for themselves. "Some of the players hope that they are" exempt from what takes place beyond the stadium walls, "and most of the sedentary members of the cast pretend that they are," he worried. "But," he promised, "you will get no such mythology here."[6] Third, Flood accounted for the complications of the well-paid slave's blackness by identifying a form of bondage provocative enough to induce the awakening of his colleagues but abstract enough to make their fight against the reserve clause seem plausible and worthwhile. This close analysis of *The Way It Is* argues that Flood attempted to make double-consciousness available to his white playing colleagues, a process that entailed shedding his blackness and defining the well-paid slave as an agent of incremental reform.

In 1969, his last season playing baseball for the St. Louis Cardinals, Flood had earned a salary of $90,000. After being traded to the Phillies, their general manager, John Quinn, made him a contract offer of $100,000 for the 1970 season, an amount intentionally designed to flatter Flood by placing him into a symbolic category of elite baseball wage earners. Flood listened politely to Quinn but rejected his proposal in favor of the lawsuit. In *The Way It Is*, Flood commented indignantly about the manner in which the press portrayed his rejection of the Philadelphia offer:

> Comparatively few newspaper, radio, and television journalists seemed able to understand what I was doing. That a ball player would pass up a $100,000 a year was unthinkable. The player's contention that he was trying to serve a human cause was somehow unbelievable. Who had ever heard of anyone giving up $100,000 for a principle? For them, the only plausible explanation was derangement. Or perhaps I was a dupe of Marvin Miller. And, in any case, I would surely show up in time for spring training. I wasn't that crazy. As a matter of fact, more than one newsman nudged my ribs with his elbow and winked conspiratorially about the money he thought I might blackmail from the Phillies with this suit. I began to wonder if the whole goddamned country wasn't infected with moral corruption. Some of the same people who criticized me for threatening the Good of the Game made it clear that they would respect my acumen if I abandoned the Players Association, disavowed honor and signed for a higher salary than the Phillies had previously offered.[7]

Flood implied that the press' preoccupation with the size of his salary was not simply indicative of a failure to understand his motivations properly but that a larger, foundational moral failure rendered the substance of his challenge incoherent in the world reporters wrote into being. *Humanity, principle*, and *honor* would always be a ruse in baseball's public sphere—how could they help unless they lined one's pockets? For Flood, these terms characterized the world in which he hoped his speech could be understood. His commentary on the press was more than a contrast in values; it was an attempt to reorder the space in which discourse about him would circulate.

From the beginning, Flood attempted to revise common knowledge regarding his lawsuit specifically by revising the public understanding of baseball more broadly. This strategy entailed establishing his perspective as a baseball insider and then presenting insights about baseball's "ideology" that were possible only from the insider's point of view. He assumed the role of an informant, a kind of whistle-blower, making his case according to a sequence of damning revelations by repeatedly characterizing baseball as "show business." Flood detailed "the mythology in which" Major League Baseball's owners "swaddle the minds of their customers and employees." He continued, "After decades of such bullshit, the loyal fan knows exactly as much and no more about the inner workings of baseball as the industry deems advisable. Which is not very much and often is besides the point. To understand baseball at all, and make reasonable demands of it, the fan must bear in mind that baseball is show business."[8] What would follow, then, emerged as the truth behind a public lie, a dirty trick meant to keep the public in the dark.[9]

John Haiman uses the stage metaphor to explain the function of sarcasm, a trope that bears close relation to irony: "The sarcast perceives only two versions of reality: that which obtains on the stage among the characters where he or she pretends to be and that which obtains for the playwright in real life, where the sarcast really stands. The sarcast's perspective is that of the know-it-all wiseguy, who rolls his eyes while he mouths the lines of his 'role,' demonstrating that he appreciates their absurdity."[10] Flood's position as a baseball insider, as a disgruntled purveyor of baseball's mythology, allowed him to fit easily into the role of the sarcast. Flood admitted, "Like other showfolk, the player usually understands the commercial necessity of kidding the public. He is willing enough to cooperate in that regard if only to be in on the joke. What burns him is the awareness that certain of his contributions to the fables of baseball strengthen the employer's position and weaken his own."[11] So weakened by the capriciousness of baseball owners and the ideological effects of their public narrative, Flood became the playwright who mouthed the absurd lines of the baseball player, thus inviting his addressees to measure the difference between the show and what was occurring backstage.

Sarcasm was, in this sense, the figurative centerpiece of *The Way It Is*. Flood offered a lengthy and acerbic description of baseball owners and the relationship they were said to cultivate with players:

> These dedicated men are custodians of a great tradition, the slightest neglect of which would plunge the entire United States into degradation. Their gravest concern is the Good of the Game. With this in mind, they maintain constant vigil over the integrity of the game—its competitive honesty and fairness. And they cultivate the Image of the Game, having realized long ago that what the public perceives, or thinks it perceives, need not always correspond to reality. If reality becomes an inconvenience, it can be camouflaged.
>
> Everyone in baseball plays a structured role in the promotional rites that emphasize the integrity, enhance the Image and consolidate the Good of the Game. On camera or within earshot of working reporters, the behaved player is an actor who projects blissful contentment, inexhaustible optimism and abiding attitude.
>
> "I'll sweep out the clubhouse to stay here," he says. "I love the game. I owe everything to baseball. I am thankful to this grand organization for giving me my big chance. I'm in love with this town and its wonderful fans. Even though I had kind of a slow start, I think I'm getting it all together now. I expect to have a big year."[12]

Flood spoke in two sarcastic voices: first, in the voice of the owners who pompously asserted their paternalist responsibilities, and second, in the voice of a player whose public persona was enacted in recitations of gratitude. Flood's mention of the press ("on camera or within earshot of working reporters") operated as the setting within which this inauthentic exchange was said to occur. Imagining a promotional conspiracy designed to shape public perception of baseball, Flood issued an exhaustive indictment of baseball's mode of circulating discourse. Flood delivered a public warning by lending sarcastic utterance to the dialogue that gave rhetorical life to a public lie.

The extent of Flood's sarcasm cannot be overstated, both in terms of its frequency and its vituperative quality. For example, the introductory chapter of *The Way It Is* closes with Flood anxious at home in March 1970, frustrated by a craving for baseball. Seeking catharsis and moving restlessly though his apartment, he settled on reading his mail, an experience he shared with graphic insight:

Three letters for me. A child begging for an autographed picture. An old ballplayer wishing me luck. And the third, on lined paper torn from a notebook, began with "Dear Nigger."

The animal informed me that if it were not for the great game of baseball I would be chopping cotton or pushing a broom. And that I was a discredit to my race. By definition, any black hurts his people if he is other than abjectly, supinely, hand-lickingly grateful for having been allowed to earn a decent living.

I assembled a martini, very dry. I probably had spoiled the animal's breakfast. I might even have ruined his day. No doubt it had started splendidly, with a front page full of grand news about undesirable elements being bombed, shot, incinerated, beaten, arrested, suspended, expelled, drafted, and otherwise coped with here and abroad. Then he must have turned to the sporting page, where horror confronted him. Curt Flood had sued baseball on constitutional grounds. If the newspaper was typical, it lied that a victory for Flood would mean the collapse of our national pastime. God profaned! Flag desecrated! Motherhood defiled! Apple pie blasphemed! The animal was furious. Them niggers is never satisfied.[13]

The details of this story may well be apocryphal, but the record of events was not the point. Flood constructed characters, with "the animal's" speaking performance defined by an expression of racist entitlement and unthinking devotion to baseball's nationalist image. The sarcasm required to reveal this figure invited a view of his antagonists at work, offering "the animal's" own words in place of a deeply repugnant truth. For a moment, Flood addressed race directly by concluding the allegory with this often underestimated observation: "I am pleased that God made my skin black, but I wish he had made it thicker."[14]

Flood's gesture toward blackness in his sarcastic rhetoric disclosed something that he believed was sustained by a thematic consonance with the racist discourses of the late 1960s and early 1970s. He said, "The hypocrisies of the baseball industry could not possibly have been sustained unless they were symptoms of a wider affliction. Wherever I turned, I found fresh evidence that this was so. Baseball was socially relevant, and so was my rebellion against it."[15] This assertion of social context, that baseball's situation was symptomatic of larger issues, helped Flood turn his sarcastic gaze toward critical ways of seeing predisposed to sympathy with his cause. Contrasting sarcasm with unintentional forms of irony, Haiman says, "the playwright sees both the message and the metamessage; so do the elect among the audience; the characters in the play itself, however, do not."[16] Personifying "the animal," Flood was not addressing baseball owners, their sympathizers, or even racists. "The animal" was a character that delivered a metamessage that, combined with ambiguous gestures toward a "wider affliction," solicited addressees in possession of critical vocabularies. *The Way It Is* operated like a discursive party crasher, speaking to those who could identify with his "rebellion" because they were accustomed to seeing the world in the same way. The cynic who knew how to roll her eyes in disgust at the hypocrisies of "God and country" might be the same cynic who would roll her eyes at the "Good of the Game." Various forms of opposition working against injustice in 1970 could be summoned to his cause if his idiomatic cynicism could find quarter in their discourses.

For *The Way It Is* to work, the players had to come to view themselves as principled and reasonable, as both appreciative of the opportunity to play ball for a living and aware of the basic need to challenge the imbalances in baseball's labor market. Flood could encourage this self-conception provided that he avoid making his racial identity a threat to the broader cause. *Are you doing this because you're black?* Tom Haller was not a racist, but he also was not Malcolm X. Exactly what motivated Flood was for the next two years subject to open debate, but the discussion rarely involved his blackness. Nonetheless, recent storytellers have attempted to reclaim Flood's racial argument. Among "three factors that emerged to influence Flood's decision," Michael Lomax argues that "the first was black rage." Lomax puts Flood's challenge into the context of Black Power. Though Lomax recognizes that "the slogan's meaning was contingent upon who defined it," he locates Flood's story next to widespread "disillusionment" among professional black athletes regarding "racism and structural inequality" in sport, asserting that "the same angry mood permeated Curt Flood's autobiography."[17] Brad Snyder makes a similar case about Flood's motivations, alternatively suggesting that Flood's end of the Puerto Rico conversation was simply disingenuous. Snyder insists that Flood's "answer to Haller's question was technically correct—the reserve clause did affect players of all races—but the answer avoided the lifetime of motivations behind his lawsuit."[18]

Other contemporary observers focus on Flood's "sensitivity" to help resolve this apparent dissonance. Alex Belth's 2006 biography of Flood situates the Haller exchange in such a way: "Flood acknowledged that being black made him especially sensitive to the inequalities of the current system. He admitted that he had become increasingly aware of this during the past several years as black consciousness influenced African Americans around the country. But he made it clear that his action was not motivated by race. He was acting as a ballplayer for the benefit of other players, for whom he was prepared to risk his career."[19] Snyder suggests the same: "Flood explained that as a black man he had experienced many hardships in baseball, hardships that made him more sensitive to injustice than the average white player. Yet, he was not suing baseball as a black man; he was suing as a major league ballplayer."[20] Though loyal to the letter of Flood's comments, "sensitivity" operates here as little more than a reason to reduce race to marginalia. But race meant much more to Flood. Or, perhaps more to the point, it meant something far more insightful: It meant that Flood could identify the discourses that signaled oppressive relationships when he heard them, and it also meant that he could perform them for show.

Calling *The Souls of Black Folk* an "incipient theoretical position about the nature of race and its pervasive role in society," Kirt Wilson argues that W. E. B. Du Bois "demonstrates the power of one individual who embraced the veil [of race] and double-consciousness and used them for critical production."[21] In the opening pages of *Souls*, Du Bois wrote,

> After the Egyptian and Indian, the Greek and Roman, the Teuton and Mongolian, the Negro is a sort of seventh son, born with a veil and gifted with second-sight in this American world,—a world which yields him no true self-consciousness, but only lets him see himself through the revelation of the other world. It is a peculiar sensation, this double-consciousness, this sense of always looking at one's self through the eyes of others, of measuring one's soul by the tape of a world that looks on in amused contempt and pity. One ever feels his two-ness,—an American, a Negro; two souls, two thoughts, two unreconciled strivings; two warring ideals in one dark body, whose dogged strength alone keeps it from being torn asunder.[22]

Du Bois's veil works well as a metaphor for the material and social divisions between blacks and whites in America. Translucently partitioning a common American space, it operates as a boundary that marks the social limits of blackness. In this sense, the veil is the structure of racism. By linking the veil to consciousness, Du Bois shows how it ensures that "the Negro" will acquire a self-image aligned with racism's demands. Du Bois allows a momentary glimmer of promise in his description. Although the veil describes the psychic condition of ostracism, "the Negro" is "gifted with second-sight in this American world." Seeing oneself through the veil provides one with the ability to see the stuff of which the veil is made. Seeing oneself through the eyes of the other permits one to see what the other sees; such is the gift of double-consciousness. By locating this condition within consciousness, Du Bois establishes an array of critical possibilities that rely on ways of seeing, ways of listening, ways of speaking, and ways of knowing. This "peculiar sensation, this double-consciousness" sees racist circumstances, hears racist discourse, is capable of uttering it, and therefore knows, through its inescapable intimacy with the other, precisely what racism is. The irony of double-consciousness, or what gives the veil its double valence, is that the "gift" comes at a costly price. Delivered by an oppressive agent, such "second sight" germinates only when fertilized by racism.

In Du Bois's poetic allegory "Of the Coming of John," the eponymous character leaves the innocence of his rural southern home to acquire an education. He works against an impoverished childhood to succeed in prep school and then college, leaving home physically and psychically. In New York, John finds himself ejected from a theater by his boyhood friend, the "white John," an incident that punctuates a series of experiences alerting John to the veil of race. In a moment of climactic indignation, John resolves to return to Georgia to educate and enlighten his family and friends. They had once spoken wistfully "of the coming of John," but hardened by his experiences with race in the North, John had discovered the veil and had come to exhibit the bitterness and cynicism of double-consciousness. Returning home, John's attempt to induce a social awakening was met with derision and scorn by a community that preferred the comforts of its religious traditions.

Wilson's account of "Of the Coming of John" focuses on a conversation between John and his sister, Jennie, after his return to Georgia:

Long they stood together, peering over the gray unresting water.

"John," she said, "does it make every one—unhappy when they study and learn lots of things?"

He paused and smiled, "I'm afraid it does," he said.

"And, John, are you glad you studied?"

"Yes," came the answer, slowly but positively.

She watched the flickering lights upon the sea, and said thoughtfully, "I wish I was unhappy,—and—and," putting both arms about his neck, "I think I am, a little, John."[23]

Although John's awakening occurs primarily as a consequence of his education in the North, his experiences help to mediate Jennie's transition to double-consciousness back in Georgia. But, says Wilson, "it is not easy to understand the discourse that categorizes you as different and labels you as a problem, but unhappiness is preferable to ignorance. If a person does not see herself through the eyes of the oppressor then she will be trapped without the knowledge of that imprisonment."[24] Seeing oneself through the eyes of the oppressor entails a self-understanding defined by one's imprisonment. Once this self-understanding is achieved, innocence is replaced by enlightened incredulity, and happiness is replaced by angry motivation to resist.

In *The Way It Is*, Flood offers a narrative of racial experience similar to Du Bois's John. Like John, Flood begins his story in a small, naive world, discovers racism away from home, and adopts a double-consciousness expressed in bitterness and cynicism. Like John, Flood enacts his double-consciousness by identifying the discourses that mark oppressive circumstances. And though the moral of John's story centers on his frustration in imparting double-consciousness to the black residents of Altahama, Georgia, the moral of Flood's story centers on his attempt to bear witness to oppression through the veil of race. At the conclusion of Du Bois's allegory, John desires to return to the North. At the conclusion of *The Way It Is*, Flood desires to return to baseball.

In early March 1970, he admitted to self-destructive behavior: "I withdrew to a couch and consulted the beer. My body protested. It was not programmed for a morning beer in a St. Louis apartment on a sunny March 2. Years of habit had established a seasonal craving for other pursuits and a different setting." He looked out his window and shared his nineteenth-floor view. After a reverent visual description of the famous Gateway Arch, erected by "leading citizens of St. Louis," Flood's prose became acidic:

> The wicket celebrates the city's geographic and historic good fortune as a gateway to the West. It stands also as an emblem of local and national priorities. A scant few blocks away are some of the most horrible slums in the United States. And barely yards from the arch is the old courthouse in which Dred Scott sued for his freedom. From the shattered windows of the worst of the slums—the government sponsored ghetto called Pruitt-Igoe—10,000 inheritors of old Dred's disappointment are free to enjoy superb views of the arch and to draw what conclusions they will. Their proximity to the city's glinting

symbol of unconcern was especially educational during the merciless winter of 1969–70, when Pruitt-Igoe heating pipes burst, ice mantled the floors and subzero temperatures punished the residents for their helplessness.[25]

What emerges from this passage is Flood's expression of poetic sadness, made possible by a combination of sarcastic insight and racialized second sight. This might have been John's description of New York.

In an early chapter, "Your Grandfather and I," Flood's recollections give voice to his childhood and offer an interpretation of U.S. social history through his experiences "in the conventionally squalid West Oakland [California] ghetto where" he grew up, where "most other households seemed worse off. To achieve these triumphs of stability, my parents held not fewer than four underpaid jobs at a time." As he looks back through the veil of race, he notices the ignorant contentment of home. Trying to remember his reaction to *Brown v. Board of Education* in 1954, he says, "By then I was sixteen. I think that I would have been aware of local reaction, had there been much. Just as the ghetto warps its victims, it also insulates and lulls them."[26] As he looked back, he saw the ghetto not as a place of angry resistance or even as a source of the rebellious spirit he would enact in 1970. Instead, the West Oakland ghetto was a place of misrecognized innocence in which the veil of race was hidden from view.

Propaganda blared in abundance, though. Now a well-rehearsed sarcast, Flood remembers, "Every child in the grammar and junior high schools was black. In the national tradition, the curriculum spared us the truth about our heritage. We had once been slaves, the teachers reminded, but now we were free. If anything went wrong, we had only ourselves to blame. Everybody rise and sing *Oh Beautiful for Spacious Skies.*" Flood's incantation of patriotic hymn demonstrates how the veil of race operated as an ideological mask. The "truth" of black heritage, Flood presumably discovered, is that race operates to distribute authority unevenly. "We saw few whites," he remembers, "none was a bearer of joy. The landlord, storekeeper, cop, teacher, meter reader and the various bill collectors were all enforcers. We accepted their presence, much as a Seminole accepts alligators. They were hazards too familiar for urgent comment. We were so accustomed to things as they were that we seldom speculated about how things ought to have been. When a teacher announced from her remote eminence that the United States was the champion of liberty and the benefactor of world mankind, we scarcely reacted."[27]

Concretely describing his position on American race relations, Flood inverts another platitude: "To be sure, black experience teaches that the American white is guilty until he proves himself innocent. No present reason exists to modify this axiom. Our country's prospects might improve if the guilty were less abundant." This gesture toward experience is pivotal to *The Way It Is*. Though uttered in passing, it clarifies Flood's sense of perspective. The essential point is that his memory of his past allowed him to measure the difference between experience and expression. Even when he found the baseball field and his talents on it, Flood refused to call it a sanctuary from racist violence; instead, baseball was the highlight of an ideologically poisoned existence: "I was headed for the crushing defeat that, in ghetto experience, awaited all strivers, all blacks who tried to better themselves. I did not think of it that way at all. I was not striving. I was just doing what I liked."[28] Experience, then, would teach him a lesson that could never be known inside the ghetto itself.

Soon after Flood signed his first professional baseball contract with the Cincinnati Reds in 1956, he was sent to Tampa, Florida, to participate in spring training. On the way there, he fantasized about the amenities at the opulent Floridian Hotel, where the Reds' team brochure promised a ballplayer's paradise. After arriving at the airport, however, Flood witnessed and experienced Jim Crow for the first time, and "the truth struck, like a door slammed in my face." After he reached the Floridian, a porter ushered him to Ma Felder's, a boardinghouse five miles away where the Reds' black players stayed. For Flood, this experience was formative and led him viscerally to social insight: "I was a good athlete and might have an opportunity to show it, but this incidental skill did not redeem me socially. Officially and for the duration, I was a nigger."[29]

In Flood's rich history of his Minor League experiences in the South, one parable from High Point, North Carolina, in 1956 stands out as a crystallized expression of his racial learning process.

> Toward midseason, when I had established myself as a star, I attended to another matter of importance. During the pregame practice one evening, a little black kid jumped onto the field, grabbed a loose ball, and climbed back into the stands. One of our lint-head pitchers screamed, "Hey you black nigger, come back with that ball!" Then he jumped into the stands, took the ball from the child and returned to the field, flushed with triumph. I was waiting for him.

"Don't use that word around me," I said. "You owe me more respect than that. White kids steal baseballs all the time without interference, you wool-hat son-of-a-bitch. If you ever come near me again you'll be sorry."

I would have killed him without regret. I was hoping that he would swing at me, but he skulked off and gave me a wide berth for the rest of the season. His peers became more civil now that they sensed my rage. By the end of the year I had even begun to adjust to the abuse from the stands. I had developed explanations for the behavior of the fans. They were little men. The opportunity to insult a baseball player made them grow a few inches. They were not worth my contempt. Who cared about them? And so forth. None of these rationalizations could have stood close scrutiny, but they worked. I became cooler and cooler. When you have answered insult and rejection with a .340 batting average, you have done something more than philosophical. Especially when you are sure that your achievements have emancipated you from North Carolina for keeps. I believe that I would have quit baseball rather than return there.[30]

Despite his physical proximity to his teammates, Flood distanced himself by producing rationalizations that allowed him to sustain his self-image. He had acquired second sight.

Flood's narrative explicitly asserts this movement from innocence to enlightenment in a way similar to Du Bois's parable of John. Says Flood, "I had spent my boyhood in the shelter of the ghetto and in the isolation of the baseball park. I truly did not know, I did not know in my bones that I had been discriminated against from birth. Fully to *know* and feel the penalties of blackness, I would have to experience something new, the onslaught of the outside world. But I did not even know that." Moreover, social awakening had made his playing baseball coextensive with social resistance. Of his year in the Carolina League, he recalls, "If I did not sabotage the team (and I never did), it was only because I had been playing baseball too long and too well to discredit myself. And I was too black. Pride was my resource. I solved my problem by playing my guts out. I ran myself down to less than 135 pounds in the blistering heat. I completely wiped out that peckerwood league. I led it in everything but home runs—although I hit 29. I played in all 154 games. I batted .340, driving in 128 runs with 190 hits. The better I did, the tougher I got. I no longer wept in my room."[31] As coolness begat toughness, Flood's response

was to turn blackness into a shelter for his identity. Refusing the dehumanization into which baseball's racism had invited him, Flood detached himself
from his social circumstances and copped a cynic's pose.

Du Bois narrates John's experience with the veil of race in terms that
foreground his entry into a racist society and that turn on the attitudinal shift
entailed by the self-understanding racism induces. Du Bois says of John,

> He had left his queer thought-world and come back to a world of
> motion and of men. He looked now for the first time sharply about
> him, and wondered he had seen so little before. He grew slowly to
> feel almost for the first time the Veil that lay between him and the
> white world; he first noticed now the oppression that had not seemed
> oppression before, differences that erstwhile seemed natural, restraints
> and slights that in his boyhood days had gone unnoticed or been
> greeted with a laugh. He felt angry now when men did not call him
> "Mister," he clenched his hands at the "Jim Crow" cars, and chafed at
> the color-line that hemmed in him and his. A tinge of sarcasm crept
> into his speech, and a vague bitterness into his life; and he sat long
> hours wondering and planning a way around these crooked things.[32]

John noticed oppression and felt the veil only after leaving his home and
entering the world. As with Flood, sarcasm became a stylistic response to
John's recognition of the veil of race. And like John, Flood plotted a way
around crooked things. As experiences with race induced the quickening
of double-consciousness, both men became individuals with expertise in
social critique.

Cal Fussman's *After Jackie: Pride, Prejudice, and Baseball's Forgotten
Heroes: An Oral History*, focuses briefly on Flood, concentrating on the
loneliness of his fight. Fussman describes what he sees as a defining moment
in Flood's changing consciousness: Flood was playing in High Point and
had to wait naked in the clubhouse before a game while his uniform was
delivered from a cleaner "on the black side of town" because the clubhouse
manager refused to wash Flood's uniform in the same machine as the white
players' jerseys. Fussman asserts that this was a defining moment in Flood's
changing consciousness: "One thing is certain: His thoughts were unlike
those of any other ballplayers in the clubhouse that day." And when none
of Flood's baseball contemporaries would testify on his behalf in federal
court, Fussman says, Flood "was as alone and naked as he had been in that
minor league clubhouse."[33]

Judy Pace, a black Hollywood icon and Flood's second wife, confirms Fussman's view of Flood's consciousness:

> When you think about it, it's not surprising that a black man did this. A white man was not going to have that consciousness. A white man was not walking around thinking, My rights are always being penalized.
>
> That's what Curt called it—the penalty of being black. There were always penalties for being black. If you never had that inflicted on you, then you might think everything was okay.
>
> If you were a white baseball player, you might think, I'm doing something that some people would give their second child for—a chance to play major league baseball. Why stir things up?[34]

She presents an important distinction between Flood and white players that both highlights the epistemic advantages of Flood's blackness and illustrates the difficulties that his public argument faced. The penalties of blackness, Flood seemed to indicate in *The Way It Is*, presented the resources for knowing unjust circumstances. In this account, white players lacked this perspective and would be prone to the fanciful and romantic discourses that secured baseball's exploitive hierarchy. Flood would be fighting formidable obstacles in justifying the way he stirred things up, particularly after he described himself as a well-paid slave; white players (and thereby Flood) could benefit from double-consciousness, but they would not come to acquire it easily.

Taken unreflectively, the slave metaphor was a symbolic accusation that implicated his white colleagues in the reserve clause's original sin and amplified the anxieties of those worried about white backlash. But the "well-paid slave" was also a symbolic invitation to his white baseball colleagues to occupy the conscious space from which racialized second sight obtained its view. Its dramatic potential offered a powerful discursive resource to the criticisms on the minds of other baseball insiders. Flood seemed to hope that both black and white ballplayers were insiders. Bound by their enslavement to enact their own subordination in disgruntled hosannas to the "Good of the Game," Flood attempted to ignite their identification of the rhetorical tricks that black Americans like he were conditioned by experience to see.

For Flood, the trade to Philadelphia was a breaking point, a critical exigency that demanded finally a righteous and unconditional refusal. The lawsuit, his failure to report to the Phillies, his refusal to sign a contract in 1970, and even his subsequent flight to Europe were certainly subversive acts relative to baseball's latest and presumably most egregious imposition. As someone willing to do something special, Flood asserted his qualifications to speak for all baseball players and to act on their behalf. In embracing his martyrdom, Flood affirmed his view of the situation from a collective consciousness gifted with second sight but now deprived of the racial content previously essential to its reckonings.

The figure of the slave helped to clarify the meaning of blackness relative to his American experiences. One of the reasons that blackness provided an exceptional form of social insight, according to *The Way It Is*, was that American slavery modeled the same type of dehumanization imposed by baseball. Flood elaborated,

> I probably cannot influence those whites who complain that they are tired of feeling guilty about what their grandfathers did to my grandfathers, but I can at least suggest that they stop making idiotic comparisons between my people and European immigrants. I think it wholesome to bear in mind that American statute and unlegislated custom not only enslaved my people but outlawed their languages, their religions and their expressions of group and individual dignity. Including their desire to form abiding family relationships. They were bred like cattle. It is inspiring that so many survived with their finer feelings intact, after a century of emancipation in which color has been the badge of ineligibility. To hell with your grandfather, baby. Just get out of the way.[35]

The distinction between Flood's "people" and European immigrants provided a historical grounding for the exceptionalism of black consciousness. Flood provides a view of slavery by illustrating its effects on the enslaved: "They were bred like cattle." Black slaves were, in other words, not just forced to work but also treated as less than human; social ineligibility paid dehumanization forward. As Brad Snyder says of the well-paid slave, "He wanted to feel like a person and not an object. As a black man, he expressed those feelings *in terms* of slavery."[36] Snyder's interpretation of Flood's feelings is well-intended and probably correct. However, Snyder easily separates blackness from the truth of Flood's argument, when it seems that from another angle, blackness made his critique of baseball possible from the start.

Moreover, Flood was not among those who valorized baseball as a mirror of racial progress or as a necessary beacon of social advancement. The racism he experienced in the minors had faded away on the Cardinals, a team, according to Flood, composed of "Latins, blacks, liberal whites and redeemed peckerwoods, the best team in the game and the most exultant. Victorious on the field and victorious off it, by God." Indeed, the Cardinals operated as a utopian image: "A beautiful little foretaste of what life will be like when Americans finally unshackle themselves." But Flood's utopia was not the same as Jackie Robinson's, located in the transforming minds of individuals witnessing the unexpected athletic achievements of a black man. Rather, Flood's allegory of racial harmony was located in the relationships Cardinals players formed through concrete social experience. Bonded by mutual appreciation for each other's fundamentally human qualities, the Cardinals achieved what Flood calls "true team spirit." But it was precisely baseball's "show," its part in the shallow politics of racial progress, that compromised the model: "Having demonstrated our ability to help win ball games, and having disproved the theory that our complexions would repel white trade, we blacks seemed to have reached our zenith. We were being allowed to play major-league baseball! We were being allowed to 'prove' that any black kid could get ahead in this enlightened society if he would only try! What more could we possibly wish? Or, as cranky whites asked when things began to heat up in the United States during the sixties, 'What do you people want?'"[37] Flood refused the standard political symbolism of his blackness because integration did not eliminate dehumanization from baseball's social composition. Instead, baseball exploited integration into an empty spectacle of progressive promises. With additional sarcasm, Flood performed the relationship of subordination and domination experienced between the black baseball player and the "cranky white." Flood essentially issued an alert to his baseball colleagues: *If you hear this, you are hearing the voice of the oppressor.*

Assuming a didactic tone in the second half of *The Way It Is,* Flood explained the epistemic privileges afforded by double-consciousness and explicitly asserted his credentials to organize a pedagogy of discursive oppression: "I was an expert in baseball's spurious paternalism. I was a connoisseur of its grossness." Armed with intellectually effective cynicism, Flood recalled his reaction to Cardinals owner Gussie Busch's diatribe on the labor disputes in the winter of 1969: "He had a fit. Profanity rattled the windows and turned the air blue (it is possible to be baronial and earthy at the same time). Labor annoyances were not what he had envisioned when he took up baseball. They could not be classified as wholesome sport. They were no fun at all. They boded ill for the future of the game. What would become of the fans? The fans! Mr. Busch decided to attack us in behalf of the fans." This characterization of Busch, which sarcastically utters the empty appeal to the "Good of the Game," finds a crucial formal consonance with the "cranky white" that demonstrates the depravity behind the owners' most trusted public argument:

> As I interpret baseball's recital of its financial woes, the [financial] situation is peachy for the fans and the players, but the owners bear a heavy load. All that stands between the Good of the Game and utter havoc is the [reserve clause]. Should a court order, a Congressional statute or players strike weaken the owners' control of their livestock, the game might perish.
> According to this pessimistic theory, if baseball players were as free to shop for employment as actors are, the richest club would hire all the stars, making a shambles of every pennant race. The implication is that some teams are too poor to compete for talent in an open market. The present reserve system protects them from that catastrophe. Reduced to its essentials, the argument suggests that baseball players now subsidize their employers by working at cut rates. And that the courts, Congress and the public should perpetuate this unique state of affairs. For the Good of the Game.[38]

The "Good of the Game" delivered on the inevitability of Flood's alert. Once again saying what *they* would say, Flood revealed that the reserve clause was a dehumanizing state of affairs. This strategy depended on a sequence of homologies: Just like the master/slave relation and the black ballplayer/racist fan relation, that between player and owner was unfair, dehumanizing, and sustained by false public claims.

Enacting the range of critical possibilities available to "the connoisseur," Flood took a view of baseball that echoed the empty promise of the brochure for the opulent hotel in 1957. Recalling his request to Cincinnati Reds management for a salary raise in 1957, Flood dramatized the logic of the conversation:

> He agreed that I had done a pretty fair job, for a beginner. But confidentially, the club's expenses were dangerously out of hand. Son, the Reds were in deep trouble. They simply did not have the money, son.

To keep the team alive, we all had to tighten our belts and be patient. At the same time we had to develop ourselves as rapidly as possible, so that we could bring a National League pennant to Cincinnati and make money for us all. Those who put their shoulders to the wheel would be rewarded. Son, make no mistake about it. He was confident that he could count on my good sense. He was confident that I would realize that I was not yet ready for the major leagues, and that my most significant contribution to the well-being of the club would come by working hard, seeing the big picture, taking the long view and not becoming impatient. The constructive thing to do was sign a 1957 contract for $4,000, accept promotion to a higher minor league and do my very, very best. I wanted to be well thought of. I agreed.[39]

In hindsight, the abandonment of his demands affirmed the rhetoric of gratitude and thus enacted his subordination. This, in fact, was exactly how baseball conditioned its employees to regard themselves.

Flood offered his conversation with management as a model of shared experience with other players. Recalling the his reaction when learning that he had been traded to Philadelphia, which Flood describes as "the nation's northernmost southern city," he expands the scope of his concern: "I was no longer bothered by Philadelphia, as such. I was thinking more clearly. The problem was no particular city but was the reserve clause, which afflicted all players equally no matter where."[40] In addition to asserting the universality of the principle for which he would sacrifice his career, Flood inserts "all players," "no matter where," into the position from which ideological discourse could be identified. Put differently, Flood sutured white baseball players into the critical standpoint entailed by double-consciousness. Every baseball player had engaged in salary negotiations with an employer, and all had been subject to indignities. Although Flood's arrival at double-consciousness was racialized and intensely personal, by sarcastically performing management's duplicitous speech, Flood verbalizes the inchoate connoisseurship of paternalism that he hoped "all players equally no matter where" latently possessed.

In February 1971, after missing a full year of baseball to his court case, Flood reluctantly agreed to a one-year contract for $110,000 to play for the Washington Senators. Because he needed to prove a monetary loss to keep his case in federal court, the attorneys involved agreed to stipulate that the new contract would not be used at trial and that the loss of the full 1970 season would constitute his claim to damages. Though he would leave the

Senators on a late-night flight to Spain in mid-April, never to return to base-ball, his signing was greeted with curious anticipation by the Washington sports press. Flood had been signed in the winter 1971 along with pitcher Denny McLain, a former all-star with Detroit who had been suspended for three months in the 1970 season as a result of his involvement in gam-bling. When asked by the press about the Senators' additions of Flood and McLain, Washington owner Bob Short reportedly said, "I never would've had any chance at all to get them if they weren't tarnished." Taking rigorous exception to this description, Flood delivered a line of rhetorical questions to reporter Milton Richman: "They have called Denny McLain and myself 'bad boys' right along. Who determines that? Is it the sportswriters? Is it the commissioner? Is it the American public?"[41] As he did elsewhere, Flood attended closely to the power of public speech. At the center of his criticism was the way that ownership imposed uninvited forms of identity on base-ball players. Calling a player "tarnished" affirmed the perceptions required to assure the owners' position of dominance.

Similarly, owners often expressed worry that the abolition of the reserve clause would lead to "tampering," a situation in which predatory owners would attempt to negotiate contracts with players currently signed to other teams. Flood closely examines the implications of this term:

> Furthermore, I resent the use of the word tampering. One may attempt to influence the play of a professional athlete, but one does not "tamper" with him. One tampers with figures or a cash register, not with a human being. As usual, baseball's terminology betrays its essential attitudes, which are those of animal husbandry. Baseball regards us as sheep, livestock with which higher forms of life may tamper at will. No wonder we are conditioned to talk the way we do. In the pregame interview and in the postgame wrap-up, and finally in his nightmares, the player dutifully recites, "Baseball has been good to me. I love the game. Baseball has been good to me."[42]

Tampering indexed the owners' regard for the players as commodities, a regard constitutive of dehumanization. Flood explained that the players were compelled to harbor a consciousness that consigned them to abject subordination. As a purveyor of double-consciousness, as a connoisseur, Flood was uniquely positioned to reveal this relationship. In essence, he worried that baseball's dehumanizing vocabulary urged players to accept their own domination.

Just as Flood cannot be counted among those who understood baseball to be the meritocracy that myth held, he also cannot be counted among those who saw sport as intrinsically dehumanizing. Brad Snyder puts Flood's use of the slave metaphor near other contemporaneous notions. Muhammad Ali once said, "We're just like two slaves in that ring. The masters get two of us big black slaves and let us fight it out while they bet, 'My slave can whup your slave.' That's what I see when I see two black people fighting." Chip Oliver, a former pro football player, said that football "dehumanizes people. They've taken the players and made them into slabs of beef that can charge around and hit each other."[43] But after having lived within the social utopia of the Cardinal clubhouse, Flood's slave can not be likened to Ali's. Furthermore, since baseball's unmediated form provided him with an outlet for exercising his individual talents, making great achievements, and centering his desire for wealth and prominence, his slave also cannot be likened to Oliver's. Flood found dehumanization in the social structure of baseball's hierarchy and in the restrained status of his employment. It was not baseball as such that degraded, but rather its precise failure to fulfill its meritocratic promise that violated human dignity. Once double-consciousness revealed the truth of things, blackness receded from view.

Baseball was, after all, Flood's preferred means of earning a living. Toward the end of *The Way It Is*, Flood signals a series of retreats from his abolitionist claim. He argues that baseball players, having dedicated their lives and careers to the sport, genuinely hold the game's best interests in mind:

> He has played his heart out. He wants the industry to prosper. He wants to share in that prosperity now, and he probably hopes to make a place for himself in the game later on, being prepared for a life in baseball and little else. Through the Major League Baseball Players Association, he and his professional colleagues (with little dissent), have attempted to negotiate an improvement in the reserve system. Not Abolition. Improvement. . . . At this writing no negotiation of these proposals has been undertaken by the laggards of baseball. The year might as well be 1881, and James Abram Garfield the president of the United States.[44]

This is where *The Way It Is* landed. Not abolition. Improvement. The old men who ran the game, Flood seems to think, just refused to see what was *really* good for the game. Abolitionism, on this score, was merely a forced hand. Nothing was wrong with baseball except that it unequally distributed the wealth.

Further contrasting his principles to those represented in baseball's public sphere, Flood says, "One of the leading wags in the baseball establishment remarked that, unless Curt Flood were another Rembrandt, he'd show up in time to play for the Phillies and collect his pay. Members of that establishment, including its wags, were entirely incapable of understanding that a basic principle of human life was involved. More to the point, they recognized no principle so basic that it could not be nullified by payment of a few extra dollars."[45] Together, these statements constituted the rhetorical function of Flood's reliance on "principle" as the positive expression of his struggle. In moving from blackness to double-consciousness to life above the veil, Flood came to occupy a fixed point—a principle of human life. This principle was absolute and universal, and Flood's claim to it consisted of his sacrifice for it. His self-nomination to lead player opposition relied on both horns of this proposition. Flood's "specialness" relied on his self-effacement; he attempted to occupy a position of universal subjectivity by offering the sacrifice of his particularity. Flood was fit to lead the fight because, as he implied, he *was* the fight. Both committed to principle and animating the principle, Flood enacted the players' resistance.

Recalling his final decision to sue the owners, Flood writes, "It had been germinating in me for weeks. Sooner or later, someone would challenge baseball's right to treat human beings like used cars. 'I want to sue baseball on constitutional grounds,' I told [Marvin Miller]. His eyebrows rose. 'I want to give the courts a chance to outlaw the reserve system. I want to go out like a man instead of disappearing like a bottle cap.'"[46] Used cars and bottle caps were only two arrows in Flood's quiver of dehumanizing tropes. Offered as variations on an underlying theme, these metaphors describe the manner in which he imagines baseball to regard him. Neither a used car nor a bottle cap, Flood insists that he is a man, thus defining principle in the affirmation. On this score, principle inhered in the defense of human dignity.

The problem of dehumanization lay at the center of his rhetorical performance, but that did not mean that Flood could dismiss the owners' argument that abolition of the reserve clause would generate financial chaos. Flood deliberately expresses his concern for the general viability of baseball as a business. To accuse baseball owners of dehumanizing the players simply by virtue of their position as owners would undermine the fundamental moral case against the reserve clause. In other words, if baseball's institutional form were intrinsically dehumanizing, then Flood would have been foolish to seek greater access to its spaces. So he stresses that the players want baseball to survive, and he idealizes the social interaction of the Cardinal clubhouse. Despite the sarcastic acid dripping from the his use of *Good of the Game*, Flood painstakingly defends a far more compromising truth: He and the other players had an earnestly vested interest in the good of the game.

Fully developed, Flood's argument for abolition of the reserve clause critiques baseball's political economy with three basic points: first, baseball players earned an unfair share of the wealth created by the sport's commercial success; second, the reserve clause produced a restrictive labor market in which players were denied economic mobility; third, the opportunity costs for a baseball player were high relative to those for people in non-sporting professions, meaning that the reserve clause was disproportionately punitive. To prove the first point, Flood asserts that "baseball players' salaries are low, not high. Baseball players' salaries compare unfavorably with those of other athletic performers, like golfers, basketball players and boxers, most of whom are paid far higher percentages of the gross."[47] True or not, Flood's rationale was common to organized labor. He implies that the players, like "the workers," are largely responsible for creating baseball's wealth and thus deserve a fairer share.

Flood advances the second point by comparing baseball's labor market to those outside of sports. Using a variety of labor analogies, Flood finds baseball to be the only profession that dehumanized as a matter of routine: "A salesman reluctant to transfer from one office to another may choose to seek employment on the sales force of a different firm. A plumber can reject the dictates of his boss without relinquishing his right to plumb elsewhere. At the expiration of one contract, an actor shops among producers for the best arrangement he can find. But the baseball monopoly offers so such options to the athlete." Prevented from exercising self-determination in an open labor market, the baseball player is regarded as a commodity to be bought, sold, or traded. "If he elects not to work for the corporation that 'owns' his services," Flood observes, "baseball forbids him to ply his trade at all. In the hierarchy of living things, he ranks with poultry."[48] This, in the end, is how baseball dehumanizes: the reserve clause transforms players into corporate possessions. He might have said, "like slaves," but slavery itself found its way back to race quite too easily. The focus on baseball's institutional form allows dehumanization to appear without reference to race, vocation, or even social class.

The third point of his critique is particularly incisive. Flood enlarges the scope of his analogical reasoning and issues his final indictment of baseball's public sphere. Sports reporters are incapable of knowing his indignities because, Flood notes, they always have the option of working for another newspaper. This section of *The Way It Is* perhaps shows Flood at his poetic finest. He points out that the reporters who vilify him benefit from a freedom he lacks, so unlike every player in baseball worried about life after the game, reporters simply cannot understand the degradation entailed by the reserve clause:

> Under the ideological guidance of baseball's proprietors, an astonishingly high proportion of our sports reporters become incensed when a young man with the career expectancy of five years undermines the Good of the Game by holding out for a $25,000 salary. Admittedly, sports reporters do not usually get $25,000 a year from their own employers and, furthermore, are sometimes capable of larger contributions to society than might be expected from a journeyman ball player. If this kind of comparison is on their minds, as it seems to be, I wish they would carry it further.
>
> For example, a young reporter's career expectancy might well be forty years. If he decides to leave newspapering, or is discharged, his education and experience qualify him to enter a related field at no loss of pay. But the ball player who does not want to continue disemboweling himself for $15,000 a year may have very few alternatives. And the washed-up player often confronts a dead end. The last I heard of Sam Jones, an excellent pitcher for twelve years, he was considering a job in the West Virginia coal mines. It was not an executive position.[49]

Underscoring his selflessness by finding common cause with baseball's young, average, or less talented players, Flood points out that because baseball players enjoy a narrow window in which to exercise their profession, they require even more employment leverage than salesmen, plumbers, and actors. The professional circumstances in baseball were singularly precarious, and relative to workers in other industries, baseball players' opportunity costs make patience and gratitude prohibitively expensive.

Flood's claim that baseball's existence depended on dehumanizing labor exploitation led him inevitably to the matter of the term *slavery*, which appears only once in *The Way It Is*. The word was used in response to the owners' claim that baseball was economically fragile and that reserve clause modification would cause basic operations to unravel:

> The whole spiel is sheer humbug, of course. No major-league baseball corporation is presently in financial straits. If any were, it seems to me that subsidies should come not from the employees but from the suffering owner's fellow monopolists. Let them pass the hat. Or, if baseball be essential to the national morale, as its proprietors claim, the government itself might support the owners with grants or tax abatements, just as it supports railroads, airlines and oil wells. Unless I misread history, we have passed the stage when indentured servitude was justifiable on grounds that the employer could not afford the cost of normal labor.
>
> Which reminds me that the word *slavery* has arisen in connection to my lawsuit. I have been needled for using the word. Who ever heard of a $90,000-per-year slave? The idea is considered farcical. I concede that the condition of the major-league baseball player is closer to peonage than to slavery. Yet I am content to stand with the sentiments expressed in 1949 by Judge Jerome N. Frank of the U.S. Circuit Court of Appeals in the case of Danny Gardella, a player who had been victimized by the reserve system:
>
> "If the players be regarded as quasi-peons, it is of no moment that they are well paid. Only the totalitarian minded will believe that high pay excuses virtual slavery."[50]

Flood's analysis evokes the duplicitous and authoritarian logic he exposed in recollecting his contract negotiations with the Cincinnati Reds in 1957. Back then, Flood's desire to be "well thought of" addled his understanding of what actually transpired in his agreement to sign a contract for less than he believed his services were worth. In 1970, Flood possessed the consciousness to ask how and why it was justifiable for the owners to earn their profits at the expense of the players. Why must the "Good of the Game" depend on the players' sacrifice? The terms *slavery*, *peonage*, and *indentured servitude* were ideal for describing the condition in which "owners" held absolute control over the labor market, a control so expansive and total that the term *labor market* itself seemed to be the metaphor rather than the literal description. Indeed, the point had been made only four years earlier when future Hall of Fame pitchers Sandy Koufax and Don Drysdale sought unorthodox contracts with the Los Angeles Dodgers.[51] Without free or at least fair access to the labor market, and bound by a reserve clause that assigned ownership of his services to one employer for an indefinite duration, Flood identified himself as a slave.

The slave's racial history mattered little to the basic public argument, even though its invocation was a pivotal feature of *The Way It Is*. As an analogy, slavery illustrated the nature of the economic relationship between owners and players: As masters are to slaves, owners are to players. The condition of bondage was the analogy's inescapable point. As a metaphor, slavery presented a rich rhetorical resource through which the imagery of dehumanization obtains its visibility. Whether described as "chattel," "poultry," "IBM cards," "used cars," or "bottle caps," baseball players could be metaphorically imagined as inanimate objects moved capriciously through a economic system designed to promote the owners' wealth. Bondage and dehumanization as, respectively, the condition and consequence of slavery similarly characterized the condition and consequences of baseball's reserve clause. Flood's argument provided that the condition of bondage was sufficient grounds for identifying dehumanization. And although dehumanization consisted of a myriad of social circumstances, such as his unwanted trade to Philadelphia, the vested privileges of the owner did not have to be exercised for the dehumanizing relation to exist. Flood saw the slave fundamentally as the figurative embodiment of this argument, the rhetorical centerpiece of his critical description of baseball.

At the same time, the slave metaphor brought with it a symbolic minefield heavily planted with racial iconography. It is easy to lose track of Flood's blackness in the shuffle of his movement from racialized double-consciousness to the expression of a universal human principle. When Flood attended a Black Muslim meeting with Bob Gibson, Flood was turned off by his discoveries, "doubt[ing] that black pride need be accomplished by racism."[52] Be that as it may, the slave narrative held a unique position in Nation of Islam rhetoric, or at least in the oratory of Malcolm X, who often distinguished between the "house negro" and "field negro" to give voice to the experiences and interests of the black masses he claimed to represent. Relying on the image of slavery, Malcolm X said that "the house Negroes— they lived in the house with the master, they dressed pretty good, they ate good because they ate his food—what he left.... They would give their life to save the master's house—quicker than the master would." In contrast, "The field negro was beaten from morning to night; he lived in a shack, in a hut; he wore old castoff clothes. He hated his master.... When the master's house caught on fire he didn't try to put it out; that field negro prayed for a wind, for a breeze."[53] In sum, Malcolm X used this difference to offer a revolutionary subject position to economically disenfranchised black masses. The house negro symbolized what he understood to be the distorted views of the integrationist civil rights movement, while the field negro symbolized the attitude toward power structures proper to a revolutionary spirit. In his autobiography, Malcolm X illustrated the repugnant dynamic between the house negro and the slave master through a sarcastic utterance of the house negro's retreating political demand: "Please, lawdy, please, Mr. White Man, boss, would you push me off another crumb down from your table that's sagging with riches."[54] Turning down crumbs and refusing the indignity of gratitude, Malcolm X rhetorically fantasized an inferno.

Flood similarly refused the indignity of gratitude, but the burning of the master's house would have been counterproductive. Though he was self-sacrificial and strategically self-effacing when he had to be, he was not prone to self-immolation. Whereas Malcolm X proposed a division within black identity as a way of illuminating the errors of black liberalism, Flood collapsed the division between white identity and black identity to advance a fundamentally liberal claim. For Malcolm X, blackness was a unifying feature of social experience whose potential for political mobilization became poisoned through its complicity with the white progress narrative. Black identity was a given in Malcolm's slave narrative, but the slave's politics depended on the coziness of one's relationship with the master. The slave narrative, in this account, was useful to Malcolm for illustrating the subordinate indignity of the white liberal's reluctant surrender of a few unwanted scraps. Read against this version of "slavery," Flood's invocation seems to be an appeal for more of the boss' crumbs. Flood sought neither the abolition of baseball as such nor a revolution that installed players into the owners' previous position. After the fall of the reserve clause, Flood hoped, owners would still own and players would still play, but the distribution of the game's wealth would more fairly reflect the players' contributions. Above all, Flood wanted some of the riches, not a reversal of fortune.

. . .

From Flood's perspective, the problem with the Players Association was its entrenched willingness to assume a subservient position relative to the owners. Speaking of a labor dispute in 1961, Flood recalls, "In those days, the Association's primary problem was ignorance of the broad principles that govern fairness in employer-employee relationships. Whatever we had, we owed to the employer with abject gratitude. Whatever else we might get could be obtained only through his paternal kindness. He was a feudal lord and we were his humble petitioners."[55] Flood knew that the situation was changing, but summoning a collective will demanded careful reassurances. "Black consciousness" offered Flood the resources to marshal the consciousness borne of black experience as a foil for constructing a pedagogy of oppressive discursive practices.[56] In one pendular swing, blackness entered and exited. It appeared to reveal the facts of dehumanization and then disappeared when the facts were debated. It placed the reserve clause onto the agenda, but then its work was done. As sure as the race question baffles his biographers, it seemed to baffle Flood. He was Hamlet on race—did it matter, or didn't it?—attempting to elide its dilemmas through a sophisticated sense of humanism predicated on racialized double-consciousness. In the end, it seemed that he did not know where his argument would circulate, so he split differences and persisted with often frustrating ambiguity on the question of race.

The circulation of public discourse is not a theoretical phenomenon; to function properly it must literally find itself in new locations. Warner's elaboration of this idea is rich with useful metaphors: "Public discourse says not only 'Let a public exist,' but 'Let it have this character, speak this way, see the world in this way.' It then goes in search of confirmation that such a public exists, with greater or lesser success—success being further attempts to cite, circulate, and realize the world understanding it articulates. Run it up a flagpole and see who salutes. Put on a show and see who shows up."[57] To work as a strategic document—to manage public opinion in a way favorable to Flood's cause—*The Way It Is* would have to audition for circulation through the places that mattered. Sarcasm was certainly part of this audition, since it created the distance necessary to see the world anew. *The Way It Is* could confirm the existence of such a public, an audience of like-minded observers, only to the extent that it found its way into spaces that might see the world in the same way: shaded by irony, dissimulation, and pretense. When Flood's blackness became part of his show, when black became a primary color in the flag being run up the pole, *The Way It Is* sought a unique and hopeful circulatory lifeworld. The black public sphere had things to say about false promises.

3

Jackie Robinson and the Rhetoric of the Black Press

One theme that persists in the contemporary retelling of Curt Flood's story is that sportswriters working for major U.S. newspapers in the early 1970s pandered to baseball owners and helped codify the claim that abolition of the reserve clause would destroy baseball. After having seen what was written in newspapers such as the *Sporting News* and the *St. Louis Post Dispatch*, Flood worried in *The Way It Is* about what the public would think about his contract for the following year with the Washington Senators: "Many fans would surely suppose that I had sold out or, at the very least, had been pressured into abandoning the fight," he reasoned. "In 1970 I had called myself a $90,000-a-year slave and now I would be playing quietly for $110,000. This would tend to affirm public belief in the invincible power of the baseball establishment. Worse, it would encourage cynicism about the durability of principles—not only mine but everyone else's. . . . Too bad. Too bad for me. Too bad for those who might misunderstand or misrepresent me."[1] Confirming Flood's apprehension about the national sports media almost forty years later, Brad Snyder points out, "During the 1960s and early 1970s, members of the press were firmly on the side of management."[2]

Perhaps the national sports press could be expected to impose an uncritical frame, but black newspapers, it might be hoped, would tell a different story. After all, they once held tremendous influence in baseball. Black newspapers were instrumental in providing Brooklyn Dodger general manager Branch Rickey with the public infrastructure necessary to execute his "secret plan" to sign a black ballplayer. Gene Roberts and Hank HanKlibanoff observe that around 1945, Rickey "had quietly begin making preparations. Looking for studies that might make the desegregation of his team easier, he had read widely in sociology, history, and race relations, including [Gunnar Myrdal's] *An American Dilemma*. . . . The Negro press was making Rickey's secret plan more plausible."[3] In this account, the successful integration of baseball depended on the serendipitous accumulation of a variety of factors, including the enlightened attention of a liberal white bureaucrat, the shifting social terrain, and the publicity given to baseball on the pages of the black press. The essence of this argument is that Robinson worked as a prototype for formulating the social justice claims that black newspapers would advance in the following decades. Over the next fifty years or so, baseball would acquire its status as a perpetual referent for both guiding and measuring national movement on the question of race. By the time that Flood was having it out in public with baseball owners, black newspapers knew well how to fight the good fight.

In 1957, Howard University sociologist E. Franklin Frazier published *Black Bourgeoisie*, a controversial and confrontational text that nevertheless established its author as "the most capable black sociologist in America."[4] Frazier advanced the thesis that the emergent black middle class faced an identity crisis. Caught between a deliberate, self-loathing rejection of black folk culture on one side and racist exclusion from white society on the other, the black middle class created a "mythological" world for the purpose of providing a safe self-definition, Frazier said: "In escaping from identification with the masses, the black bourgeoisie has attempted to identify with the white propertied classes. Since this has been impossible, except in their minds, because of the racial barriers those identified with this class have attempted to act out their role in a world of make-believe." Frazier argued that black newspapers constituted the public space in which the "world of make-believe" found expression. In a scathing analysis replete with critical cues, Frazier explained the function of the "Negro press":

> It is the chief medium of communication which creates and perpetu-
> ates the world of make-believe for the black bourgeoisie. Although
> the Negro press declares itself to be the spokesman for the Negro
> group as a whole, it represents essentially the interests and outlook of
> the black bourgeoisie. Its demand for equality for the Negro in Amer-
> ican life is concerned primarily with opportunities which will benefit
> the black bourgeoisie economically and enhance the social status
> of the Negro. The Negro press reveals the inferiority complex of the
> black bourgeoisie and provides a documentation of the attempts of
> this class to seek compensations for its hurt self-esteem and exclusion
> from American life. Its exaggerations concerning the economic well-
> being and cultural achievements of Negroes, its emphasis upon Negro
> "society" all tend to create a world of make-believe into which the

black bourgeoisie can escape from its inferiority and inconsequence in American society.[5]

At least two problems arise with an unqualified acceptance of this exhaustive indictment. First, like all radical social theory, it speaks from the assumptions of its time and therefore resists an easy mapping over history. Second, it relies on claims about group psychology that are sometimes difficult to accept as generalities, even for its time. But to the extent that Frazier spoke with prominence in his historical moment, he provides a narrative of the black press that cannot be written today, and to the extent that his generalities ring true, he gives good reasons to challenge a view of history that always identifies black newspapers as heroic protagonists. What many take to be Flood's primary source of support (often with references to Jackie Robinson) may not, in fact, have been much help at all, especially for those conditioned to notice the differences between the facts of social inferiority and the "world of make-believe."

When Flood appeared in the black press, his supporters' arguments reflected the "interests and outlook" of the members of Frazier's black bourgeoisie not only by extending their investments in Robinson but also by rendering those investments through the kind of speech that enacted the irrelevance of race. I first consider the similarities between the black press and what Nancy Fraser calls "subaltern counterpublics" by reading black newspapers' reflexive discourses to discern the ways in which they imagined their own purposes. Second, I conduct a brief rhetorical history of Robinson, demonstrating the exclusive features of "black unity" in urging black newspapers to lose their formal affiliations with radical speakers. Third, I explain an important implication of the Robinson model of public address—that "radical," "militant" or racialized speech was very often subject to disciplinary rhetorical countermeasures. Finally, I show what these phenomena meant for Flood: Their unanimous advocacy of his case was disjoined from the facts of his experience and his racial identity. Situated in facts and explained in axioms, Flood would win, black newspapers insisted, if reason prevailed.

Some scholars argue that as a crucial organ in the black public sphere, the black press constitutes a "counterpublic." Todd Vogel, for example, urges critics of black newspapers to "ask how identity and counterpublics became intertwined in trying to bring change to society," asserting that, "black newspapers' messages assume their full meaning only as we revise the public sphere and the ways it works with marginalized peoples."[6] By cultivating resistant discourses, counterpublics might be defined as constructs that widen the scope of democratic participation. According to Fraser's frequently cited definition, subaltern counterpublics are "parallel discursive arenas where members of subordinated social groups invent and circulate counterdiscourses to formulate oppositional interpretations of their identities, interests, and needs." Engaging what Robert Asen calls "collective imagining," which, "occurs in situations where advocates explicitly call upon their audiences to rethink relations to one another," the black press seemed to possess a self-understanding defined by its oppositional potential.[7]

Ronald Jacobs argues that "by establishing an independent black press, African-Americans were able to secure a space of self-representation: not only to craft common identities and solidarities, but also to develop arguments which might effectively engage white civil society."[8] But "engagement," according to Fraser, has a dual character: "On the one hand, [counterpublics] function as spaces of withdrawal and regroupment; on the other hand, they also function as bases and training grounds for agitational activities directed toward wider publics. It is precisely in the dialectic between these two functions that their emancipatory potential resides. This dialectic enables subaltern counterpublics partially to offset, although not wholly to eradicate, the unjust participatory privileges enjoyed by dominant social groups in stratified societies."[9] Fraser's "dialectic" can be imagined as an oscillating movement whereby subordinate social groups alternately retreat into counterpublics to organize politically effective forms of collective identity and will—a kind of intrapublic activity—and pivot to engage "wider" publics (with more or less success) in moments of interpublic interaction. By holding the idea of "counterpublics" in synchronous analytical suspense with the black press' self-imagination during Flood's historical moment, we might come to learn something about what happened to Flood when he appeared on the pages of black newspapers, which understood their purposes in ways that echoed Fraser's description of subaltern counterpublics.

At the fourteenth annual meeting of the Broadcast Promotion Association,[10] a month after Flood was traded to Philadelphia, John Sengstacke, editor and publisher of the *Chicago Defender*, spoke to the organization about "ways to relate to the black community." His comments were published in the *Philadelphia Tribune*, like the *Defender* a black newspaper: "From the day of the first Negro newspaper, Negro readers were drawn to it by a common background of disenfranchisement, segregation, and exploitation. The readers have been dependent upon the black press because for over 100 years it has been a champion, friend, advisor, and confessor on a scale matched by no other agency."[11] Sengstacke's observation, delivered in a speech to an organization seeking models with which to engage black television audiences, identified the black press as a discursive arena, formed according to a subordinate social identity, that develops alternative interpretations of blackness. Most notably, this discursive arena ran parallel to the wider public sphere in that it was oriented along a crucial axis of difference precipitated by racial segregation. Sengstacke continued, "Racial stress and strain have forced the Negro to develop a different line of thought, different emotional reactions to issues and problems that affect his basic interest. . . . [T]he incidence of segregation has compelled them to be oriented differently, so that different views and messages which appeal to whites may fall on deaf ears so far as black people are concerned."[12] Moreover, the black press styled itself as an authoritative black public voice by virtue of its unique connection to black readers. The *St. Louis Argus* claimed that black newspapers "have a believability that other newspapers do not have, for they are the only media that express the black point of view on community affairs which is recognizable and accepted by black readers."[13] And in August 1972, Charles Rangel, who represented Harlem in the U.S. House of Representatives, wrote a laudatory letter to the *Baltimore Afro-American* in celebration of its eightieth year of publication: "For 80 years, you have provided an invaluable public service to Baltimore's black community. During most of the history of the Baltimore Afro-American, the news of greatest interest to black people was nowhere to be found except on your pages." Rangel stated further, "Today, the black community turns to you each week for your excellent coverage of the events and issues which affect their lives."[14]

In the early 1970s, black newspapers continued to imagine their activities in terms that resembled Myrdal's "fighting press." They offered self-descriptions through various expressions of opposition, attempting rhetorically to constitute the black press as a field of agitational activity. In a 1972 column that provided an updated rationale for the existence of the black press eighty years after the founding of the Baltimore paper, the *Afro-American* declared, "We are still and will continue our major efforts in the aim to upgrade the quality of life for all American people. As a minority member of the press, we know that we are only a small voice in the cry for the liberation of our readers in this complex democratic society, but we know that the voice provides a viable wedge in the fight for equality and we intend to keep it loud and clear."[15] Myrdal had proclaimed in *An American Dilemma* that *"to get publicity is of the highest strategic importance to the Negro people,"* adding that "a great majority of white people in America would be prepared to give the Negro a substantially better deal if they know the facts."[16] Myrdal's suggestion undoubtedly was infused with naive optimism—the color-coded and often violent social clashes of the 1950s and 1960s attest powerfully to the strength of racist conviction unbent by the self-evident call for justice that the "facts" might have revealed. Nevertheless, Myrdal's faith in the facts worked as a hopeful call to throw two dimensions of the "dilemma" into public view: the sheer rawness of the deal black Americans had been handed and the contributions to American democracy that blacks had to offer.

The effort to "upgrade the quality of life for all American people" described a political impulse that did more than simply revalue blackness. The black press's self-imposed role was to insert black identity into a mode of address that enacted the broader meaning of American life. The fight of the "fighting press," then, was bound up with its assertion of its own hopeful irrelevance. Jacobs notes that around 1970, "a number of African-American leaders were beginning to believe that racial integration would remove the need for a separate black newspaper and began arguing that the black press should fight for its own disappearance."[17] One such African American leader was James D. Williams, who in 1970 directed the office of information and publication for the U.S. Commission on Civil Rights. Williams said that "in a fully integrated society, the black press would shrink and eventually vanish."[18] Recognizing, in any case, that oppositional activity was still necessary in 1972, the *Argus* asserted the black press's role in unequivocal terms: "So long as inequities exist *in the framework of American justice,* the black press will remain the most strident voice in the crusade of freedom."[19]

The black press' aspiring ephemerality implied the desire to destabilize the rigidity of social hierarchies by being more universal than the public sphere against which it set itself. As Jacobs puts it, "Excluded groups successfully transform their subordinate position by making more substantial and more deeply institutionalized—more real and less utopian—the universalistic solidarity promised by the dominant civil sphere."[20] In this sense, the expressly pyrrhic victory sought by the black press made sense. By orienting the rationale of their forum as if participants hoped that it would soon be assimilated out of existence, black newspapers generated a space from which to critique not the ideal of universal justice itself but the failure of the "wider public" universally to protect the promise of social justice. Indeed, the existence of the black press bespoke this critique. "As a black newspaper, printed primarily for black readers," wrote *Afro* editors, "the AFRO-AMERICAN is proud that it has been on the firing line for 80 years and has never reduced the force of its firing power in the cause of freedom for all, civil rights, and justice. It never intends to lessen its power in this direction."[21] The *Chicago Defender*'s Sengstacke appropriated the notion of the watchdog to make a similar point in a published letter to the *Afro-American*: As a result of the newspaper's "commitment to the democratic process . . . a high tide of change is rolling through America today. In the scale of human values, there are no decent alternatives to social justice. The persistent struggle to achieve such an end fully sustains the conviction and the rationale that Black America has no greater watchdog than the black press."[22] All at once, the black press indicted the universality of the public sphere and claimed to more faithfully represent "freedom for all" through the "democratic process." Thus, the plot and subplot of the black press, which paradoxically announced its necessity and planned for its own demise, achieved coherence in universality, the meaning of its life articulated in the conditions of its death. America may have been richer because the *Afro* lived, but its auspicious mortality signaled the "real" value of the riches: redeeming the universal potential of the framework of American justice. This rationale, however, contains a dilemma.

Frazier had described in historically specific sociological terms a situation similar to the one that Asen put in the theoretical language of the public sphere. Asen says, "Emergent publics cannot articulate all possible perspectives in public debates without asserting a dubious discursive totality that presumes knowledge of the needs and interests of others prior to discursive engagement. Exclusion thus appears as a recurrent feature of public discourse, in that new formations of publics engender new exclusions."[23] Frazier's critique of the "Negro press" seems to have foreshadowed the "dubious discursive totality" that Asen describes as recurrent exclusions. Asen suggests that new publics entail new exclusions, which may produce new counterpublics, which entail new exclusions, and so on—a kind of spiral of participatory exclusion structured into the idea of a public. If the black press built a liberal political imagination through a rejection of blackness itself, then Frazier and Asen direct critical attention to the exclusions occasioned in and through its formation.

As the *Afro-American* celebrated its eightieth year, it articulated the complementary goals of fighting for social justice and achieving black unity:

"As we mark another birthday, we simply pause to let our readers know that we intend to continue to build an effective communication instrument that will create unity in our fight for full justice and freedom. It will be this unity that will make the difference."[24] The *Argus* asserted the importance of black newspapers along similar lines in 1972: "The chief aim of the Black press is to maintain a united front to protest and expose every condition inconsistent with democratic concepts we all treasure, and to give coverage to that news of the black population that is ignored and distorted by the white papers."[25] Similarly, Whitney Young made the case for black unity as a precondition for negotiation with "white America" in August 1970. At the time, Young was the executive director of the National Urban League and a regular columnist in the *Afro* newspaper chain. Young's argument was two-pronged. First, he stressed the need for unity as a strategic response to a "divide and conquer" strategy of oppression: "Black leadership and organizations should muster the courage and the strength to make one last effort to stand united. Oppressors have always followed a divide-and-conquer policy. Minorities have only been able to succeed when they stood together and refused to let their differences obscure their basic goal."[26] If, as Frazier instructs, we look suspiciously on Young's claim to be the spokesperson for "the Negro group as a whole," the notion of the "basic goal" is fraught with difficulty. In addition, when differences are subsumed for the "basic goal," the consequent political strategy acquires a unique character. Young then continued with the second prong of his argument, the goal of such unity:

> What's the purpose of a strategy of unity and coalition? Negotiation. The opportunity for a united black community and its allies to negotiate a peace that will settle the issues that have split this country for so long. It is in the self-interest of all concerned to adopt such a strategy for the seventies. And the key to the success of this effort is the achievement of black unity, for we have been the most wronged against and the most self-conscious and organized of America's dispossessed. This could be America's last opportunity to deal with black Americans and to negotiate with leaders responsible to their people before the terrifying prospect of internal strife and armed suppression descend upon us.[27]

Young's alarmist tone evokes the realities of the shifting goals and alliances expressed by the various civil rights organizations that had been at the front of a broadly visioned social movement until the late 1960s. With the

1970s upon him and the fight becoming more complex, Young can be read as attempting to invigorate the aging momentum of civil rights leadership. But on the pages of the *Afro-American*, Young demonstrated the problem of the "dubious totality." One is left to wonder exactly what negotiation might entail when the "self-interest of all" collapses into a unified black community within which differences have been successfully eradicated.

"Negotiation," after all, was not a transparent or self-evident synonym for political action but was instead the public expression of a form of political action designed to solve a dual problem. Frazier wrote, "As a result of the break with its cultural past, the black bourgeoisie is without cultural roots either in the Negro world with which it refuses to identify, or the white world which refuses to permit the black bourgeoisie to share its life."[28] This statement evokes the dual character of Fraser's subaltern counterpublics. On the one hand, they serve as spaces of withdrawal and regroupment; on the other hand, they serve as training grounds for agitational activities aimed at "wider publics." This process may look "emancipatory" in theory, but it is only so to the extent that this oscillating movement offers participation to those represented in a carefully delimited and manicured emancipatory ideal. Stated simply, the identities generated by counterpublics must be fit for the pivot from "withdrawal and regroupment" to engagement and agitation; the meaning of blackness must make possible interpublic interaction. On this score, the notions of withdrawal and regroupment begin to look illusory, because counterpublic engagement with the "wider public" is just another name for the type of co-optation that occurs as subalterns come to terms with collective identities qualified for inclusion. This was the essence of Frazier's argument. The black press bespoke "the inferiority complex of the black bourgeoisie" through the way it organized its discursive space and coordinated its movement; in the early 1970s, the black middle class defined blackness according to the promise of entry into the public sphere. The black bourgeoisie, in other words, thought it could negotiate. Seen this way, the black press did not so much oscillate as spin its wheels establishing the credentials to be included in public life.

One of Frazier's most fully developed arguments for the estranged class-consciousness of the black press focused on the "society pages." Frazier insisted that although the basic notion of "'society' was not created by the Negro press, it is the Negro press which feeds and perpetuates the illusion of this element to the black bourgeoisie." Most important, said Frazier, "The activities of 'society' serve to differentiate the black bourgeoisie from the masses of poorer Negroes and at the same time compensate for the exclusion of the black bourgeoisie from the larger white community."[29] Magazines such as *Ebony* came under Frazier's most intense scrutiny, preoccupied as they were with reporting on the growing wealth of chosen few, glorifying the incomes of black celebrities, and advertising Cadillacs and "products which will remove or modify Negroid characteristics." As part of this criticism, he noted the "exaggerated" attention given to Jackie Robinson, both in terms of his high baseball salary and as evidence of the press giving "lip service to pride in being a Negro."[30]

Perhaps closer to the point, sport (and baseball in particular) produced a salary spectacle. In the black press in the early 1970s, salary milestones were reported with fanfare and urgency. When Oakland rookie pitching sensation Vida Blue asked owner Charles Finley for a $92,000 contract before the 1972 season, the *New York Amsterdam News* strongly defended Blue, asserting that without him American League attendance figures would drop sharply: "What happens if, perchance, the AL didn't have Vida?"[31] In March 1970, the *Pittsburgh Courier* argued that "the best proof of black supremacy in the major leagues today resides in the fact that of the 15 historical stars who have signed minimal $100,000 per year contracts, nine of them are black."[32] In 1972, Chuck Andrews reported with glee in the *Amsterdam News* that Hank Aaron's $200,000 contract provided him a higher salary than President Richard Nixon.[33] And in April 1970, the *Baltimore Afro-American* produced a magazine insert focused on "Color in Sports," in which the lead article was titled, "Color of Sports: Black Blends Well with Green." "Since money is the name of any professional game," the *Afro* asked, "what would be wrong with considering first the people who are worth the most in the eyes of the club owners?" The article compiled a formidable list of black names: Aaron, Willie Mays, Willie McCovey, Frank Robinson, Bob Gibson. When did the valuation of black athletes begin, wondered the *Afro*? When "the late Branch Rickey shocked the baseball establishment by signing Jackie Robinson to a contract, and announcing that the modern majors were destined to get their first black player. They did in 1947."[34]

Until the early 1940s, the *Pittsburgh Courier* had an informal agreement with the *Daily Worker*, the Communist Party newspaper, whereby the publications would print each other's stories on the racial integration of Major League Baseball. The Communist Party criticized a highly visible American enterprise on the basis of a concrete social justice claim, and papers such as the *Defender* and *Afro-American* secured a partner in the pursuit of agitational activities very much in the spirit of Fraser's "multiple public sphere." As Jules Tygiel suggests, "The *crusade* waged by the Communists, the black press, and a small coterie of white sportswriters helped to alleviate the apathy that nourished baseball's segregation." Indeed, the Communist Party emphasized a point that would be made dramatically about thirty-five years later by Flood, claiming that "professional athletes, too, were workers, who labored but did not receive a fair share of the fruits of their labor."[35] But as soon as the black press began to achieve gains relative to baseball's legitimate structures—specifically through the attention of Rickey—the convenience of this relationship became less clear to black editors and publishers.

The "communist" argument would be reconfigured by Flood and his advocates, but the mutual disavowal of communist participation in baseball's public affairs made by *Afro* editor Sam Lacy and the *Courier*'s Wendell Smith would have broad effects, particularly in relation to what such disavowal made possible—a working relationship with Major League Baseball. In August 1947, Smith wrote a *Pittsburgh Courier* column in which he completely reversed his position on the *Worker*, insisting that "the Communists did more to delay the entrance of Negroes in big league baseball than any other single factor."[36] Smith and others in the black press apparently learned that one must choose one's friends wisely. Baseball's communist purge, initiated in 1943, complete by 1947, and executed institutionally by the black press's "most influential" voices, signaled a strategic course correction for the 1950s into the atmosphere saturated by postwar race politics. Risky associations—even those built on common interests—were abandoned and deliberately maligned. Black newspapers did not want the Communist Party to participate in their public spaces after Rickey became an ally.

In pursuit of negotiation strategies with professional baseball, black newspapers left communism and communists such as Paul Robeson behind. The result of the disjunction from communism in the early 1940s was a template for political action drawn as an explicit rejection of communism and deepened investment in American national identity. Above all, black journalists derived two crucial learning experiences from the mid-1940s: a divorce from radicalism could purchase effective negotiation, and the right symbolic representative could make a public splash. With these two ideas in mind, the black press found an ideal black citizen through whom to construct an activist ethos and wage a crusade in sport: Jackie Robinson. He was both the spoils of victory and the discursive means through which more victories could be achieved. Black newspapers' termination of their relationship with communist media, such as the *Daily Worker*, is a history that has been written and seen within a frame that takes the liberalism of black politics for granted, these developments seem to be naturally occurring by-products of a process affirmed by history. In the context of contemporary anxieties regarding the status of the black activist-athlete, though, one wonders if the side effects of the Robinson moment in the mid-1940s were not more consequential than they initially appear to be.

Investigating this proposition requires reading Robinson's public address against the most sacrosanct dimension of the Robinson memory. In 2008, *New York Times* columnist Dave Anderson reported on a rare event in Cooperstown: the alteration of a player's Hall of Fame plaque. The story goes that when Robinson was inducted in 1962, he refused to allow any mention of integration on his official plaque. Of course, this deferral of race only heightened the colorblind ethos for which Robinson already stood, but forty-six years later, a remarkable sentence was added to the list of Robinson's statistical accomplishments: "Displayed tremendous courage and poise in 1947 when he integrated the modern major leagues in the face of intense adversity."[37] Authorized by his widow and daughter, the change merely registered in the Hall what serious public address repeats ad infinitum, that Robinson was not just the first black Major Leaguer but an icon of virtue in the fight for reform. Robinson did what needed to be done with "courage and poise." Without explicitly saying so, the change reminds new audiences that Robinson experienced overt, venomous racism both on and off the field in his first year with the Dodgers. Robinson sensed before his first game that the experience would tax his spirit to previously unknown depths, and he certainly qualifies as a courageous person. "Courage and poise," however, not only narrate his status as a pathbreaker but also mythologize his response to the threats and epithets: two years of public silence on race. Robinson was famously silent about the racist abuses he suffered with the Dodgers in his first two years, preferring to follow Rickey's dictum that Robinson turn the other cheek.

The story of Robinson's silent years delivers drama, explains his profound effect, and canonizes him. The rhetoric of Robinson's courage, in other words, works to abet his hegemonic presence in public discourse and buttress the rhetorical constraints set by the black press' liberal progress narrative. Robinson was surely not, as he once put it, a "patient black freak." But the steady application of virtue to his suppression of internal conflict set the threshold at which speech, as either an expression of anger or mode of resistance, acquired its political warrant. Robinson had plenty of things that he wanted to say, but he waited. Mediated by Rickey, liberalism's white embodiment in baseball, Robinson's voice acquired broad importance. Every time he spoke in public, he performed the advantages of patient interracial cooperation and thereby enacted liberal integrationism's foundational requirements. Robinson modeled blackness to white audiences whose racism could be rebuked only by distinguished humility, and he modeled interracial cooperation to black audiences who might come to see the pragmatism of fastidiously planned reform. As loyalties were redrawn, the moment to speak was postponed.

At the end of the 1948 baseball season, Robinson's second as a silent symbol, Rickey and Robinson met personally in Dodger offices. As Robinson remembered, "I was relieved when Mr. Rickey finally called me into his office and said, 'Jackie, you're on your own now. You can be yourself now.'" As might have been expected, Robinson soon discovered that his suddenly outspoken persona had perilous effects: "I learned that as long as I appeared to ignore insult and injury, I was a martyred hero to a lot of people who seemed to have sympathy for the underdog. But the minute I began to answer, to argue, to protest—the minute I began to sound off—I became a swellhead, a wise guy, an 'uppity' nigger."[38] Despite the obstacles, Robinson spoke eloquently and passionately on questions of racial justice, both in and out of baseball, beginning in 1949 and through the remainder of his life. In *I Never Had It Made*, his 1972 autobiography, he revealed what had finally authorized his transition into a speaking subject: "I wanted to be Jackie Robinson, and for the first time I would be justified because by 1949 the *principle* had been established: the major victory won. There were enough blacks on other teams to ensure that American baseball could never again turn its back on minority competitors."[39] The moment to speak had arrived, but only after the principle of integration had been established and Robinson had secured what he took to be an irrevocable pathway for black players into baseball.

In this narrative, Robinson's "principle" bespoke a political strategy and form of expression proper to liberal integrationism. In 1949, Robinson was summoned to testify before the House Un-American Activities Committee (HUAC) to "give the lie to statements by Paul Robeson," who had allegedly claimed that racial injustice would prevent conscientious black Americans from fighting the Soviets. Though Robinson admitted in 1972 that he would "reject such an invitation if offered now,"[5] he explained that at the time he was compelled to provide testimony primarily because "people shouldn't get scared and think that one Negro among 15,000,000 of us, speaking to a Communist group in Paris, could speak for the rest of his race." Like his advocates in the black press in the mid-1940s, Robinson worried that the imagined connection to communism would be used to discredit "blacks in the eyes of whites," thereby interrupting the progress Robinson had been instrumental in producing. In response, Robinson's testimony before HUAC displaced Robeson's voice, refused the errors of communism, and strengthened the bonds of commitment between progressive black politics and the promises of American national identity:

> I am a religious man. Therefore I cherish America where I am free to worship as I please, a privilege which some countries do not give. And I suspect that nine hundred and ninety-nine out of almost any thousand colored Americans you meet will tell you the same thing.
>
> But that doesn't mean that we're going to stop fighting race discrimination in this country until we've got it licked. It means that we're going to fight it all the harder because our stake in the future is so big. We can win our fight without the Communists and we don't want their help.[40]

From Robinson's perspective, Robeson seemed to represent a challenge to the formation of a black public ethos. But as word of Robinson's testimony spread, Robeson became central to establishing Robinson's public identity. Just like black newspapers, who found the coalition with the *Daily Worker* to be bad publicity after Major League Baseball began listening to their protests, Robinson found that however righteous, Robeson's politics were ill-suited for contextualizing an argument in favor of integration, which required a performance of blackness that represented an investment in American democracy and its political culture. Relative to the way that this performance was received in the country's most widely circulating daily newspaper, the *New York Times*, Robeson was a foil, Robinson's negative instance, crucial to his emergence as the idealized embodiment of black public address.

In those infamously paranoid times, the issue was one of "black loyalty," especially following widespread *Times* reports that Robeson had "said that he loved the Russians and asserted that American Negroes would refuse to fight in a war against the Russians." HUAC Chair John S. Wood invited Robinson to testify so that he might "give the American people an idea of how the Negroes stand in the event of war which we hope will not develop."

When asked about it by the Associated Press, Robinson said, "Paul speaks only for himself."[41] On July 13, 1949, Robeson's comments were slated as the only topic in public HUAC hearings intended to provide "minority groups with a forum on which to defend their patriotism and declare that Communist drives to dominate them had failed." The same day, Thomas Young, publisher of the black newspaper *Norfolk Journal and Guide*, assured committee members that Robeson had "'betrayed his race' and could no longer be declared a spokesperson for it." When asked if Robeson ought to be subpoenaed, Young worried that "very little useful information" would be gleaned and that HUAC testimony would merely provide Robeson with a counterproductive "sounding board" for his distortions of black opinion.[42] Robinson's July 18 testimony qualified as front-page news in the *New York Times* under the headline, "Jackie Robinson Terms Stand of Robeson on Negroes False."[43] The paper reprinted the full text of Robinson's statement, in which he reinforced the link between progress and public perception: "We're going to make progress in other American fields besides baseball if we can get rid of some of the misunderstanding and confusion the public still suffers from."[44]

The full weight of Robinson's testimony evinces a curious tension in his persona, one that might be traced to a basic irony in the liberal public sphere. On the one hand, Robinson attempted to quarantine the scope of his comments relative to both the significance of baseball and the limits of his own speech. He opened his statement by insisting that baseball "is as far removed from politics as anybody can possibly imagine," and he extended the point by attempting to deliberately undercut his authority to speak about politics: "I don't pretend to be an expert on communism or any other kind of a political 'ism.' Going to college at UCLA, helping to fight a war with about ten million other fellows, trying to break into professional baseball and then trying to make good with the Dodgers, and trying to save some money for the time when my legs lose their spring—all this, together with my family life, has been enough to keep me busy without becoming an 'expert'—except on base-stealing or something like that." On the other hand, Robinson acknowledged his status as a symbolic representative, asserting to the committee that, "you can put me down as an expert on being a colored American, with thirty years experience at it. It's true that I've been the laboratory specimen in a great change in organized baseball."[45] The tension here resides in attempting to discern exactly what Robinson was trying to accomplish. Was he muting or recognizing the importance of his racial achievement in baseball? Was he speaking on behalf of "colored

Americans" or refusing to speak for them? The answers here, of course, are both. Accepting the invitation to speak before HUAC thrust Robinson into politics, whether he liked it or not, and despite all contrary stated intent, his voice boomed with authority through the eager ears of a curious nation as he rejected Robeson's statements about black (dis)loyalty.

This was Robinson's public moment, the signature rhetorical event in constructing Jackie Robinson as a subject of national public address. Coming in the heat of the summer in which he broke his silence and "spoke his mind," some in fact would see him as a rabble-rouser. But Robinson accomplished a number of things that would for years follow his persona through the news cycles and remembrances that constituted his life as a political symbol. Robinson affirmed his story as a crucible of progress in baseball (while bracketing its significance), he disjoined black politics from communism through a negation of Robeson's authority to speak for others (while claiming to speak for no one but himself), and enacted liberalism's black civic ethos by indexing his stake in idealized images of America (while assuring integration's position on the national political agenda). Robinson's initiation into publicity, sterilized by his mute mediation through Branch Rickey, performed a spectacle of blackness that was fundamentally fit for politics: black but loyal, determined but measured. About a week after Robinson's performance at HUAC, Democratic New York Representative Arthur G. Klein asked Congress to print half a million copies of Robinson's testimony, declaring that it should be made available "to schools, churches, libraries, and other groups," including Congress. Said Klein, "This great American athlete has spoken successfully for all minorities—and for all Americans."[46] Despite—or perhaps precisely because of—his insistence to the contrary, Robinson operated as a symbolic representative for black America, performing civic perfection in virtually every manner necessary to make the case for racial integration. Every time Robinson said that he spoke for nobody but himself, he enacted the self-abstracting individualism on which both integration and the public sphere were predicated and secured his credentials as America's symbolic representative of black political opinion.

Later in the fall of 1949, Robinson was named the National League's Most Valuable Player; he had been the key player on a Dodger team that lost the World Series to the Yankees. Against unfair rumors that Robinson's racial identity had secured an award more deserved by perhaps Stan Musial or Enos Slaughter, *New York Times* columnist Arthur Daley mounted a spirited defense of both the award and the color-blind qualifications of the sportswriters who conferred it. "Prematurely curious outsiders frequently asked this reporter," Daley admitted, "'Will the Baseball Writers' committee vote for him, though?' The answer was obvious: That they were honest, objective reporters. If Jackie deserved the award, he'd get it." Daley vaguely referenced Robinson's silent patience, insisting that "Jackie has won for himself complete freedom as a ball player, with the right to be judged only as a ball player." Thus set free to play and speak, Robinson was baseball's most meritorious individual, and the problem of race, concluded Daley, was neither here nor there: "He didn't win the MVP honor because he is a Negro or in spite of the fact that he is a Negro. He won it because he was the most valuable ball player in the National League. And don't let any professional rabble-rouser try to tell you differently."[47] When everyone was color-blind—Robinson, his teammates, the press who covered him, the nation, the public—the pragmatism of patience transformed "rabble-rousing" into the dishonest vocation of those, black and white, who spoke superfluously about race.

Chris Lamb and Glen Bleske observe an important difference between the coverage Robinson received in black and mainstream newspapers during spring training in 1947: "For the black press, the Robinson story transcended sports and touched on racial issues neglected by both the mainstream press and society at large. The mainstream press, on the other hand, rarely gave the story the social or cultural context it deserved."[48] William Kelley offers a similar comparison of the coverage of Robinson's signing with the Montreal Royals: "Negro publications tended to focus more on the Robinson event as a significant historical occasion. They showed an energetic job of emotionalizing the story, in particular the Pittsburgh *Courier* and the Chicago *Defender*. . . . The metropolitan newspapers tended to take the story as another occurrence in the sports world."[49] The point of these comparisons, generally speaking, is to disclose the racial bias of the nation's largest daily newspapers. Be that as it may, the comparisons also illustrate the influence of Robinson's story on the strategies employed by black newspapers to inaugurate new forms of black publicity. As the black press began to direct its discourses toward inclusion, black heroes in black papers, in the words of Gunnar Myrdal, "achieved something extraordinary . . . in competition with whites," offering "every Negro a gloating consolation in his lowly status and a ray of hope."[50] Robinson emerged in 1947 as a racial "competitor" of vast importance to the black press's effort to stage politically useful racial performances.

This proposition runs the risk of reductionism. Robinson, after all, did not individually determine the direction of race politics after 1947.

Nevertheless, the space Robinson occupied and continues to occupy cannot be overemphasized. Contemporary observers easily draw a comparison to Martin Luther King Jr. to explain Robinson's influence on history. For example, the *New York Times*'s Dave Anderson recited a line of reasoning applied commonly to Robinson, writing in the summer of 2008, "More than a decade before Rev. Dr. Martin Luther King put the phrase civil rights into the nation's vocabulary, Jackie Robinson taught millions of baseball's white fans that black was beautiful."[51] This argument of prefiguration does double duty: It invests each individual with the other's symbolism and asserts a lineage from Robinson to King. Moreover, it places baseball history and civil rights history into an ancestral relation, with the former as a precursor to the latter. Robinson, many people are quick to remember, "came first." Along these lines, Tygiel, Robinson's most prominent biographer, wrote, "In 1954 when the Supreme Court declared school segregation illegal in the famous Brown v. Board of education decision, a majority of major league teams already fielded black athletes."[52] In addition to all of this, Jackie Robinson refused an order to the back of the bus while in the U.S. Army in 1944 (an offense for which he was court-martialed), eleven years prior to Rosa Parks's famous gesture. As a purported figurative antecedent to the civil rights movement, Robinson is many things to many advocates, and as these memories of his significance accumulate, a binding assumption becomes visible beneath them: Jackie Robinson was a central character in the national drama of racial integration that unfolded on the pages of black newspapers in the mid-1940s.

Into the late 1960s and early 1970s, Robinson remained a powerful scene maker. In December 1969, about a week before Flood met with player representatives in Puerto Rico and then filed suit in federal court, Robinson appeared on New York public television to discuss a problem in sport that was receiving increasing attention. The *Amsterdam News* reported that "Jackie Robinson, the first black player to be admitted into major league baseball, has noted 'little,' if any, progress on the coaching lines and managerial offices for black men since he broke the color line on the playing field a quarter-century ago."[53] Though not the first of its kind, the *Amsterdam News* article signaled the placement of managerial and executive positions in sports onto integration's political agenda. The front office was taken to be a logical extension of the path Robinson had blazed in 1947, the next phase of progressive reform. In characterizing Robinson's position, the *Amsterdam News* was careful to highlight the significance of sport to achieving larger goals. Robinson appeared on television with Fritz Pollard, a star professional football player in the 1920s who had also become the National Football League's first black head coach in 1922. The *Amsterdam News* reported, "Both men underscored the importance of athletics as a means for black men to get into the mainstream of the nation's economy and as a common denominator for integrated living." Robinson was quoted as saying, "I believe that athletics offers a lesson in human rights. It shows that people must work together to be successful and what can be accomplished when they pull together as a team."[54] For Robinson and others, the problem of black coaches and executives in sport constituted the next barrier in the ever-expanding quest for interracial progress not just within sport but also relative to the promise of integration writ large.

Thus, the *Los Angeles Sentinel* offered an optimistic report in 1970 that detailed the findings of the Race Relations Information Center (RRIC), a "nonprofit journalistic research agency in Nashville." Among the many findings of the report, which included an analysis of black sports participation in the intercollegiate Southeastern Conference, the *Sentinel* stressed one hopeful prediction in particular: "Major league baseball's first black team manager is likely to be named within the next three years, possibly as early as 1971, according to an exclusive." Moreover, the *Sentinel* named names: "The report raises the possibility that three National League stars, Willie Mays, Ernie Banks, and Maury Wills, could be likely 'first black manager' candidates."[55] The first black baseball manager, Frank Robinson, would not be hired until 1975, but the Sentinel report was surely encouraging to those, like the *Chicago Defender*'s Doc Young, who saw baseball as both a locus of political activity and mirror of racial progress.

Nearly two years later, Young again compared the situation to Robinson's. Asking, "Who will have the guts to make the next move?," Young remembered Rickey's importance to the fable. He cited Roger Kahn's contention that Rickey's desire to integrate baseball could be traced to a 1938 conversation with St. Louis Cardinals pitcher Preacher Roe. Rickey was a Cardinals executive at the time, but he would have to join the Dodgers to execute his integration plans. According to Young, in Brooklyn, "the racial climate was better," and "the primary club owners also had guts." As Young summoned nostalgia for the courage of Rickey and Robinson, he pointed toward what he took to be a largely ignored feature of the 1971 World Series, which marked the twenty-fifth anniversary of black participation in the fall classic: "The black player had become so commonplace by now that nobody remembered to note the anniversary year. But both managers and the coaches and the top front office executives were white." Young thought such circumstances problematic, especially given the significance of anniversary that had just passed without notice: "When Robinson joined the Royals in the spring of 1946, he—and Rickey, of course—brought an end to the vicious practice of racial discrimination in major mass-appeal American sports."[56] Decades after Robinson joined the Dodgers, memories of his partnership with Rickey were still operating in the service of integrationist reform rhetoric.

These memories, which for Young revealed the truth of integration, imposed limits as well. As debate about a black manager in baseball proceeded into 1972, Young became anxious about Robinson's contributions to the conversation. With caution, Young wrote in the *Defender* that he had "to be critical of 'my hero.' I have to be critical about him because he is wrong in the way he constantly puts down the leading black candidates for managerial posts in major league baseball." Young noted the conspicuous absence of Wills's name from list of potential black managers offered by Robinson in response to a question from a white reporter. From Young's perspective, Robinson had violated the color-blind principles he had supposedly established in 1947. When it came to accomplishing an important racial goal, Robinson, Young feared, was being too "militant," judging "black managerial potential on the basis of militancy. That cannot be the primary role of the first black manager in major league baseball. This man, whoever he is, must be able to manage black and white players alike, all players, regardless of race, creed, or color. Jackie sometimes seems to forget—though he DOESN'T forget—that for an important racial goal, he, himself, made personal feelings secondary. If he is going to be true to the cause he must give the Maury Willses every conceivable break."[57] Robinson apparently was not enacting the Jackie Robinson ethos in a manner consistent with the black press' political imperatives: inclusion, integration, and symbolic representation. By 1972, the abstraction of Robinson into public space had outpaced the particularity of his beliefs. Put differently, Robinson established a burden of racial representation that was, by the 1970s, too heavy for even him to bear: His scene-making power had exceeded even his own rhetorical command. Through, because of, and, as Young's last point demonstrates, sometimes even in spite of himself, Robinson modeled a form of political activity in the black press characterized by the relentless pursuit of inclusive, color-blind institutional reform. Just as black newspapers premised their existence on the telos of their disappearance, they established Robinson as a frame of reference that structured the black public subject.

Warner argues that the public sphere is oriented around the performance of speech protocols that enact the transformation of one's particularity into a universal speaking subject. The problem with "rational debate" is that it secures an asymmetrical privilege for those whose particularity can be easily shed in public address—white, male, heterosexual, middle-class, and so on. If race is a particularizing mark of difference, then racialized subjects must engage rhetorical strategies that establish and project the public sphere's requisite frame of reference. These critical assumptions help to recast Frazier's psychosociological observations about the black middle-class into an insight about black public address. The "pathological struggle" and the "craving for recognition in the white world" expressed the black press's contradictory effort both to assert black interests and to achieve inclusion. As Frazier notes, using terminology that anticipates Warner, "Despite [the black bourgeoisie's] attempt to escape real identification with the masses of Negroes, they can not escape the mark of oppression any more than their less favored kinsmen."[58] So marked, a rhetoric of disincorporation was required. This rhetoric was frustrated, however, by precisely the fight for justice that the black press claimed to be fighting. Consequently, the nature of the fight came to be determined by that which could accomplish the abstraction of blackness into publicity and allow black newspapers to speak to mainstream politics.

Roy Wilkins, whose leadership of the National Association for the Advancement of Colored People earned him the Presidential Medal of Freedom in 1967, was a regular columnist for the *Afro* newspaper chain, challenged the "black militants" in a September 1969 article on the question of strategy: "The truth of the matter is that the black militants have not moved with much strategy except the shock-'em-and-sock-'em kind. Apparently they have never analyzed their position as a minority in America. They have not considered tactics by which they could not only win new ground but build themselves in the eyes of the general public." Wilkins's criticism of the unnamed "militants" linked political practice to a preferred speaking style. The crucial factor for him was to act politically in ways that conferred public legitimacy, an injunction that bespoke the rhetorical imperatives of the bourgeois public sphere. Wilkins, in fact, painted the militants in broad strokes, wondering how race-inflected discourse would influence political action: "There are smarter ways of advertising the just cause than staging shouting matches with public officials, using four letter words, organizing racial clashes in schools and robbing and killing people. . . . Does one use the same slam-bang black racism in a town where black votes total only 10 to 30 percent of the electorate as one does in a town where blacks outnumber whites? Is any racism good politics?" Though grounded on stereotypes and unfair generalizations of the behavior of the "militants," those problems simply underscored the black press's impulse to discipline political speech in ways that attempted to ensure a color-blind rhetoric proper to electoral politics, where, presumably, the important action was. According to Wilkins, political speech needed to "adapt itself to the performatives" (in Warner's terms) of good, rational debate in the public sphere.[59]

Similarly, Whitney Young complained in his regular *Amsterdam News* column that although his strategy of negotiation with Richard Nixon represented the interests and views of most blacks, his ideas were often shouted down by an unruly few:

> If black people are to make the changes needed in our society, such divisiveness must be replaced with the unity and true brotherhood that will allow us to negotiate from strength and from power.
>
> Above all, we must not be diverted from the real struggle by phony issues. In certain quarters, you're considered irrelevant if you don't mouth the current slogans and don't endlessly repeat the same anti-Establishment jargon over and over. For example, after nearly two years of bitter criticism of the [Nixon] Administration's policies, I ventured the opinion that it was time to sit down with the powers that be and, from a position of strength, negotiate black advances.
>
> Most black people agreed with me that restricting ourselves only to endlessly repeated criticisms wouldn't break the deadlock between blacks and the Administration, and that willingness to negotiate doesn't signify approval. But others were satisfied to try to score some cheap verbal points and distorted our position for the sake of grabbing a few headlines.[60]

Young can certainly be read as an individual attempting to justify his position of leadership: His statement gives the impression that he saw himself becoming unfashionable. In any case, Young established binaries between the "phony" and the "real," with "slogans" and "jargon" on the one hand and power and negotiation on the other. From Young's perspective, black particularity, when asserted publicly, was a distraction from the authentic struggle. Thus, he policed the boundaries of political discourse through a careful definition of political speech circumscribed by the call for unity.

The effort to discipline black discourse extended even beyond direct claims about political ineffectiveness; the same point at times could be made indirectly. Once again enunciating the theme of reverse racism, Wilkins extended his argument to the effects that racialized slogans could have on black children. Citing a study by two black psychiatrists covered in *Redbook* magazine, he admitted in his *Afro* column in 1971 that the "pet philosophy of some younger colored people" had its advantages. "The obvious dividend," he said, "has been a restimulation of pride and race and a healthy curiosity about African origin." But the pet philosophy came with a worry: "The real danger in a population hungry for recognition and angry at the restraints is that black arrogance may supplant black pride with reverse racism the unhappy result." Quoting the study, Wilkins continued, "However, those who teach by rote the slogans of black dignity—'I am Afro American,' 'Black is beautiful,' may be too extreme in their approach. It is possible that drilling black pride into a child's head in a stereotyped and isolated manner may actually have a reverse effect. . . . Whatever his thoughts, this false sense of power is making it difficult to initiate and enlarge a black-white dialogue." Above all, Wilkins worried about Black Power's ability to engage white society in a way that would encourage progress. "There is power in the black community which, if used smartly, can help make progress. But some of the braggadocio by colored people is tragic in its patent ineffectiveness," he chided, "a little like the naked emperor who believed he was clothed."[61] The key to black-white dialogue—meaning "realistic" political discourse—depended on the commitment to progress expressed in rhetorical moderation.

In January 1970, the *Los Angeles Sentinel* published an opinion by Lin Hilburn, a regular columnist, striking not just for its disciplinary tone but also for its explicit attack on what Hilburn called "the whole new rhetoric of blackness." The article declared prematurely that "the black power pimps, for the most part, are no longer with us. For that, there is thanks." To illustrate the new "rhetoric of blackness," Hilburn targeted the "Black Nationalists," who "are always yelling about their blackness, the 'I am blacker than you' bunch, . . . reflecting, for the most part, a civilization they cannot identify, let alone identify with." He presented a hypothetical dialogue between himself and a "young black chap, . . . wearing a Buba, necklace of seal tusks, Lucien Picard watch, Aquascutum trench coat and black horned rim glasses." The dialogue parodied the speech patterns of the "chap," who calls Hilburn "Baby" while asking for a job. "Me: 'Alright my man, just what kind of gig did you have in mind?' He: 'something cool.'" Put off by the young man's appearance and speech, Hilburn offered his reply: "Your bag seems to be one of talk loud and black and then in anger either walk away or try to bring [the establishment] down. My bag is not to hate or allow my anger to control me, but to stop getting mad and getting even." The difference between their "bags" resides squarely in opposing styles—sartorial style, labor style, political style, and rhetorical style. After responding to the Black Nationalist's accusation that Hilburn is "just like all these other Uncle Toms. You have been brainwashed by the Man," Hilburn concludes his column with an observation he hopes provides insight into a problematic way of speaking: "And there you have a taste of the rhetoric of the ghetto."[62]

The black middle class had in mind a specific mode of speaking that it hoped would translate into political agency, provided that the problematic aspects of black identity could be sequestered when engaging the public sphere. This mode of address constituted an appeal by the black bourgeoisie to represent blackness in a manner that was, above all, *reasonable*. Fundamentally liberal in its rationale—in search of progress, laboring to avoid offense—its exhortation to "Black Nationalists," "militants," and other "young black chaps" to adopt a universal speaking protocol was simultaneously a petition submitted to the white middle class. It was an entreaty for inclusion, a promise that if the doors of politics were open to blackness, blacks would be willing to play by its speaking rules. Even if Frazier overstated his psychological and sociological reading of the black press as evidence of black self-hatred or as a "world of make believe," his critical observations lend credence to the idea that black newspapers occupied a middle space, fighting a discursive battle on two fronts, one internal to black speaking styles and the other directed toward the levers of economic, social, and political power that guarded the entry points into public life.

Wondering why Curt Flood has not become "a politicized sports hero for a new generation of blacks," Gerald Early describes Flood as "fighting a particular legal advantage that baseball owners had that was not explicitly racial. In other words, what was done to Flood in trading him against his will, was not done to him because he was black, nor was it something that was only done to black players."[63] Early's point is that there was nothing intrinsic to Flood's cause that lent itself to an argument about racial injustice. Brad Snyder supposes that organized civil rights groups ignored Flood at the time because "they lacked sympathy for a small group of athletes perceived to be spoiled and overpaid, rather than subjugated and oppressed. The reserve clause was not strictly a racial issue."[64] Flood may not have echoed through history as Robinson did, but Flood's cause was ideally suited for coverage by the black press in the early 1970s. Even down to the salary spectacle of sport in black bourgeois "society," the fact that Flood's case was not "explicitly racial" resulted in the kind of advocacy that affirmed the liberalism that underpinned black newspapers' strange dual movement. In other words, Flood did not put his public at risk; his cause—especially as it relied on a solidarity with white players—occupied public space according to the inclusive principles that animated the black press's awkward self-understanding.

Though reporters knew the Players' Association was meeting and would certainly be interested in their decision to fund the lawsuit against the owners, Flood spoke extensively on the details of the meeting only in *The Way It Is*. In the first chapter, Flood presented himself in a philosophical mood, moving between sarcastic observations on the St. Louis slums, bitter judgments of baseball ownership, and pessimistic predictions about what would happen to him. Near the end of this chapter, Flood reveals Haller's question:

> A fascinating question, well-meant. If I were white, would I be less sensitive to injustice? Was it inevitable that, of all baseball players, a black man would be the first to rebel? Robert Brown Elliot, of South Carolina, was one of twenty blacks elected to the U.S. House of Representatives during the brief period of democracy that followed the Civil War. Arguing in the House for passage of the country's first civil rights law, Elliott said: "I regret, sir, that the dark hue of my skin may lend color to the imputation that I am controlled by motives personal to myself in my advocacy of this great measure of national justice. Sir, the motive that impels me is restricted to no such narrow boundary, but is as broad as your constitution. I advocate it, sir, because it is my right." I told the meeting that organized baseball's policies and practices affected all players equally and that the color of my skin was besides the point. It occurred to me later that the answer, while valid, had by no means exhausted the subject. Neither can it be exhausted in this book or even in our time. As I have already suggested, it heartens me to realize that my dispute with baseball will affect more than baseball. I like to believe that I would feel the same way even if I were white. To diminish the established insanity in one area of life is to undermine it elsewhere as well. In due course, the quality of justice changes. Values alter. Priorities improve. At the very least, the poor get glass for their windows. One need not be black to appreciate that.[65]

For good reasons, Flood refused to call the question racist: He claimed to understand where Haller was coming from, a fair recognition of his white colleagues' concerns. As Warner says of counterpublics, "Ordinary people are presumed not to want to be mistaken for the kind of person who would participate in this kind of scene."[66] As Flood seemed to see it, Haller did not want to participate in that kind of scene, at least not in public.

Flood's allusion to Elliott is remarkable, not just in the sense that it bespoke a keen knowledge the history of black oratory but also because of the rhetorical invention contained in the invocation. In an analysis of the desegregation debates in the U.S. Congress during Reconstruction, Kirt Wilson examines the public address of speakers such as Elliott and Alabama's James Rapier, both of whom were elected to Congress immediately following the Civil War. These speakers, argues Wilson, engaged "enactment" as a rhetorical practice—that is, they embodied their arguments for African American equality in eloquent performances. The very fact of speaking well demonstrated their claims regarding social equality. According to Wilson the metaphor and imagery that Elliott marshaled on the House floor in 1847 "enacted the speaker's equality. Elliott's speech was praised on the floor and in the press. Within the debate his rhetorical performance was used as proof of black equality."[67] Flood similarly shows how enactment is a strategically self-effacing move. Calling attention to the speaker ultimately so that he or she may fade from view, enactment's power lies in its ability to deliver force to a better argument uttered by an ostensibly universal subject, a move made possible and necessary in a public sphere that requires disincorporation. In this situation, enactment functions as a kind of rhetorical qualifier that means to erase something problematic but that must be admitted because it is in full view. Flood knew that his blackness was in full view; Haller had made that much obvious. Flood's attempt to acknowledge his blackness and move on was never complete. He assigned himself social influence that reached beyond baseball and refused to close the question of race. There and not there, black but uninfluenced by blackness, sure of his race but unsure of its significance, Flood tiptoed the same boundaries drawn by the public sphere's requirement that he abstract his identity into a speaking voice that performed the irrelevance of race.

That the public sphere demanded a rhetoric of disincorporation was never made more explicit than by influential *New York Times* baseball writer Leonard Koppett. In 1967, Koppett had written *A Thinking Man's Guide to Baseball,* a classic text that has seen several editions and is still in print under the title *The Thinking Fan's Guide to Baseball.*[68] As the *Times*'s lead baseball writer, Koppett took a keen interest in Flood's case and its developments between 1970 and 1972. Koppett's coverage began with a January 31, 1970, *Times* article in which he addressed the owners' accusation that Flood had violated his contract by refusing to report to the Phillies. Koppett went straight to the contract language for answers, promising that "none of what follows is intended to be a wise-guy comment. I am not interested in making any sort of point by ridicule, exaggeration, or striking an attitude." Before concluding that Flood did not seem to have violated his Cardinal contract, Koppett offered a word of sincere caution: "I am trying to be straightforward and serious, and if the points I raise are invalid, it is because I really do not understand them."[69] Three weeks later, Koppett acknowledged a "facet of journalism, one worth calling attention to because it will arise again and again." What followed was a recitation of the journalistic canon that is illuminating in approaching the histrionic speech coming from both Flood and the owners: "Each antagonist, naturally, states his side of a question as forcefully as he can. A journalist does his best to give as accurate a picture as he can of the real situation—which, invariably, falls somewhere between the view either side would prefer to sell the public." After explaining his relief at discovering that the owners were not accusing Flood of an emotional betrayal, Koppett enacts the essentials of disincorporated public address: "I am glad my suspicions are unfounded, because I want to think well of the baseball establishment. And it will be a pleasure to follow the Flood case through to its conclusion in an atmosphere of dignity, mutual respect, logical argument, and sweet reason. I expect no less, of course, from the player side."[70] The point here is not that Koppett failed to be as neutral as he thought he was but that the demand for neutrality— dignity, mutual respect, logical argument, sweet reason—was simultaneously a demand for a disciplined speaking style, an official announcement that being "straightforward and serious" meant placing faith in journalistic objectivity and legal facticity. One certainly did not need to be black to appreciate that.

Matters were less straightforward for the members of the black press, but their rhetorical aims hardly differed. In a novel configuration of the power relations between dominant publics and counterpublics, Warner asserts, "Dominant publics are by definition those that can take their discourse pragmatics and their lifeworlds for granted, misrecognizing the indefinite scope of their expansive address as universality or normalcy. Counterpublics are spaces of circulation in which it is hoped that the poesis of scene making will be transformative, not replicative merely."[71] There is no question that the black press did not take either its discourse pragmatics or its lifeworld for granted.. Black newspapers could not; after all, the marked particularity of blackness forged the shared identity of its speakers. But the black press strived to take its address for granted, using those speech protocols as an index of good political discourse and hoping that when this strategy accomplished its goals, the black press would find its dissolution in a universal public sphere. With the particularity of black identity both always present and always under threat, the process of scene making was an elaborate rhetorical exercise in bourgeois public sphere replication.

As his response to Haller's question illustrates, Flood's rhetorical performance in *The Way It Is* is thoroughly accented by the public sphere's requirement that he manage the meaning of his racial identity. In a sense, he had to say, "Yes, I am black, and yes, my blackness matters to me, but for the problem I'm trying to solve, blackness plays no important part." So went black newspapers. Responding to the transformed labor relationship that a successful conclusion to Flood's lawsuit would initiate between baseball owners and baseball players, Sam Lacy observed in his regular *Afro* column, "From A to Z,"

> Flood sees the need for restraints on the part of employer and
> employee, but he also sees what football and basketball have done to
> bring the two sides closer together. . . . And he and his colleagues in the
> players association are wondering why they, as baseball players, should
> be victims of discrimination. Use of the word discrimination, of
> course, brings in the matter of race, although that is not what this col-
> umn had in mind at the outset. As a colored athlete, Curt must feel the
> restraint more than his white counterpart. . . . But, as I have said, this
> is not to be construed as an A to Z complaining on the basis of Flood's
> complexion. . . . It has to do with the reserve clause, its irritation to the
> stomach of the player and its balm to the mind of the owner.[72]

As Flood had attempted to do, Lacy made race present and absent at the same time, invoking the political watchword of racial justice (discrimination) only to stretch its meaning beyond its familiar context and then fore-close serious questions about the matter of race. Baseball's discriminatory practices could be understood as unfair relative to football and basketball, but not on the basis of color.

Generally, however, such explicit gestures away from the question of race, in terms of either the facts of Flood's identity or the anatomy of these newspapers' audience, were uncommon. Instead, writers in the black press often asserted, as Koppett did, the weight of reason as evidence of the justness of Flood's claim. Major League Baseball had gained its exemption to federal antitrust law from a 1922 Supreme Court ruling that baseball's business operations did not constitute interstate commerce. The existence of the reserve clause in the standard player contract depended on this antitrust exemption; if bound by the Sherman Antitrust Act, Baseball's reserve system would likely qualify as an unlawful, collusive labor practice. Writing in the *Philadelphia Tribune* in February 1970, civil rights activist Bayard Rustin offered the counterargument in Flood's defense: "Baseball's income from television now exceeds what is taken in at the local box-office by $10-million. In addition, the traveling and communication that are required to stage a baseball game cost over $1-million a year. Baseball is clearly an interstate enterprise."[73] Lacy offered the same argument, but it came straight from a neutral place of rational critique. In an *Afro* column that anticipated the sense of neutrality envisioned by Koppett, Lacy admitted, "My knowledge of the law is minimal, but I learned away back in freshman high school that all law is founded on reason. . . . I find it very difficult, therefore to understand how anything in baseball can be protected because it is said to escape the restrictions of interstate commerce." Lacy continued, "If 33 workers are flown from Baltimore from Seattle to do a job they are paid to do, before spectators who pay six dollars apiece to sit on wooden benches, they are in interstate commerce . . . unless, of course, I am all fouled up on my interpretation of what is reason."[74] Lacy obviously was not "all fouled up," and it would be a fair reading to say that his point about "reason" was made with tongue in cheek. Nevertheless, he did not end by saying that his interpretation of baseball's *commercial practices* might be erroneous. Instead, he implied that the error of those who defended baseball resided in their inability to grasp the wisdom contained in a self-evident proposition. The force of this argument was treated as undeniable unless, Lacy implied, one's understanding of it was influenced by self-interest. Lacy was making the point that baseball's status as interstate commerce should be plain to anyone who could think. This idea involves more than assuming the disembodied requirements of public debate; like Koppett, Flood, and even Elliott, Lacy reflexively observes those requirements in staging his claim.

Moreover, as Lacy observes and performs the rational imperatives of public deliberation, he inscribes them onto the notion of law itself. Extending his argument about interstate commerce into commentary on the meaning of the legal system, Lacy writes, "One doesn't need a law degree to assume that somebody is looking the other way when: transcontinental trips are made each year via chartered jetliners; players are transported from one city to another, along with equipment that is essential in pursuit of their work; radio, television and newspaper reporters relay the happenings into the 50 states of the union, and athletes are traded from teams in New York and Boston to teams in Illinois, Minnesota and California at the whim of their employers. If there isn't enough 'reason' to make one suspect that the reserve clause vitality has spent itself, the observation made two centuries ago about the main component of 'law' appears to be a frivolous one."[75] Lacy's concluding assertion implied an analogy in form between the mode of public debate he performed and the procedural rationality of law. This homology foreshadowed a line of reasoning that operated from a similar distance: Were Flood to lose his case in court, the response demanded by Lacy's appeal to reason would find expression not in embodied self-interest but rather in the "law's" struggle to disguise the interests of those who derived its benefits unfairly. That is to say, Lacy implied that Flood's loss could be possible only if the partisan public discourse governing baseball mythology found its way into a juridical system already prone to predatory and improper influence. This was not a rhetorical strategy that rooted for Flood per se, but instead a strategy called attention to the universal interests that the legal system must unavoidably protect if it were to pursue the inerrant line of reasoning expected in sincere public debate. This rhetorical practice also guided a prediction recorded by the *Pittsburgh Courier*'s Jess Peters in April 1972. In a passage inserted under the heading, "Flood Fighting Slavery," Peters wrote, "Curt Flood is fighting that exact battle before the Supreme Court right now. A decision on his test of the reserve clause is due in June. It is inconceivable to this column, that the court will allow the cancerous clause to enjoy the protection of the law."[76] Of course, Flood's loss in court was perfectly conceivable, but by stressing its inconceivability, Peters invested forthcoming (and inevitable) criticism of the court with the distancing judgment of unfettered rationality.

As Lacy moved his argument from a technical point about interstate commerce to the basic problem of labor freedom, self-effacement again proved a useful rhetorical device. In 1972, with the Supreme Court about to hear Flood's case, Lacy wrote, "As I noted at the outset, I am not a lawyer. But it is a long-held declaration that the law is based primarily on reason. And, if that is the case, I am convinced that time has outgrown the mood of subserviency, no matter how much money is spent to preserve it."[77] On this point, the weight of reason carried less argumentative weight but obtained similar rhetorical advantages: It clarified the self-evidence of baseball's unfairness. Peters took a similar line in defending Flood against the charge that he was too well paid to complain about his circumstances: "The fact that major league baseball players are fairly well paid during their big league careers is really irrelevant. Anyone who follows a normal path of logic can't ignore the fact that a man who makes $20,000 a year is enti- tled to no less Constitutional protection than a man who makes $5000."[78] Here, the universality of the claim and the universality of the speaker were crucially linked: Anyone who followed the rules of logic would know that anyone deserves the same protection under everyone's law. Liberalism was hard at work. Flood in his book, Koppett in the *Times*, and Lacy and oth- ers in the black press had found ways to participate, as Manning Marable might say, in a universalist dialogue that could, were it insisted upon, tran- scend the ancient barriers of race.

· · ·

The explicit move away from a racial argument combined with the rush to rationality to form a speaker and object being spoken of that conformed to the disembodied discursive norms of public debate; the social fact that Flood was a black individual whose cause was being advocated in the black press entailed a neutralizing rhetoric, a mode of address that found discur- sive protection in a universal subject unburdened by the risks and com- plications of racial identity. Along these lines, Warner sees a problem with labeling a public *counter* or *oppositional* on the basis of "its claim to be oppo- sitional," because "there would be no difference of kind, or of formal media- tion, or of discourse pragmatics, between publics and any other publics." Referring directly to Nancy Fraser, who makes the case for subaltern coun- terpublics through a reading of the history of feminist discourse, Warner asks, "Is the feminist counterpublic distinguished by anything other than its reform program?"[79] The same question might be asked of the black press. It certainly claimed to be oppositional, but black newspapers were centrally concerned, even to the extent of fantasizing about their own disappearance, with imposing the speaking protocols that would erase racial symbolism. Talk the way *the public* talks, insisted speakers in the black press.

Frazier wrote that the black middle class' "feelings of inferiority and insecurity are revealed in their pathological struggle for status within the isolated Negro world and craving for recognition in the white world."[80] This assessment typifies the argumentative tenor that made his text an object of outrage and derision by a number of black readers when it was released in the United States.[81] But however anachronistic his criticism might appear, he pointed incisively toward the narrow social vision expressed in the black press in the early 1970s, a vision constituted by liberal arguments expressed, perhaps by necessity, in disincorporated forms of speech. The thirteen years between the publication of Frazier's book and Flood's trade render comparisons prone to the objection that the time between, which might be labeled the apex of black protest rhetoric in the United States, fundamentally recast the terms of the debate Frazier had initiated. But not only did black newspapers seem to evoke his basic concerns, they appeared to cope with the 1960s in ways that vivified Frazier's original critique. These black newspapers, the only public space in which Flood received vociferous and largely unqualified support, demonstrated a commitment to disciplining the discourses that ran afoul of their liberal imaginary. The bourgeois world of make-believe came into being along with Robinson's exemplary performances and had an unmistakable influence on the black public sphere in which Flood found himself.

4

The Disappearance of
Curt Flood's Blackness

Recent scholarly interest in Curt Flood has generally taken the form of revisionist history targeted at disclosing the dimensions of his challenge to the reserve clause that were influenced by race. Working from various assumptions, including the idea that Flood was vilified in the national press, these critics try to recover a narrative that connects the "principle" for which he claimed to fight to the fact of his blackness. Michael Lomax, for example, counts "black rage" as Flood's primary motivation to file suit, attributing Flood's decision to "Black Power," which "exemplified a mood, a disillusionment and alienation from white America, race pride, and self respect or 'black consciousness,'" a historical construct out of which Flood's "sensitivity" tends to emerge.[1] Gerald Early offers a more nuanced analysis of two basic features of the public rhetoric both from and with regard to Flood: the slavery metaphor and the pointed resistance to the owner's rhetoric of gratitude. For Early, these themes fit historically within the kinds of civil rights discourses that enabled a principled critique of baseball's investment in American democracy: "In the velvet glove of the myth of baseball as the Great American pastime, the game of heroes, the sport that symbolized our democratic impulses, was the iron fist of its absolutist corporate power, a power it enjoyed for far too long in the form of the unrestrained exercise of its reserve clause."[2] This line of reasoning is incisive, but in the same allusive manner that the insistence on Flood's "sensitivity" makes race visible only at the margins, Early advocates Flood most persuasively once the error of the reserve clause becomes something larger than racial injustice.

Lomax and Early engage one side of a contemporary debate about where Flood fits in American history. Located in mismatched popular and interdisciplinary locations, advocates such as Lomax and Early attempt to thicken the political context that surrounded Flood in an effort to draw out a denser understanding of the role his blackness played in the case's unfolding. The other side seems to argue that Flood was sensitized by experiences with racism to challenge organized baseball in a way that had nothing to do with race. Perhaps the most interesting and provocative such instance comes from David Leonard, who measures recent memories of Flood against the historical record to conclude that Flood "was hated then because of racism yet now loved because of and evidenced by the fact that we see him as a baseball player first and as a black man in America second."[3] This is a fair analysis, but Leonard overstates both sides of his case: Flood was not universally vilified then, and he is not beloved now. In particular, the *New York Times*'s Leonard Koppett and several columns in the *Sporting News* offered plenty of favorable opinions. By skipping over the black press while dismissing Flood's mainstream support, Leonard misses a crucial connection in his central claim that Flood's case represents "the continuity of demonization, denigration, and denunciation of blackness in the name of protecting whiteness." The whiteness story rings true, especially if one dwells closely on what it means to be a baseball player first. But in calculating that "much of the media erased [Flood's] place within a larger revolt of the black athlete," Leonard overlooks the way that support for Flood in the early 1970s may have enabled that erasure in ways that had little to do with racist demonization.[4]

The effort, in any case, to fix Curt Flood into the black public sphere or to demonstrate, in Leonard's terms, "the centrality of race,"[5] belies the strategic ambiguity of Flood's rhetorical performance in *The Way It Is* and the earnestness with which others took up his cause in fundamentally race-neutral ways. Like Jackie Robinson (whom Leonard ignores), Flood was a fighter for "principle." But, unlike Robinson, who spoke his mind after the principle of integration had been established, Flood's principle was never grounded explicitly in a claim about racial injustice. Looking back, it might be fairer to say that Flood's principle was prudently equivocal on the question of race. For those who still saw baseball as a vestige of racism or sport as a dehumanizing social institution, Flood's principle summoned the surrounding discourses of racial (in)justice, and for those who looked at matters with the enabling distance of liberalism and color blindness, Flood's principle summoned emerging criticisms of baseball's ownership plutocracy, nascent conceptualizations of sporting labor, and anxieties regarding the inevitable modernization of sport's economic structure. For members of this group, Flood's race and salary were beside the point; fair was fair, and Flood was being treated unfairly by a system designed to enrich the overprivileged few. The principle could be one of two things, then, each of which attracted support: a racial principle or an economic principle—a "black thing" (as Tom Haller had put it) or an economic thing. Both might have been understood, as in Flood's equivocation, to be a "basic principle of human life."[6]

For many contemporary narrators, Flood's representative detractor was Bob Broeg, the *St. Louis Post-Dispatch*'s baseball beat writer whose articles on the highly successful 1960s Cardinals often appeared in the nationally circulating *Sporting News*. In January 1970, Broeg delivered the most direct attack on Flood's position that gained widespread attention. Calling him "a bit overdramatic," Broeg insinuated through a pithy play on words that Flood was just pouting for more money: "It is difficult indeed to be sympathetic to the little man, particularly when it really is not a matter of principle, but of principal." Broeg expressed brief reluctance at personalizing the reserve clause debate but then alluded to Flood's salary: "It is difficult not to get personal in Flood's case because Curt benefited from a large measure of personal consideration." Here, Broeg made the argument that seemed to bother Flood the most: that he was too well paid to complain. "If the legality of the baseball reserve clause were being contested by a player less affluent than Curt Flood," Broeg insisted, "the sympathy would be considerably greater." Instead, citing the $3 million in damages that Flood sought in litigation, Broeg tested Flood's limits: "If principle were really involved in his legal assault on baseball's reserve clause as violating the federal antitrust laws, Flood would have asked for $1 and the right to negotiate for himself." Though it is possible to read through Broeg's paternalism to what Leonard calls a "modern form of lynching," his obtuse defense of baseball's status quo ignored Flood's blackness until *The Way It Is* was released in December 1970. In a book review published in both the *Sporting News* and the *St. Louis Post-Dispatch* in the spring of 1971, Broeg wrote that Flood "emerges as a cynic and as an unforgiving guy whose racial resentment runs deep." And quoting Flood's assertion that "black experience teaches that the American white is guilty until he proves himself innocent," Broeg issued a tired scolding about color blindness, saying that Flood "penned what has to be the most discouraging sentence to all who think they've learned to accept a man for what he is and does, not for what he looks like." That Broeg ignored what Flood took to be meaningful racialized experiences became obvious in the review's final sentences: "Through most of the 236 pages of 'The Way It Is,' whether bedding, boozing or playing ball, Curt is indeed curt. I never knew he was so damned unhappy."[7] Even the fairest historical interpretation of Broeg's commentary would have to admit that he entirely missed Flood's point.

Such an admission fails to shed any light on precisely what Flood's point was, especially since he often left the "principle" for which he was fighting up for the public to supply. Despite his ambiguity, one eventuality was certain: Flood's lawsuit would drive him out of baseball. His "basic principle of human life," however defined, as enacted in the lawsuit would entail sitting out the 1970 baseball season. In this sense, Flood did not stand for *a* principle as much as take a principled stand, and since he demonstrated the sincerity of his cause by refusing to play ball, Flood's supporters found ways to animate the "basic principle of human life" with arguments, narratives, and themes that may or may not have been faithful to the sophisticated humanism Flood attempted to formulate. The stand authenticated the principle, which was then elaborated in terms that reflected the interests, motivations, and political imaginations of his supporters. In suing and refusing to play, Flood had put his money where his mouth was, so his commitment to conscience could only be challenged disingenuously. Flood's supporters from the black press to the *New York Times* to the *Sporting News* easily and dramatically falsified Broeg's uncharitable accusations of greed.

Nevertheless, according to Broeg and others who shared his views, Flood's wealth delivered the lie to "the basic principle of human life."[8] Perhaps, then, it is reasonable to say that the most stable principle that Flood embodied revolved around the notion of freedom. This is the point at which observers such as Leonard tend to overstate the influence of racial politics. Although Flood's rhetorical performances evinced an interest in finding common cause with agitational black discourses, Flood's description of himself as a "well-paid slave" to Howard Cosell's national audience also demonstrated a strategic understanding of public argument. The figure of the slave performed double duty, simultaneously evoking racial imagery and analogizing baseball's basic institutional moral error. Anticipating the color-blind platitudes (which Flood had learned to identify and disdain) that would be repeated by numerous detractors, the "well-paid slave" could be regarded, if deployed skillfully, as intrinsically raceless. His self-characterization certainly would attract little sympathy from Broeg and other critics, but supportive commentators attended closely to the basic structure of Flood's slave metaphor—Flood was a freedom fighter with the conviction and sincerity to act on principle. The pricelessness of freedom, by contrast, made Broeg's lecture look distasteful and churlish.

The slave metaphor proved itself to be racially slippery and symbolically perilous. The "well-paid slave," though evoking graphic racial imagery for those who wanted to see it and seeming absurd to those who marveled at Flood's paycheck, paradoxically contained both symbolic difficulties and built-in symbolic solutions relative to the race and class identifications that sometimes vexed his advocates. For Flood, slavery was a flexible resource that rhetorically condensed what he took to be an abject social position. Once released into public circulation, however, the slave metaphor forced his advocates to cope with the complicated representational obstacles imposed by the facts of his salary and blackness. Broeg's columns gave voice to a naive populism that used Flood's class and race against him. Broeg said, in essence, that Flood was not poor and therefore should not be talking about race. Why, Broeg ultimately asked, should one root for Curt Flood? Who did he represent other than himself? The answers here revealed the ingenuity of the slave metaphor: Freedom as a principle rested on the abstract condition of Flood's slavery; once regarded as a freedom fight for which Flood was willing to sacrifice, many observers saw the principle as trumping the size of his salary and the color of his skin. The slave metaphor, which might have symbolized systemic articulations of race and class, became in baseball's public sphere precisely the symbol through which race and class were disarticulated from principle.

It was easy, then, for public speakers to lose sight of Flood's blackness when addressing the challenge to the reserve clause in the early 1970s. Supportive public discourse turned its rhetorical activity toward universalizing Flood's case and figuring out a way to save baseball. Race became superfluous, part of the story but not part of the argument, something for which his advocates would have to account so that they could set it neatly aside. The black newspapers and the national sports press made three basic discursive moves. First, Since Flood's condition of supposed bondage extended to his white teammates, the argument from blackness—incipient in the imagery of slavery and inflecting Flood's speech—was safely quarantined in Flood's consciousness and removed from the social and structural facts of the case: Flood was "sensitive" and "principled." Second, the labor dimension of the slave argument became the locus of extended discussion and analysis. Well-paid slavery had piqued the interest of black newspapers eager to establish baseball as a measure of progress (an achievement for which Robinson can be credited), and the comparison had certainly drawn the attention of a national sports press already narrating baseball's economic minutiae. Third, any abolitionist spirit of well-paid slavery gave way to the rhetoric of reform: Flood's advocates moderated his claim and pointed out where interests converged. In both black newspapers and the national sports press,

Flood indeed found support, but along the way, the symbolic significance of blackness to the slavery argument got lost in the commotion.

The owners insisted that Flood was an agent of destruction. In late January 1970, Joe Cronin and Chub Feeney, presidents of the American and National Leagues, respectively, issued a press release concerning Flood's federal lawsuit. The concise statement summarized baseball's official public position in defense of the reserve clause, and it set baseball's preservationist discourse into motion. In various press outlets nationwide, such as the *New York Times*, the *Sporting News*, and black newspapers such as the *Chicago Defender*, Cronin and Feeney's statement characterized Flood's legal action as a potentially fatal threat to baseball's future. They scolded Flood for selfishly refusing his "reassignment" and spoke in catastrophic terms regarding a successful lawsuit's potential consequences:

> When a player refuses to honor an assignment, he violates his contract, in which he agrees that assignments may be made, and he violates the fundamental baseball rules, including the reserve clause, which experience has shown to be absolutely necessary to the successful operation of baseball.
>
> The court action commenced by Curt Flood attacks these fundamental rules and makes the same charges that have been made in the past and rejected by the Supreme Court of the United States. We have complete confidence that the rules of professional baseball, which have been central to the success of the game over many decades and which have permitted players such as Curt Flood to reap rich personal rewards, will withstand this new attack. . . .
>
> A congressional committee, after an exhaustive study of baseball and weeks of hearings, concluded as follows:
>
> "Baseball's history shows that chaotic conditions prevailed when there was no reserve clause. Experience points to no feasible substitute to protect the integrity of the game or to guarantee a comparatively even competitive struggle."[9]

Given what would follow, a detailed and bulleted list of the chaos that would result if Flood were to win in court, Cronin and Feeney's "complete confidence" that baseball could withstand attack reads like petty, misplaced bluster:

> The chaotic results that would be created without the reserve clause should be obvious:

1. Without the reserve clause the wealthier clubs could sign an unbeatable team of all-stars, totally destroying league competition.

2. Clubs of more limited resources would be stripped of their stars and their ability to field a team which the public would accept.

3. The integrity of the game would be threatened as players could negotiate with one club while playing for another.

4. Clubs could no longer afford to spend millions of dollars to scout and sign new players and to subsidize their development in the minor leagues. No club could build with assurance and no intelligent person would continue to invest the large capital required for player compensation, an unmatched pension and benefit plan costing $5,450,000 per year, minor league subsidies and other costs of operating a minor league club.

5. The minor leagues, which exist only because of major league support, would be destroyed. Professional baseball is the only team sport that finances the development of its players.

6. Mutually advantageous trades would become impossible if the players' consents were required, thus preventing contract assignments which have been beneficial to both clubs and players and which are exciting to those who support the game of baseball.

7. Professional baseball would simply cease to exist.[10]

This statement can be read in various ways. One possibility is that it is an honest declaration from baseball's chief bureaucrats in a panic over the security of the institution they had been installed to protect. Another is that it is a set of alarmist talking points meant to induce public panic about baseball's demise. From a more critical perspective, one might also call it a detailed (albeit unintentional) analysis of the political economy of Major League Baseball, a naked iteration of the slavelike conditions described by Flood and a performance of the kind of dehumanizing rhetoric Flood had identified as necessary to the preservation of the owners' power. In any case, Cronin and Feeney's statement officially summarized the terms of baseball's public position, which put "chaos" and "collapse" at the center of its unabashedly dystopian vision.

Koppett and other observers critical of baseball, however, pointed to such statements as evidence of the owners' traditionalism, painting baseball as out of touch, stuck in a different time, inherently conservative, and most tellingly, "obtuse." A predominant narrative held that sport was undergoing massive shifts relative to the desires and expectations of its athletes, the spiking growth of its economic structure, and its public image.

Koppett's columns turned frequently to a trope that resonated with general announcements of shifts in the national psyche and that was a favored term of Flood's: the "sports establishment." In a late January 1970 *New York Times* piece, Koppett offered a history of baseball's labor organizations in an effort to make sense of the Flood case. Naming this history a "Brotherhood of War," Koppett dramatized the nature of the false choice presented by ownership on the matter of the reserve clause:

> The hardest thing to understand, for most outsiders, is the apparent obtuseness of the baseball establishment in resisting any and all change. . . . After all, it sounds silly for supposedly responsible businessmen to hint at "total destruction" of their affairs if so much as a comma is changed.   But everything has its origins, even unreason. It's easy enough for mid–Twentieth Century lawyers to say "devise a less restrictive reserve substitute." Driven into baseball consciousness, however, is the idea that the present system, which did evolve gradually, has worked profitably; that alternatives tried in the past—even if it was the dim past—did fail; and "alternatives" presented in theory can lead to numerous booby traps in reality.
>
> In this light, the reluctance of the establishment to confront change is more comprehensible, if not necessarily more justified. Perhaps the real criticism of today's baseball brass should be on other grounds. Its rigid stance implies timidity, a self-confessed lack of confidence in its ability to act imaginatively, constructively and with goodwill, to devise improvements.[11]

In adopting a reformist line of reasoning, Koppett provided a reading of Cronin and Feeney that simultaneously exposed the "baseball establishment" as on the one hand bellicose, blustery, and foolish and on the other hand acting expectedly (however irrationally) to secure its self-interest. At the same time that Koppett demystified the owners' dystopia, he recognized the symbolic advantages that the dystopian vision conferred.

Owners operationalized their catastrophic rhetoric through shamelessly frightening terms such as *chaos, destruction*, and *cease to exist*, choices that carried with them at least three benefits. First, the owners were able to expand the scope of the problems associated with reserve clause abolition coterminously with Flood's rhetorical escalation to "principle." Beset by the charge that they were slaveholders and tyrants, owners enumerated the catastrophes that would ensue if the disloyal subjects had their way.

Second, "chaos and destruction" helped to reclaim the public ground that had been undermined by the revelatory rhetoric emerging from Flood and his advocates. Flood claimed to be showing "the public" a truth obscured by an ideological trick, and the owners responded with a "public" victimized by Flood's threatening gestures. After all, the owners had said, modifications to the reserve clause would erode competitiveness beyond the point of public acceptability. Finally, baseball's dystopia concretized the emerging malaise in sport in a way favorable to the "sports establishment." As critics groaned about the increasing influence of big money in sports and the loss of baseball's iconic national status, baseball owners contended that Flood was exacerbating baseball's demise as an idyllic pasture of American life.

Critiques similar to Koppett's circulated widely but also abetted ownership's effort to construct a dystopian scene animated by labor disagreements. "Chaos and destruction" fit easily within the national sports press's controlling thematic at the beginning of 1970. Flood's case had become a matter of public attention as December 1969 turned to the new decade, which occasioned a variety of predictable articles attempting to make sense of the 1960s and speculate on the 1970s. On January 4, 1970, Joseph Durso wrote the lead article in a special section of the *New York Times* on sport at the dawn of the decade. Durso's column, "Color the Next Decade a Lush Green," observed the effect that money would have on sports: "It's green, it's abundant, it's inflated. It buys oats for race horses, llama rugs for quarterbacks, domed stadiums for cities. It's money, and it will make the sports world go round in the seventies as never before." It was not all bad, though. Durso saw economic reasoning as the price of progress: "Economics—the 'dismal science'—will bring more teams to more cities in more areas of the world at higher prices and on more artificial surfaces with the color of currency. But economics will also bring more lawsuits by athletes, unions for umpires, boycotts by players and strike deadlines for all sides." As Durso depicted sports in a mythic fall from innocence, his first case in point was hardly surprising: "Curt Flood, an outfielder famous for catching the ball, may become even more famous as the man who attacked the 'reserve system' that governs most major spectator sports. As the seventies begin, he is suing for his 'freedom' from baseball's reserve clause, which binds a player to his team until he is traded or quits." Moreover, as Flood, his advocates, and the owners insisted for various purposes, "the public" was left to watch helplessly as matters spiraled out of control. Durso saw Flood's case as "part of the scramble for the public's growing leisure time and leisure cash. And sports in the seventies will spiral upward with the economy into the chase for big money, big security, big pensions, big investments, big payoffs. The gold rush is on."[12]

Baseball commissioner Bowie Kuhn gave a March 1970 interview to the *Sporting News* that was quoted extensively in an editorial about baseball's "chief concern." Under the headline "We Believe . . . ," summarizing the position of the newspaper, editor and publisher C. C. Johnson Spink helped Kuhn lend voice to the establishment's version of events: "Kuhn is facing some serious problems, but the most serious, he believes, is the damage being done to the game's public image by the lack of rapport between the clubs and the players and between the players and the fans." Against this backdrop, Flood's case was reduced to a trivial annoyance: "'These other things are important,' [Kuhn] said, referring to Denny McLain's troubles and Curt Flood's suit to abolish the reserve clause, 'but the image is more vital than the legal aspects.'" Spink expressed concern that baseball must "convince a new generation that the game is both 'now' and 'relevant.' It won't be easy, especially if some of the people in the game keep blackening baseball's eyes."[13] With Kuhn in command of baseball's public image, Flood was simply another "black eye," further evidence of the erosion of public confidence that Kuhn was charged with preventing.

Similarly, a February 1970 *Sporting News* article (published originally in the *Los Angeles Times*) presented both a diagnosis and cure as understood by Walter O'Malley, president of the Dodgers. The *Times*'s Ross Newhan cataloged O'Malley's concerns, including his assertion that "what is needed in baseball is an 'era of goodwill,' a restoration of the rapport between owners and players rather than the negativism produced by Marvin Miller, executive director of the Major League Baseball Players Association."[14] "Goodwill," in Flood's view, was a ruse that sustained the owners' paternalism, particularly when they claimed that organized labor intervened in otherwise amicable management-player relations. O'Malley cited Flood's case as expressive of the Players Association's deleterious influence: "Formerly a practicing attorney, O'Malley said he did not care to participate in the judicial semantics of the Flood case. 'I can only say that I'm disappointed in the methods he's used. He's created an aura of negativism that has harmed the image of the sport.'"[15] In contrast to the kind of careful analysis issued by Koppett, O'Malley saw the details as mere "judicial semantics"—nonsense. The image of baseball was under assault from an interloper using unbecoming methods to chase false causes. O'Malley externalized the causes of "negativism," reifying the image problem through a dismissal of baseball's principled critics. Such statements may have been what led Koppett to call the owners "obtuse"; one is left to wonder how labor might have protected the players from the predatory desires of ownership from behind closed doors. After all, O'Malley used the catastrophic possibilities of Flood's case as an opportunity to reassert benevolence: "Selfishly, [the Dodgers] would benefit by removal of the reserve clause. Realistically, there would be such an imbalance that the game couldn't exist."[16] In this common establishment view, only the sagacious selflessness of the owners sheltered baseball from destruction by shortsighted, carpetbagging union agitators.

With nostalgia and regret, the nation's papers narrated the evolving relationship between money and professional sports, developments that were taken to be contrary to public enjoyment and in some cases detrimental to the health of society. Of course, this is precisely why Flood had regarded the owners and the press as cohorts; they worked together to elevate the primacy of the game's public image beyond the point of constructive labor relations and, perhaps more important, humane labor standards. And just as obviously, this pattern urged the Players Association into existence as a useful public instrument; in private, nothing ever changed. Regardless of how forward-thinking observers such as Koppett may have regarded themselves in supporting Flood's cause and authenticating new player demands, the underlying story of regret, a wistful goodbye to the golden era, blended Flood seamlessly into the fog of baseball's preexisting war.

In January 1970, days after appearing on national television with Cosell, Flood was featured in an occasional *New York Times* column called "Man in the News." Sportswriter George Vecsey's profile appeared under a large photograph of Flood standing next to an oil portrait of Martin Luther King Jr., which Flood had painted for an Atlanta charity auction. Although the *Times* sensationalized the case in typical fashion with a headline that read "$90,000-a-Year Rebel: Curt Flood," Vecsey offered a sympathetic, nearly tender portrayal. The image of Flood next to King presented a clear racial cue, however oblique. But much in the same way that the slave metaphor performed double duty in *The Way It Is*, the *Times*'s photo of Flood with his painting of King brought race into view so that it might be pushed out of focus. Vecsey's column coped with Flood's blackness but did so in a way that rendered its meaning unique to Flood's individual experience and conscience. Vecsey depicted Flood as a kind of Renaissance man, contextualizing the rhetorical appearance of the slave. As Vecsey put it,

> The wiry little center fielder was known to return to his apartment
> after a night game and take out his oil brushes and work until dawn.

The shoulder healed in due time, but the Cardinals never got him to change his hours.

This is the man who filed a suit yesterday against baseball and its so-called "reserve clause." Flood had resented being traded to the Philadelphia Phillies last October, partly because he hated to leave "Cardinal-land," as he calls St. Louis, but also because he felt he had put too much time into his profession to be shuttled around "like a slave."

Out of this proud reaction, Flood is mounting one of the most serious challenges ever made on baseball's control of its hired hands. Flood is in a more independent position than most players because of his future as an artist and his business interests in the United States and Denmark.[17]

In this characterization, Flood appears as a man equally committed to baseball and to his creative pursuits, thoughtful enough about both to remain loyal to a principled professional ethic, and successful enough at both to assert his independence with a steady and confident temperament. The slave was just Flood's way of putting things.

As Vecsey came to terms with Flood's blackness, he considered the way that racism may have influenced the development of Flood's baseball career: "While playing in the Carolina and [South Atlantic] leagues in 1956–57, he encountered southern bigotry, living in a Negro college dormitory and often going hungry after night games because there was no place that would serve him. But, he has recalled that the experience made him play better, in an inspired rage." A generation later, Lomax would call this "black rage," but for Vecsey in 1970, Flood's "rage" inspired his individual success. So, in 1958, "the little man proved he belonged with the Cardinals." When asked about the King painting, Flood told Vecsey, "This is one of the rare instances where I integrated my feelings about the subject. This is more expressive because there's more of me in it."[18] Bigotry made Flood play baseball better, and thinking about King made Flood paint better (or at least more expressively). In the end, Flood emerged from Vecsey's profile as thoughtful, intelligent, and sensitive, as someone who knew how to properly channel the anger of racialized experiences into an acute professional instinct. As an international businessman, world-class ballplayer, and portrait artist who held King close to his heart, Flood was ultimately a remarkable individual—well qualified, in the eyes of the New York Times, to be a "man in the news."

Vecsey's article, published just as the slave metaphor began to appear in the sports press, helped to initiate Flood into public discussion. As the story took shape, other similar profiles would appear, in, among others, such nationally circulating publications as *Sport* and *Newsweek*.[19] Generally speaking, these articles, even when parroting the owners' concerns about the destruction of baseball, constructed a persona for Flood similar to the one in the *Times*. The result was a kind of professionalization of Flood as an insightful and principled individual, as a newsmaker, as a bona fide public citizen. To be sure, this depiction would not always hold up. The detractors would have their say, and cynics would moan about the loss of baseball's innocence, but Flood possessed a business professional's ethos. After all, Flood never got anything for free. He excelled at his job despite long odds, was rewarded as such, claimed roots in the St. Louis community, dwelled creatively on King, and fairly felt punished for having done everything right. Is this, some supporters wondered, how you treat a pro? Just as Flood had expressed passionately in *The Way It Is*, the whole business was an insult to a dignified man of substance.

In the black press, Flood found a similar advocate in Bill Nunn Jr., the sports desk editor of the *Pittsburgh Courier*. Like other black newspapers, the *Courier* had covered Flood's case from its initial moments, the most notable being the January television appearance in which Cosell had quoted Flood's salary to a nationwide audience. In May 1970, a few weeks before Flood's federal trial would begin, Nunn asked Cosell's rhetorical question: "Why would a man want to rebel against a contract that could have meant $90,000 in salary and fringe benefits for the year 1970?" The question set Flood's rebellion against his contract, not against baseball, and the answer sounded much like the one that appeared in the *Times*: "To understand that you would have to know Curt Flood the man as well as Curt Flood the ballplayer."[20] Such characterizations attempted to offset and reverse the confounding aspects of the "well-paid slave." The unusual size of the salary he refused made him neither spoiled or ungrateful but instead dramatized the depth of his character and demonstrated the sincerity of his personal and individual sacrifice.

Moreover, Flood had earned Nunn's endorsement by virtue of the player's commitment to the Cardinals, and his keen sensitivity was indicated in the persona that contextualized that commitment: Flood was a serious businessman. "As a major league star Flood had always been a manager's dream. Day in and day out Curt performed his duty with class. He had a keen desire to win. He never shirked his duties. He could be counted on when the chips were down. Curt Flood, in other words, came to play. Off the playing field, there is another side to Flood. Soft spoken, articulate and a smooth dresser, he could easily be taken for a 9 to 5 business man on Wall Street. A successful businessman we might add. Curt Flood is also a sensitive man. He's sensitive to the problems that surround us everyday. He's sensitive to the cast in which he wants to mold his life."[21] Nunn's sketch evoked sporting clichés of team play that might have been (and still are) applied to any number of pro athletes: Flood was a classy guy, Flood was dependable, Flood came to play, Flood wanted to win, and so forth. Even further, however, as Nunn emphasized in triplicate, the same Flood who put the team first possessed a rare personal sensitivity. Similar to Vecsey's Renaissance man, Nunn's Flood was profiled through the individualism and individuality of his character.

Unlike Vecsey, however, Nunn did not explicitly account for Flood's racial identity. Instead, Nunn simply offered an iteration of the slave metaphor linked to Flood's personal sensitivity and individual impulse to rebellion. Flood was not someone to take mistreatment lightly, Nunn insisted: "Instead of accepting the news that he was no longer a Cardinal in good graces, Flood rebelled." Nunn saw the figure of the slave as appearing out of Flood's emotional reaction as a comparison befitting his bitterness over the insult: "One day he was a Cardinal. The next day he had been peddled down the river. Slaves, Curt felt with bitterness, were treated the same way. He decided to fight."[22] Among Flood's supporters, profiles such as Vecsey's and Nunn's cooperatively stitched a persona that countered Broeg's infantilizing portrait of an impetuous ballplayer in a fancy suit pouting over a trivial and manufactured injustice. Having performed his professional duties in baseball with class and pride, Flood operated as an exemplar of the kind of self-determination that could be achieved through the offices of vocational excellence and individual talent. Baseball had, in essence, punished him for his success, and Flood, as a sensitive man, was remarkable for his refusal to stand for it.

This approach probably represented the best argumentative strategy for addressing the rhetoric of gratitude that Lomax, Early, and Leonard identify as racist. Why, many advocates asked, should Flood be grateful for what he had rightfully earned? Early is certainly correct to insist that the owners' paternalistic tenor and line of reasoning seemed to emerge from the same discursive well that produced the racist rhetorical question, "What do you people *want*?"[23] In this instance, however, determining that the argument from gratitude was "racist" in the way that Early intends depends on a puzzling counterfactual. Had the reserve clause's first "serious challenger" been white, would baseball owners have responded differently? Would a white player have faced the accusation that he was ungrateful for what baseball bosses had benevolently provided? Such questions are hard to answer, but such a thorny scenario becomes even more difficult to address in a rhetorical context that consigns race's meaning to Flood's individuality. National publications such as the *Times* and the *Sporting News* accounted for Flood's blackness by rendering it a private concern, and the black press followed a similar theme in avoiding any positive elaboration of its meaning. Depictions such as Nunn's individuated Flood at the same time that they conferred an intrinsically raceless professional identity: Flood's blackness was left to speak for itself as the black press highlighted the valor in his path to individual success. Together, the *Times*, the *Sporting News*, and black newspapers professionalized Flood's ethos and privatized his blackness, removing race from both public debate and the modes of identification into which Flood could be inserted. Questions of freedom and dignity were imagined to be universal as the case developed in the news, erasing blackness from the image of the slave and encouraging forms of collective identity better fit for public discussion. Race was part of Flood, not part of the Flood debate. But if you were curious to know how anyone could turn all that money down? Well, for that, you would have to know Curt Flood the man.

Unlike the awkward character of the fight for racial inclusion, which was replete with internal tension, Flood's case inverted the logic that often strained to establish forms of black identity fit for racial inclusion. Flood offered the black press the means by which it might formulate and defend the upwardly mobile aspirations of the black professional class in the context of shared national interests. From black journalists' perspective, the details of Flood's particularity—his blackness and his wealth—dissolved into an encompassing bourgeois imaginary. Flood's $90,000 salary became neither a marker of baseball's inevitable collapse nor a factor that alienated him from average folks. Instead, everyone's interests seemed to converge quite nicely.

The *Chicago Defender*'s Doc Young managed the problem of Flood's extreme wealth by imbuing Flood's principle with a notion of freedom premised on Flood's earnings as an employee: "Flood's salary is irrelevant. The Cardinals paid Flood $90,000 only because he was an outstanding fielder. Flood earned the money. It was no gift." In fact, insisted Young, Flood's freedom fight had baseball's interests in mind: "What he is fighting is a clause in baseball law which ties a player to the club with whom he signs initially and permits the club to sell or trade him, at will, regardless of his feelings about the matter. He is seeking, in a broad sense, more freedom for the professional athlete. He is not attempting to wreck organized baseball, nor does he object necessarily to joining the Philadelphia Phillies."[24] The assertion that Flood did not object to Philadelphia was slightly inaccurate: Flood had called Philadelphia "the nation's northernmost southern city"—meaning, of course, that he expected to experience racism there.[25] Young's point (supported by this inaccuracy) was that the size of Flood's salary bore no relation to the abstract principle for which he stood. "Chaos and destruction" were not Flood's goals: What mattered most, since he had earned his money fairly, was that he be treated fairly according to professional standards.

Similarly, the March 1970 issue of *Ebony* magazine featured a full-page, full-color photograph of Flood next to a full-page editorial headlined, "Found—An 'Abe Lincoln' of Baseball." *Ebony* asked its readers to consider a hypothetical scenario:

> Imagine yourself with a great talent for doing plumbing and, at the age of 17 or 18, signing a contract with a plumbing firm for a bonus of $1000 and the chance to work at perhaps $100 a week. Three years later you are one of the best plumbers in the business and your contract holder has raised your pay to $500 a week. But you feel that you are worth $1000 a week and, in fact, a number of other plumbing firms would gladly pay you what you want or even more. Then you find you cannot leave your job—your contract is for life. You cannot change jobs when you wish but your contract holder has the right to sell your contract to another plumbing company in another state without consulting you and—if you want to continue as a plumber— you have to go no matter how much the move might inconvenience you. In addition, no matter what price a contract is sold for, you will not realize a penny for the sale.

Comparing this situation to the circumstances in which baseball players found themselves, *Ebony* asserted that baseball was "able to enslave its players in plush fetters." Baseball players, the magazine pointed out, "are still bought and sold like property." But, said the editors, "This year, before the long, long season is over, there just might be some changes made. It just might be that baseball's long needed 'Abe Lincoln' has finally shown up in the person of Curtis Charles Flood."[26] *Ebony*'s analogy incorporated Flood's impressive salary into an imaginary labor subject and offered Flood as Lincoln's negative racial instance. Lincoln, of course, was a white hero who set black persons free; Flood, *Ebony* hoped, was a black man who would set his white colleagues free. Concretizing the principle in the figure of the plumber, Ebony abstracted Flood's labor identity and disconnected blackness from the figure of the slave.

The suggestive interplay of racial identities at work in *Ebony*'s argument underscores the way in which black press accounts of Flood managed his blackness in public address. After the Supreme Court ruled against Flood in 1972, *Baltimore Afro-American* sports columnist Sam Lacy made this interplay explicit: "Generally overlooked in the comments of both sides following last week's 5–3 ruling ... is the fact that a young black man from the ghetto voluntarily committed suicide so that his teammates—the majority of whom are white—might have a better life. . . . He assailed the [reserve clause] as an instrument which denied him the civil right of controlling his own destiny." Lacy's column, which reads like an epitaph, emphasized the racial interchangeability—or universality—of Flood's "sacrifice": "The challenge was in the nature of a suit against baseball which was designed to free not only himself, but all his fellow athletes as well. . . . Yet, while any benefits derived from his action would be shared by all his colleagues, a loss would be suffered by him alone. . . . That is the supreme sacrifice."²⁷ Lacy's complaint turned out to be too true. An early version of free agency was incorporated into Major League Baseball's collective bargaining agreement when an independent arbitrator released two white players, Dave McNally and Andy Messersmith, from their contracts.

An unattributed opinion piece in the *New York Amsterdam News* understood Flood's situation in similar terms, putting an explicitly colorblind spin on employment freedom in baseball. "The reserve clause is Willie Mays, $165,000. Bob Gibson and Robert [*sic*] Clemente, $150,000 each. Frank Robinson, $140,000. Ferguson Jenkins and Willie McCovey $125,000 each and Billy Williams $115,000." In listing baseball's highest-paid players, the newspaper insisted that the reserve clause did not curtail the salaries of the players but instead "curtailed the free movement of players. It stopped them from taking the highest bid which is the American way. It stopped free enterprise."²⁷ Race and class were bracketed together as the *Amsterdam News* made its pitch. Worry not, it seemed to say, black players are profiting from baseball, so it is not that baseball is racist; rather, the problem is that baseball is obstructing everyone's path toward wealth. The operational telos in this defense of Flood was the fair play of equal antagonists on a field of free enterprise, a process expressed under the ostensibly inclusive sign of the "American way."

This narrative of free American enterprise precipitated a rhetorical shift, whereby Flood's specific identity as a wealthy ballplayer was replaced in political and economic terms with more identifiable forms of labor, including those that in another context might not have found common cause with a person making $90,000. The plumber metaphor was popular among Flood's public advocates perhaps not just because it worked as an illustrative analogue relative to baseball's economic structure but also because its mode of illustration was defined by the way in which the problem of socioeconomic class could be resolved: Rich baseball players could be represented as sharing the interests of the working class.[28] The *Pittsburgh Courier* similarly compared Flood to an auto worker:

> Look at the situation for example, or even more so, this analogous stupor. Imagine an auto mechanic employed by General Motors whose salary is determined by annual review. On Jan. 1, he is offered a new contract for the new year at a salary of $1,000 less than he received the previous year.
>
> The mechanic is not allowed to offer his services to Chrysler or Ford. If he quits, he may not work at his trade for any employer. If he has not signed by Feb. 1, GM is entitled to tell him: "Sign now for what we've offered or go dig ditches, Buddy."
>
> Major league baseball players, of course, are rewarded more handsomely for their services than are auto mechanics. But their career expectancies are far shorter. The tiny minority of players who get to the big leagues only last for an average of four years.
>
> The real point is that the professional athlete is the only civilian in America who cannot bargain for his service with any employer he chooses. He is the only American who does not work in a free market economy.[29]

In addition to the face value of the analogy, the *Courier* offered an analysis of the career window for baseball players, resolving the problem of Flood's high salary by both comparing his aggregate earnings to that of the auto mechanic and pointing out that the average baseball player did not earn what Flood did. Unlike auto workers, these Americans—baseball players—were unfairly prohibited from availing themselves of the general labor market.

In the *Philadelphia Tribune*, Bayard Rustin pointed out that Flood's lawsuit was significant not because of Flood's identity as a baseball player but because of his identity as an employee working to expand the rights of others: "All of the points of contention in Flood's suit may not, at first, seem relevant to baseball as a sport. But it is also an enterprise and a profession, and Flood, in addition to being a player, is an employee. His suit, therefore, represents an attempt to expand the rights of a specific group of employees who are now at the mercy of their employers."[30] In the *Baltimore Afro-American*, Lacy explicitly compared baseball to "any other job" despite Flood's high pay: "On any other job, although he doesn't get paid nearly as well, the worker does his best or gets fired. . . . If he is dissatisfied with conditions on the job, he quits and goes elsewhere."[31] Both Rustin's and Lacy's arguments relied on the premise that Flood's principle consisted in a group identity dissociated from the facts of his race and the size of his salary.

Nunn emphasized Flood's career sacrifice in an analysis of his salary:

> By fighting the structure upon which baseball says it exists, Curt could be through as a player. There is no certainty how long his case will be allowed to drag on in the courts. It could be months or it could be years. At age 32 any years Flood gives away are being done at a terrific sacrifice. As a player Flood has made over $20,000 only during the last six years. While his salary has expanded tremendously during that time so have his taxes. It has been estimated from one source that over his first nine years in professional baseball Flood had averaged $11,500 a season. At that time he was rated as one of the top players in the game. That is why I believe Flood should be commended for the battle he is waging. He isn't doing it for personal gain. He's fighting for something he believes in. Few men are willing to pick up the sword of battle under such circumstances.[32]

Nunn's analysis presented a catalog of factors mitigating against the criticism that Flood was too well paid to complain: Flood was an aging player, his salary increases had come only recently, his taxes had also increased, and he was underpaid while an established star. Instead of merely dismissing the salary debate, Nunn engaged in it directly, refuting Broeg's sanctimonious accusation that Flood's real interest was "principal, not principle."

Black newspapers' basic rhetorical strategy in covering Flood's case between 1970 and 1972 was to assert a sequence of transpositions that exchanged Flood's particularity for forms of collective identity that

reflected the press's political interests and self-imagination. When addressing Flood's blackness in public, journalists did so to show that he was the
inverted racial image of Lincoln or that he was a poor black kid from "the
ghetto" fighting for rich white athletes' freedom. Of course, Flood was a
wealthy baseball player, but as *Ebony*, the *Courier*, and the *Amsterdam News*
attempted to show, he might as well have been a common laborer. All at
once, black newspapers rebutted the contention that Flood was stalling
for a bigger contract, moved the reserve clause debate back to the abstract
ground of principle, and redoubled their rhetorical investment in both
baseball and the American way. For this reason, Flood's case was ideally
suited for black press uptake and advocacy. As a public subject, he could
be emptied of the racial particularity that problematized the struggle for
inclusion, and his labor identity could be abstracted in a way that demonstrated the consonance between black politics and the national interest.

As events began to unfold publicly in late 1969 and early 1970, much of
the country's sports press attended to the details of his case carefully and
thoughtfully. In particular, the St. Louis–based *Sporting News* followed the
case diligently, and though it would be an overstatement to call the *Sporting
News* unconditional in support of Flood's cause, this national paper advocated Flood conscientiously within a news frame that put Flood in relation
to ongoing labor disputes between baseball owners and players. The *Sporting News* and other advocates, such as Koppett, moderated Flood's appeal
to principle by offering suggestions for reserve clause "modification" and
"improvement." As they observed the modernization of sport's economic
structure, they defended some adjustment of the reserve clause as an essential and inevitable reform. This position implicitly accepted the owners'
contention that abolition of the reserve clause would cause irreparable
damage to the game. News coverage of the case repeatedly emphasized that
reserve clause alteration would be enough to mollify Flood and the Players
Association, thereby saving baseball's basic economic structure.

At the time Flood filed suit, baseball's players and management had
already discussed the reserve clause. Most of the conversation had been
unproductive, but it had allowed each side to offer something in the way of
a public position in the newspapers rather quickly. The main disagreement
by January 1970 centered on a common negotiation dilemma: The owners
said that the players had not offered any plausible alternatives to the reserve
system, and the players said that the owners had refused to take seriously
any recommendations. In an editorial following reports that Flood had
filed suit, the *Sporting News* summarized the situation:

Commissioner Kuhn says major league club owners feel the players have failed to offer any acceptable changes in what most baseball
men consider the heart of their administrative apparatus. It should be
emphasized that the players have never demanded complete freedom
to negotiate with any employer. They are asking for modification of
the reserve clause. The Major League Players Association contends
the owners foster the impression that the reserve clause is an all-or-
nothing device: Change it one iota and all is chaos. The owners have
not, the Association claims, offered a single counter-proposal to any
idea the players have broached. The players have suggested, the owners have rejected, and there the matter apparently stands.

In the context of this standoff, the *Sporting News* offered a few underde-
veloped ideas, including a variation on the contract system in the National
Football League, but also expressed grave concern (keeping oddly in theme
with all the talk about plumbing) about what might happen if matters were
allowed to proceed in the court system: "While baseball is saying no to
these proposals, the courts might well rip out the whole plumbing system,
not merely divert a bit of the flow in the players' direction."[33]

The *Sporting News* generally expressed sympathy for Flood's case but
attempted to push the issue away from the courts and toward collective
bargaining. Wondering "what would happen if baseball granted Flood free-
agent status," the *Sporting News* wrote that a court decision "could prove
devastating if the reserve clause were knocked out completely, which the
courts might very well do." Nevertheless, "the players want the reserve clause
modified, not torpedoed," and "Flood says he'll drop his suit if the reserve
clause is altered to the satisfaction of the Major League Players' Association." Instead of the courts, the *Sporting News* suggested "some genuine
bargaining now between players and owners over possible revisions which
both sides could live with."[34] But the problem with moving the reserve
clause dispute to labor negotiations was that owners used Flood's case as
a reason to further stall meaningful debate. The *Sporting News* reported at
the end of January 1970 that Cincinnati Reds president Francis Dale took
the Players Association decision to support Flood's case to mean that the
players had lost interest in negotiation: The head of the Players Association, Marvin Miller, "asked whether he should keep bargaining or did the
players want to support Flood's action. They voted to back Flood. So, this
would infer they're taking the reserve clause off the bargaining table. How
can we negotiate anything that's in the courts?"[35] Dale's rhetorical question

indicated the owners' willingness to play chicken with the players in court as they heralded the specter of baseball's collapse.

The national sports press nevertheless continued to insist that Flood had no interest in the game's destruction and that "Flood is on record to the effect that any negotiated modification to the reserve system, satisfactory to the Players Association, will lead him to abandon his antitrust suit."[36] Furthermore, reporters seemed firmly to take Flood's side. A May 1970 *New York Times* editorial that appeared about a week before the first federal court trial affirmed all of Flood's essential points in the antitrust suit, noting that "there is no question that baseball today is big business" and that "the interlocking system of player contracts and club rules may well come within the jurisdiction of Federal anti-trust and various civil rights laws." At the end of the editorial, the *Times* fully advocated a change to the reserve clause: "Some modification of the reserve clause—which Hank Greenberg, who was both a player and a club owner, testified is 'obsolete, antiquated and definitely needs change'—is in order."[37]

The *Times*'s Koppett, whose columns also often appeared in the *Sporting News*, was perhaps Flood's most consistent supporter throughout the various stages of his challenge. Koppett's position embraced the inevitability of baseball's changes and maintained that since neither the owners nor the players were foolishly self-destructive, the two sides were likely to figure things out in a way that would benefit everyone. Taking the long view, Koppett asserted that "despite the alarming and fearful cries of the baseball establishment, it is inconceivable that all concerned are so lacking in ingenuity and common sense that they will fail to work out appropriate arrangements." Believing that the situation would balance out satisfactorily in the end and that ownership was expressing unfounded alarmism, Koppett asserted "plain facts": "Baseball, like everything else, changes all the time and always has. And for each change, some response re-establishes a suitable equilibrium."[38] After learning about a year later that the U.S. Supreme Court had agreed to hear Flood's case, Koppett reiterated his beliefs that the owners were wrong about "chaos" and that changes to the reserve clause were Flood's only real demand: "It is highly unlikely that chaos will result from any decision. A victory for Flood will only begin the process of working out new contractual arrangements between club owners and athletes, and these new arrangements will be arrived at gradually. The suit itself argues for modification of restrictions on free movement of players from club to club."[39] By the time the Court had ruled against Flood,

Koppett credited Flood with having forced the kind of collective bargaining both sides had known all along would be necessary:

> As it is, the terms of a modified reserve system must be hammered out across the table, and the players can get as much modification as they are willing to fight for.
>
> But even this is possible only because Flood's case was pursued. Until Flood raised the issues, the club owners flatly refused to consider any kind of modification. They offered to bargain only in an attempt to get the case dropped. Then, in arguing the case before the Supreme Court they adopted the defense that the reserve system was really a matter of compulsory collective bargaining and therefore not an anti-trust matter at all. They can't retreat from that position now. They must bargain. But it was the Flood case that moved them into that position.[40]

Occasionally and in passing, the national sports press would mention the matter of "human rights" or would point out that Flood thought of himself as a slave. But the overriding and persistent approach for Flood's advocates in venues such as the *New York Times* and the *Sporting News* was to place Flood's case into the context of a preexisting player/owner conflict. For these outlets, the image of baseball's chaotic implosion was merely a productive illusion the owners used to defend their negotiating ground, and the business about slavery was a similarly useful counter-ruse. Cooler heads, these journalists figured, would prevail. The essence of their advocacy took the form of repeatedly emphasizing the necessity of modifying the reserve clause, an approach that made Flood the figure who might frighten the owners out of their obstinacy. In this view, Flood hastened (or at least helped to realize) the inevitable.

The black press adopted a similar emphasis on pragmatic reform. In late December 1969 and early January 1970, a United Press International (UPI) article that appeared in a variety of black newspapers, including the *Chicago Defender*, the *Pittsburgh Courier*, and the *Baltimore Afro-American*, effectively announced the beginning of the Flood debate. The article, built on quotations from Miller, Joe Torre, and the infamously provocative Jim Bouton, essentially reported on the proceedings of the Players Association meeting in Puerto Rico. Though the UPI warned that Flood's suit might "strike at the very heart of organized baseball," it quoted Miller's understanding of Flood's motivations: "Curt felt he had the rights of any other citizen. He has nothing against Philadelphia as a city or a team, but saw no basis for being confined to a limited market." But asserting the "rights of any other citizen" seemed to entail a recognition of the reserve clause's constitutive importance to baseball: "Miller, Torre, and Bouton emphasized that the players were not attempting to create chaos in organized baseball by simply out-lawing the reserve clause but wanted certain changes in it." More directly, the UPI promised that Bouton was speaking about "certain modifications [that] would retain the structure of baseball but at the same time enable players to have negotiating privileges which they now do not have."[41] And days after Flood and Miller appeared with Cosell, the *Philadelphia Tribune* quoted Flood as saying, "I cannot be bought. I have too much integrity for that." The statement was a rejoinder to the possibility of a financial settlement to drop the suit, but the paper emphasized that "it is doubtful that Flood will go beyond the goals of the Players Association" and that "Miller will be happy to get [an] option clause [similar to that in the National Football League] for major league players. He would settle for less as a start."[42] Later in January, after the details of the lawsuit began to circulate widely, the *Afro-American* printed another UPI article explaining that Flood had the support of at least one white player, Baltimore Oriole third baseman Brooks Robinson. Above all, the story of his endorsement operated as a pledge that Flood would not ruin baseball: "Major League players don't want destruction of the reserve clause, only modification of the rule, veteran Baltimore third baseman Brooks Robinson said. . . . The All-Star Oriole infielder . . . said elimination was not the intention of the club representatives who voted support of Curt Flood's suit challenging the controversial reserve clause."[43]

The reports and UPI articles about Flood that appeared in the black press in early 1970 consistently offered reassurances that although Flood's cause was principled and righteous, a fair recalibration of the reserve system would be sufficient to mute the threat posed to baseball by the lawsuit. Affirming Flood's status as an employee or worker entailed an appreciative recognition of the basic economic architecture of sport. Defining Flood's principle in terms as various as the American way, "free enterprise," and the "free market economy" and asserting a collective labor subject on whose behalf Flood was fighting, black newspapers simultaneously critiqued baseball ownership and inscribed the game itself with institutional legitimacy. In rhetorical strokes that shadowed the logic of liberal inclusion, baseball was characterized as a path of opportunity obstructed by recalcitrant gatekeepers. However, this argument offered little rejoinder to the gatekeepers' alarmist claim that abolition of the reserve clause would devastate baseball's economic foundation. Relative to this position, the rhetorical problem for Flood's advocates in the black press turned on the choice between Flood's "rights" and the collapse of the institution they venerated—unless the terms of the debate could be shifted. Thus, constructs such as the American way, free enterprise, and the free market brought with them the basic vocabulary of reform, expressed variously as *modification*, *alteration*, *adjustment*, or *improvement*. In any case, *abolition* became terministic anathema to those in black newspapers voicing support for Flood.

The compromising impulse of the black press raises questions about the moral force implied behind the assertion of Flood's principle and demonstrates the extent to which the owners' catastrophic spectacle determined the rhetorical choices of Flood's public advocates. With "chaos" and "collapse" looming in the background, many opinion columnists in black newspapers found themselves conceding the owners' anxieties. When news of Flood's suit began to spread among players in early 1970, the *Chicago Defender* registered the dissent of Minnesota Twins star Harmon Killebrew, who warned, "This is just the way baseball is. There has to be control. Without control there would be no baseball."[44] And, a March 1972 *Amsterdam News* piece worried that a Supreme Court decision in Flood's favor might deal a deathblow to all of the major professional sports: "The Supreme Court may not give a decision and then again they may rule the reserve clause a slave master. Then again, if the Supreme Court rules against the reserve clause it may lead to the end of the major sports like football, baseball, and basketball as we see it today."[45]

The *Chicago Defender*'s Young backed both Flood and baseball owners on the way to making the case for modification of the reserve clause. "Baseball, to be sure, has a legitimate argument," Young proclaimed. "Owners and teams are entitled to some protection for their investment." With almost the same dehumanizing vocabulary Flood had identified in *The Way It Is*, Young parroted the owners' anxieties: "Total abolishment of the reserve clause very well may cause some chaos in the game, with the richer clubs grabbing off the best players." The solution, then, consisted in an observation from "Chet Walker, player representative of the Chicago Bulls, [who] admitted that there is need for some sort of legal tie between player and club when he said, 'I don't think the reserve clause should be abolished. It should be modified so as not to bind a player to one team for his entire life.'"[46] Like the *Amsterdam News*, Young suggested that the effects on baseball could ripple outward in a way that threatened other sports. Young regarded players as "investments" that the owners had the right to protect. Moreover, Young used the owners' favored term, *chaos*, to describe the results Flood's victory might produce. In the end, the quotation from Walker balanced the argument back in Flood's favor: the reserve system ought to be modified. Young and others supported Flood, in essence, through an argumentative retreat: If the reserve clause were adjusted to meet reasonable standards of professional respect, baseball's error could be resolved and the game could go on.

At its core, however, the modification compromise indexed the flexibility of Flood's "basic principle of human life" not just relative to its moral force but also in terms of its applied scope in public address. The call for modification rather than abolition of the reserve clause revealed cracks in the commitment to principle opened by the need to preserve the progressive legitimacy of baseball's institutional existence, which in turn involved stretching Flood's principle past his individual interests to fit it over the collective interests of professional baseball players as a group. In the *Philadelphia Tribune*, Rustin illustrated this maneuver:

> Over 80 years ago John Montgomery Ward, a star outfielder with the New York Giants, called the reserve clause a form of "slavery." The term is still appropriate. Flood was traded to the Phillies last October after twelve successful years with the Cardinals. The years of work he put into his profession, his desire to remain in St. Louis, his well being as an employee were all irrelevant beside the wish of some top management official to send him somewhere else. He was being treated, as Flood appropriately put it, "Like a slave." Out of a sense of violated rights, he is mounting a campaign which in the end may benefit not only himself but all of his colleagues.[47]

Echoing Young's point about professional "equity," Rustin enacted the tropological elasticity of slavery. Ward was a nineteenth-century baseball player who became disgruntled with the "reserve rule's" effects on the innocence of the "pastime" and thus attempted to start a "players' league" that would operate according to the model of a cooperative.[48] Rustin's reference to Ward, a white player, removed the facts of Flood's racial identity from the basic structure of the slavery argument. Moreover, by locating the consequences of the reserve clause in the violation of Flood's professional "rights," Rustin preserved baseball's ground and observed Flood's potential to protect the interests of a labor class broadly construed. Baseball treated

its players like slaves, implied Rustin, but not in an exercise of racial prejudice; instead, encouraged by a system rigged to enable their abuses, owners
and management treated employees like possessions. Flood's importance,
then, lay in his potential to set his colleagues free.

The national sports press and black newspapers pursued routine coverage of Flood's case in rhetorically congruent ways. The *New York Times*
and the *Sporting News* fit Flood within the broader unfolding of baseball's
labor relations events, apprehending his lawsuit as the latest and maybe
even most formidable indicator of the Players Association's accumulating
influence. Change was inevitable, these writers said, and each side had overstated the situation. The *Times* and the *Sporting News* offered the inevitability of a negotiated compromise in place of either side's extremist rhetoric;
they replaced both the owners' consequentialist dystopia and Flood's deon-
tic appeal to slavery with the pragmatism of adjustment and reform. The
black press narrated events similarly, accepting and promoting the reformist dimension of Flood's challenge with a vested symbolic interest in the
protection of baseball. "Modification" operated to domesticate the racial
hubris of Flood's slavery argument. The black press's interpretive charity
extended to the recognition that Flood's lawsuit was a matter of principle
behind which Flood stood conscientiously but ended at the concession that
baseball owners might have been onto something with "chaos." In elaborat-
ing a principle that resided ultimately in Flood's professional identity—in
the unique labor subjectivity of the ballplayer—the black newspapers that
covered his case regularly urged a path of sensible reform. Players were
recognized "investments," whether black or white, "slavery" was printed in
quotation marks, and the racial symbolism of slavery was safely neutralized by the practical wisdom of compromise. For the *Times* and the *Sporting News*, Flood symbolized change already under way; for the black press,
Flood was a worthy agent of institutional amelioration. In any case, the
owners were purveyors of a false choice, and Flood was no mortal threat.
Flood was right, and baseball would flourish.

• • •

Ultimately, Curt Flood lost in court. Despite the apocalyptic rhetoric
employed by both Flood and the owners, the games in fact went on. In at
least this sense, Koppett was right to suspect both sides of engaging in self-
indulgent rhetorical brinkmanship. In the spring of 1973, owners locked the
players out of camp for about a week before agreeing, among other things,

to salary arbitration and to the "ten and five rule," which gave players the right to veto trades provided they had ten years of Major League service and at least five years with a particular team.[49] In March of that year, the *Baltimore Afro-American* announced that the agreement "gave everyone remotely connected with sports cause to breathe relief." The *Afro*'s editorial, however, focused not on a rhetorical exhale but on Flood, to whom "the players owe a debt of gratitude" and "who, after only two years, is virtually forgotten." Under the headline "Curt Flood Pointed Way" on page 2 of the paper, the editors wrote,

> Curt Flood turned his back on $95,000-a-year—and a career esti-mated at a quarter-million dollars—in order to battle singlehandedly against the reserve restriction that impales a player to the whim of a club which holds his contract.
>
> Flood went all the way to the Supreme Court, with no Mar-vin Millers, no threat of strike, no nothing. He lost, but it must be acknowledged that the battle they were forced into by him had a dis-tinct softening effect on the owners.
>
> It is true that the Players' Association supplied the money for Curt's suit, but that means little. It is like the boxing promoter who furnished the gloves for two guys to fight to fill his pockets.
>
> Besides, of what value is martyrdom?[50]

Such ultimately was Flood's early legacy. Even the *Afro*, which through Lacy had categorically supported Flood, strained to remember him through baseball's labor haze, assailing the error of the reserve clause. In this view, Flood's importance rested on his status as a martyr to a compromise—he had a "softening effect"—even if the case had destroyed him personally. Echoing Koppett's assertion in the days after the Court ruling, the *Afro* insisted that baseball players benefited from the negotiating position in which Flood had put them.

The *Baltimore Afro-American* no doubt perceptively noted the value of martyrdom to Flood but failed to recognize the value of Flood's mar-tyrdom to the public claims of the black bourgeoisie. Flood helped the black press record three achievements: First, supporting Flood meant sup-porting a black player whose blackness could be relegated to the margins of the cause, thereby enacting the political rhetoric of color-blind justice with rare effectiveness. Having prudently inserted the meaning and signif-icance of Flood's racial identity into the limited confines of his individual consciousness, black newspapers fit Flood into a mode of representation that was explicitly nonracial. Speaking in a rhetoric consistent with that found in outlets such as the *New York Times* and the *Sporting News*, they removed the question of race from serious public debate. Nevertheless, the black press, marked by its blackness and accustomed to fighting injustice, still found ways to advocate Flood's cause with demonstrable principled intent. Second, then, Flood's circumstances were abstracted not relative to a collective black subject but instead relative to a universal labor subject with righteous claims to free enterprise, the free market, and the American way. All at once, black newspapers rebutted the bellicose accusation that Flood was acting greedily and identified his circumstances as representative of an upwardly mobile black middle class. The plumber and the auto mechanic, as Flood analogues, were crucial to this process, since they collapsed the differences internal to blackness in a transpositional movement toward universality and redoubled the black civic commitment to a shared—that is, integrated—national interest. Third, once professionalized and emptied of racial and class-inflected meaning, the principle for which Flood stood and the slavery metaphor, both of which contained embryonic threads linking freedom to race, labor, and human rights, became subject to the political discourse and logic of liberalism. The value of "principle" was cashed out in terms of institutional reform, and "slavery" was exposed as a mere expression, a dramatization, or a regrettable rhetorical gambit essential to pushing the two sides closer toward acceptable reform. In essence, black newspapers had it both ways: They advocated Flood in a persuasive defense of universal justice and simultaneously fought to protect an institution—baseball—with nearly unmatched symbolic importance to liberalism's progress narrative. All things considered, Flood served elegantly as a protagonist. He was a black man fighting for the right cause against the right establishment, and through it all, his blackness could be made to disappear.

5

Race, Slavery, and the Revolt of the Black Athlete

Ebony's March 1970 editorial on Flood was as brazenly self-congratulatory as it was enthusiastically supportive in defense of his cause. The same magazine that had discovered Abraham Lincoln "in the person of Curtis Charles Flood" and described baseball as restraining its players in "plush fetters" took the space (the opening words, in fact) to document its foresight six years earlier on the question of the reserve clause: "In April 1964, Ebony published an editorial entitled, 'Needed—An Abe Lincoln of Baseball.' The editorial took up cudgels for what may be the highest paid group of slaves in all history—the players in that All-American Game called professional baseball." *Ebony*'s foregrounding of slavery, however, did not entail the foregrounding of Flood's racial identity, except at the very end, where the magazine offered him its best wishes: "So, best of luck to you, Curt (Abe Lincoln Flood). It will be a bit of poetic justice should it turn out that a black man finally brings freedom and democracy to baseball." *Ebony*, like the black newspapers that narrated his case on their sports pages, issued another reassurance that baseball would survive: "But don't worry about baseball disappearing from the American scene if Flood is victorious. . . . It will be with us for a long time—as long as people will pay to get into ballparks and TV and radio will pay for the privilege of bringing it into the homes of literally millions of baseball fans."[1] Just as black newspapers had moved rhetorically between the slave metaphor and analyses of sport's labor structures, *Ebony* pointed out that baseball was now big business. This point was crucial to Flood's lawsuit and was a recurrent feature of pro-Flood advocacy: If baseball were interstate commerce, then it would surely be subject to the prerogatives of antitrust law.[2]

Despite a reflexivity that tended to discipline radical discourse and shelter the political imaginary of liberalism, the black public sphere played host to a discursive contest over the constitution of a collective black political voice, a struggle over the meaning and importance of blackness to political action. Generally speaking, political effectivity was defined according to the logic of inclusion as the black newspapers regulated the movement of rhetorical currency in their discursive marketplace. My choice of the market metaphor is intentional; in the spirit of the marketplace of ideas through which American democracy is often imagined, black newspapers offered themselves as spaces of deliberation modeled on the liberal public sphere. They idealized the spirit of protest as essential to democratic action while aligning the substance of protest with the progressive success of integration. Accordingly, the injunction to speak courageously resolved the tension between the facts of internal difference and the perpetual assertions of unity. Flood, standing "in the tradition of Robinson and Ali" and "Jim Brown, Arthur Ashe and Bill Russell"—in spite of the ways in which these men's individual ambitions may have been at odds—deserved support and respect for being a principled participant in public life. In speaking, such men added to an ongoing conversation. Regardless of what they stood for, they stood for something. All were admirable black public subjects, even if, as Bill Nunn Jr. had asserted, one did not agree with Flood. The canonical lists of courageous black athletes that began to emerge in the late 1960s provided what Michael Warner might call a "utopia of self-abstraction," a rhetorical mechanism that symbolically collapsed the internal differentiation of blackness. Figures such as Robinson and Flood were rendered politically vital precisely through their commitment to speak, a rhetorical move that worked to mask meaningful differences and discontinuities not just relative to a political project but also in relation to the way that blackness was presumed to function in a political project. Black newspapers expressed the corporeality of blackness, to be sure, but they also decided its meaning according to its irrelevance and contained poetic expressions of blackness through the logic of the public conversation.

"Poetic expressions" of blackness refer to the kind of discourses whose further circulation depended not on the abstraction of blackness into a racially unmarked public sphere but instead on pointed and elaborate assertions of black identity as the basis of one's experience and political expression. In the black press, the significance of racial experience to the truths contained in their public arguments was subject to constant disavowal. At the same time in the early 1970s, however, sport figured prominently into an emerging discourse that alternatively placed urgent demands on blackness as a rhetorical resource. As Harry Edwards demonstrated in the late 1960s and early 1970s, corporeal expressivity helped to constitute a form of public address in which being black meant something more than being devoted to inclusion. Being black in this public entailed a form of speech that positioned black identity as the starting point of one's political impulses, which challenged the instinctive demand for institutional reform that came along with the commitment to color blindness. Treating differences within collective black identity not as a regrettable indicator of unity unrealized but instead as determinative of one's politics, Edwards and others offered rhetorical performances that forced "the poetic-expressive character of counterpublic discourse to become salient to consciousness."[3]

The distinction between the two types of public discourse I am proposing here is illustrated most vividly in the different ways that Flood's slave metaphor found mediation in public argument. If it is fair to say that the errors of slavery reside in at least two problematic relations of domination and subordination, one grounded in the exploitation of labor and the other grounded in racist dehumanization, then it is also fair to say that Flood's slave narrative produced coterminous lines of reasoning that emphasized these power relations differently. All of these lines could work in Flood's favor. On the one hand, black newspapers seized the opportunity to demonstrate the reciprocal benefits of integration. As a black man fighting to bring justice to a racially unmarked class of exploited laborers, Flood represented both the universal advantages of color-blind justice and the urgency of labor reforms that would accelerate the arrival of a racially neutral economic meritocracy under the sign of the American way. On the other hand, public rhetors such as Edwards saw in Flood's slave metaphor a dramatic expression of integration's limits and errors. As a black man treated like the subhuman property that had historically characterized the social identity conferred on blacks by whites, Flood dramatized the invitation to indignity that integrated sport had become. In this version of the slave narrative, Flood disclosed the fallacious intent of appeals to meritocracy and the entire system of dehumanizing social relations on which the predicates of incremental reform rested. Flood's blackness was neither incidental nor ironic—not simply "poetic justice"—but enjoined the insistence on justice poetically expressed under the sign of what being black in America meant. The former version of Flood's slave narrative eagerly concealed the importance of Flood's blackness to his cause, and the latter version was expansively poetic in making political meaning out of Flood's racial identity.

This chapter illuminates the racialized dimensions of Flood's case that are systematically occluded in public memory: the ways in which Flood's case might have resonated within a social and political imagination that was deeply racialized and unapologetically committed to a world-making project informed by black experience. First, I present an analysis of the rhetoric of revolt. Edwards and cohorts such as Floyd McKissick issued a critique (as Flood did) of the sportswriting establishment, undermined integration as a self-evident social objective, and confronted black athletes with conflicting loyalties. Second, I show how Flood's "argument from blackness," as opposed to being confined to his consciousness or spread thinly over the amorphous "mood" of the 1960s, consisted in discernible rhetorical consonances to the radicalism of Edwards's *Revolt of the Black Athlete*, especially as it appeared in a new academic journal, the *Black Scholar*. Such radicalism posed a symbolic threat to the color-blind political imaginary that underwrote the existence of the black press. To stabilize the rhetorical volatility of radicalism, black newspapers positioned Flood in relation to the "new black athlete," proudly announced the emergence of a new ethos of protest, and then rhetorically constituted that ethos through the principles proper to liberalism. Third, then, I explain how black newspapers appropriated Flood and domesticated the threat he posed by fitting him into the political rationality of liberalism.

The potential energy produced by the appearance of the new black athlete found its most elaborate expression not in the ephemeral calls to conscience smattering black press coverage but rather in the fresh memories of the 1968 Olympics undergoing useful configuration at youth conferences, in the shifting texture of the black intelligentsia, and in the rare press pieces that in their immediate contexts may have resonated as little more than angry slogan shouting or, in the words of Lin Hilburn, as "the rhetoric of the ghetto."[4] With unmatched depth, the new black athlete was narrated in Edwards's *Revolt of the Black Athlete*. Originally written in 1969, *Revolt* attempted to organize and concretize the ideas that emerged from the Olympic Project for Human Rights. By the spring of 1970, however, Edwards was more sociologist than activist, and the circulatory fate of *Revolt* might be described better as a seminal work in the sociology of sport than as a founding document for a social movement.

Nevertheless, Edwards had quite a bit to say and created spaces in which to say it not only by publishing *Revolt* but also by helping to formalize, in places such as the *Black Scholar*, an image of the black activist-athlete quite different than the one generally appearing in the black press. He personally had little to say specifically about Flood, but much of what Edwards and others speaking like him had said strikingly resembled much of what Flood had said. Within the rhetorical context characterized in and through *Revolt*, Flood had only a few explicit advocates. But relative to the way in which Flood imagined race's significance to his cause, his challenge to baseball evoked Edwards's *Revolt* with heretofore unexplored depth. In contrast to the way Flood's story was told in black newspapers, and expressing political conviction in a language modulated heavily by corporeality and racialized affect, the public space projected by Edwards resisted false assertions of black unity under the banner of color blindness and readily labeled reformers as Uncle Toms.

In *Revolt*, Edwards attempted to open a critical space through which an intervention regarding the prevailing wisdom about race politics might be mounted. As Flood had shown in *The Way It Is*, this move relied on a critique of the sociology and political economy of sportswriting. Howard Cosell, whose support of Muhammad Ali had conferred on Cosell the reputation of a maverick, reenacted his outsider status with his criticism of the "sports establishment." Flood had devoted sustained attention to the damage done to players by sportswriters, and Cosell similarly saw that exposing sanctimonious pretense was crucial to understanding the determinate dynamic of the emerging age. After a sarcastic rendering of the "sports sanctuary" in the *New York Times*, Cosell addressed the source of the mythology: "The legend never had much truth behind it, but it has persisted to an astonishing degree largely because of the daily propaganda of many of the nation's sports writers and virtually all of the nation's sports announcers." And Cosell saw Flood as fitting here because he had provoked a reactionary response: "How else can one explain so much indignation in so many places over the recent books by Jim Bouton, Dave Meggysey, Curt Flood, and Johnny Sample—books that disturbed the establishment by dealing with such un-American matters as drink and drug and racism and blackballing in American sports?"[5] Cosell shed critical insight on a point in lending voice to propaganda, which often reveals its coercive nature in institutional responses to acts of conscience. His observation called attention to the constitutive and contingent features of sport's public sphere: Its trusty mediators were lying, and Flood was among those helping to spot the lies.

Edwards did not specifically name Cosell in *Revolt* but offered a list of trustworthy exemplars—synecdochically labeled "the black sportswriter"—who spoke in genres similar to Cosell's. In fact, the figure of the sportswriter gave Edwards the opportunity strategically to structure the kinds of divisions into black politics that might produce new demands and thus help to reorganize the political imaginary of blackness itself. In *Revolt*, Edwards conceded the bygone benefits of white media coverage to the black liberation struggle but insisted that "the mass media has on frequent occasions been harsh, insensitive, and indifferent to the plight of black people," remaining "an unofficial arm of the establishment in America." When it came to sports, Edwards asserted that "most news reporters in America . . . are towers of morality, ethics, and truth when compared to this country's sports reporters."[6] Flood had tiptoed a difficult argumentative line in issuing his sportswriting critique: It was not easy both to give voice to "the player" and to avoid making the players feel like fools. He tended to solve this problem by claiming to say aloud what all of them already knew, but Flood had to speak, of course, for all of them. Edwards was under no such rhetorical constraint. He would instead become expansively poetic in describing what race meant to the quality of one's public expression. Thus, he established a sportswriting hierarchy to disclose accurately the politics of his antagonists and protagonists.

"The White Sports Reporter," according to Edwards, committed three errors. First, he *became* a white sports reporter. It was, in other words, fallacious to assume that the practice of journalism, the canons of journalism, or journalism school transformed one's social consciousness. According to Edwards, "A racist white man who becomes a journalist becomes nothing more than a racist white journalist." Such a claim took obvious aim at the "objectivity" often underwriting the specious "common sense" of race politics. Second, sports reporters were beholden to counteroppositional interests and thus subject to co-optation: "Sports reporters must be responsive to the desires and needs of the sports industry. This is roughly analogous to a situation where the jury is chiefly responsive to the needs and desires of the criminal." This idea looked to both reverse the valorization of sport as a "big business" (a stipulation through which black newspapers had sought to protect baseball's legitimacy) and invert the rhetorical criminalization of black athletic protest. Third, the white sports reporter promulgated the representational logic of tokenism, exploiting black athletic heroes in a stroke of self-congratulation over continuing progress.[7]

Edwards's criticism of the "Negro Sports Reporter" was far more damning. *Revolt* gives the impression that as detestable as he may have found the activities of white sports reporters, he regarded them as perfectly rational extensions of racism and corruption. Negro sports reporters, however, had "deluded many of their own followers with fanciful myths that belie the truth about the world of sports." In terms that seemed to draw directly from E. Franklin Frazier, Edwards said that the "chief concern" of Negro sports reporters was to "keep everyone happy, though deluded. Most of the time they are too busy looking the other way, keeping the boat steady, to report objectively and with conviction."[8]Edwards obviously meant something different by "objectivity and conviction" than did most sportswriters in the black press. The insidiousness of tokenism gained strength in the kind of sports reporting that glamorized the achievements of the black bourgeoisie through the effacement of black identity. Edwards's position reads as an even sharper iteration of Frazier's black press critique in *Black Bourgeoisie*:

> A publication, of course, is no better than the people who write for it—black or white. Many high-circulation magazines that purport to speak for America's Blacks actually are more concerned with maintaining a "respectable Negro image," meaning the image that portrays black people striving as hard as possible to be like white folks. At the very best, such publications take a middle-of-the-road position when it comes to approaching and handling critical racial questions. Invariably, in their worst guise they fill the pages with irrelevant, defensive drivel about the social life of the Bourgeois Negro, the latest wig crazes, the experiences of the "only big-time Negro hunting master," the only Negro airline pilot, and so forth. But when it comes to socially, politically, and economically relevant issues, most of them play it right down the middle or worse. For they have their white advertisers to consider, who buy pages of space to advertise bleaching creams, hair straighteners, wigs, and other kinds of racially degrading paraphernalia. In the area of sports, one generally encounters innocuous stories about Willie Mays' ability with a bat or the speed of halfbacks Walt Roberts and Nolan Smith, little men in a big man's game. But seldom, if ever, has the truth about the sports industry in America and the situation of black athletes found its way to the pages of these publications.[9]

In essence, Edwards argued that Negro sports reporters—presumably operating in the black press—performed the nastiest of all ideological tricks: They gained false bourgeois status by performing ugly forms of tokenism and black self-hatred in the service of racists. White-controlled public expression was bad enough, but white-mediated public expression—that is, "Negro" expression—was worse: It collaborated with the enemy. Hence, Edwards often intoned, "Uncle Tom."

Above all, Edwards utilized the Negro sports reporter as a lens through which to challenge the prevailing representational logic of black politics. The

Negro sports reporter, like the white sports reporter, made spectacles out of limited achievements. The division that Edwards attempted to forge within black collective identity turned on how one represented black experience in political discourse. From his perspective, the Negro sports reporter represented blackness in the same manner as the white sports reporter—that is, as simultaneously damning and irrelevant. The black sports reporter, by contrast, represented blackness assertively, unapologetically, and in a manner appreciative of human dignity. Color blindness as practiced in the black press seemed to Edwards to do the work of the establishment. Alternatively, the black sports reporter was characterized by "certain qualities" that generally positioned "him outside of, and in many instances in opposition to, the sports establishment." Edwards sidestepped the specifics of those "certain qualities" but promised that the black sports reporter "differs significantly in attitude, philosophy, and guts level."[10] Edwards seemed to be describing a kind of "guts" precisely opposite to that which Jackie Robinson had enacted. In a direct refutation of guts' transformation into "turning the other cheek" through the mediation of Branch Rickey and Robinson, Edwards's black sports reporter possessed a discursive tendency presumably unmediated by the corrupting forces of the racist establishment.

Alluding not to specific political aims but instead to competing modes of political expression, Edwards conducted a shrewd maneuver: "Neither the designation 'black' nor the differentiating qualities are necessarily directly related to skin color or racial heritage." He presented a list of six sportswriters "on the contemporary sports scene," including Dick Edwards of the *Amsterdam News*, before revealing "the last-mentioned four just happen to be white."[11] The ingenuity of this maneuver consisted in its dual work. It helped to recover some of the color-blind argumentative ground that underwrote the hegemonic absurdity of reverse racism. (Whether or not this strategy works is unclear even today.) At the same time, the collapsing racial distinctions led him not toward an affirmation of the black press's "color-blind" reckoning but instead toward the elaboration of an authentically oppositional voice informed by blackness, or a willingness to speak in an idiom uninfluenced by the diluted (and deluded) discourses of the establishment. Said Edwards,

> The black sports reporter writes not only about developments on the field of play, but also of those influences that might affect athletes off the field. He does not pause to consider how the sports establishment will respond to his story. If his editor refuses to print it, he may

soften it, but he always presses to maintain its central focus. The black reporter is undeterred by risks to his job or personal attacks against his reputation. For him such considerations are secondary to justice, fair play, personal character, and conscience. For the black reporter actually believes in all the principles and ethical considerations supposedly fostered by sports. His fight is against those who have violated these standards and sought to profit from their debasement. It will be men of dispositions and persuasions such as these who will write the true history of American athletics.[12]

Undeterred by personal risk, holding sport accountable to sporting values and not to their corrupted economic versions, black sportswriters, regardless of their skin color, would write a true history.

The cleavage between racial identities was transposed into distinctions in how one spoke about justice. Racial particularity consisted in the quality of one's public voice, not in the facts of the body. White persons could be black sports reporters if they characterized the world in the right way. Edwards's approach was poetic and productive; he forged a means of inserting black corporeality and affect into public discourse out of a slippery equivocation on what black newspapers seemed to regard as color blindness. His critique, as Cosell's criticism perhaps reveals, was not limited to speakers who identified themselves as "white," "Negro," or "black" but instead traced an individual's racial constitution to his or her function in public address. Whiteness, Negroness, and blackness referred to speech genres and their connection to antiestablishment political interests, not to observable physical differences. In *Revolt*, Edwards explicitly put the meaning of blackness onto the political agenda, and the case of the black sports reporter who just happened to be white illustrated that authenticity, objectivity, and conviction were expressed in only one kind of idiom and not another.

From the beginning of his project, Edwards carefully secured the legitimacy of his organization. In 1968, Edwards held a meeting with "as many recognized leaders as possible" to "strengthen the forces behind the Olympic Project for Human Rights" (OPHR). In attendance were Edwards, Louis Lomax, Floyd McKissick, and Martin Luther King Jr.—a recognizable crew, to be certain. Moreover, Edwards took extra effort to ensure (and explain) that the OPHR would be oriented with the proper philosophical disposition: "Leaders of other organizations that we regarded as primarily 'Negro oriented,' such as the Urban League and National Association for the Advancement of Colored People, we purposely avoided." Once again separating revolutionaries from sellouts, Edwards reinforced the distinction between Negroness and blackness operant in his alternate racial typology: "Negro flunkies" would not speak for the OPHR. Lomax, King, and McKissick "agreed to become formal advisors." Edwards pointed out that a complete black boycott of the 1968 Olympics was plausible. The idea, he said, had come from King, whom Edwards said had advocated deepening the protest's commitment level: "Dr. King stated that perhaps the conditions of race relations in the United States today demanded a total boycott of the Olympic games by black people for little else in the way of nonviolent protest was left to them."[13] This telling of history in *Revolt* worked, in essence, to announce the OPHR's authenticity and legitimacy.

Douglas Hartmann points to a number of factors that secured the OPHR's legacy, including the enduring image of John Carlos and Tommie Smith's medal-stand protest, the prosecution of lingering struggles (among them Flood's), destabilized notions of labor and national identities set in motion by a new orientation toward "human rights," and the enactment of Title IX, which presumably initiated a process by which gender equality could be achieved in sport. Hartmann's discovery of a vibrant and enduring Edwards "legacy" bespeaks the ways in which Edwards made a new political vocabulary of sport publicly expressible. He places a large emphasis on "style," noting Edwards's tendency to appear, as the Black Panthers often did, in dark sunglasses and a beret.[14] Edwards's style certainly indicated the desire to hang with the right kind of radicals, but his approach also entailed innovative rhetorical strategies designed to both divide blackness from the inside out and reverse the symbolic power of integration. *Revolt* attempted to reconstitute sport as a publicly mediated political terrain, moving it from its sacrosanct position in dominant progress narratives to a dominant position in an oppositional narrative inflected, above all, by what it meant to be black.

In 1969, Edwards's announcement of the "athletic revolt" amounted, then, to a synthetically articulated invitation to action motivated by three basic factors: deep resentment over continued racial violence, a mounting sentiment of race-conscious obligation among black athletes, and the emergent recognition that the racial meritocracy of sport was a depressing, fitful sham that black athletes had been used to perpetuate. In *Revolt's* impassioned introduction, Edwards explained,

> The athletic revolt springs from a disgust and dissatisfaction with the same racist germ that infected the warped minds responsible for the

bomb murders of four black girls as they prayed in a Birmingham, Alabama, church and that conceived and carried out the murders of Malcolm X, Martin Luther King, and Medgar Evers, among a multitude of others. The revolt of the black athlete arises also from his new awareness of his responsibilities in an increasingly more desperate, violent, and unstable America. He is for the first time reacting in a human and masculine fashion to the disparities between the heady artificial world of newspaper clippings, photographers, and screaming spectators and the real world of degradation, humiliation, and horror that confronts the overwhelming majority of Afro-Americans. An even more immediate call to arms for many black athletes has been their realization that once their athletic abilities are impaired by age or injury, only the ghetto beckons and they are doomed once again to the faceless, hopeless, ignominious existence they had supposedly forever left behind them.[14]

Edwards said that the source of the revolt was a dissatisfaction with both establishment conservatism and the errors of gradual reform. Waiting was no longer possible in a "desperate, violent, and unstable America." Summoning the symbolism of recent martyrs, Edwards lent presence to the presumably unmediated realities of daily black experience. And in sport specifically, the disparate social conditions and economic opportunities afforded to black and white athletes indexed the dehumanized relation on which the use and abuse of black athletes was predicated. Worst of all, this sad state of affairs was sold as the hope for social mobility.

Anticipating the worries of contemporary critics regarding the damaging allure of sports as a path for success among black youth, Edwards took aim at the myths surrounding black athletic achievements, which depended on the dehumanization of the machinelike black athletic body: "So thoroughly has this myth been perpetuated that athletic excellence, even today, looms second only to education as a prescribed path for blacks to follow in escaping the humiliations and drudgery of their 'second-class' citizenship. But what has integration really meant to the black athlete? What has this move really meant psychologically, socially, and educationally for him? Is the Afro American athlete significantly better off in predominantly white schools than he was in all black institutions?"[16] The integration of college and professional sports had, in Edwards's view, created a false spectacle that merely invited indignity and mistreatment, so his line of questioning challenged dominant assumptions about the benefits of racial integration.

In a December 1969 *Amsterdam News* column headlined "Is Integration Necessary?" McKissick, who had served in an official advisory role to the OPHR, doubted integration in no uncertain terms, asserting that it had merely "reinforce[d] the myth of white racial superiority." Using integrated education as an example, McKissick argued that "Helpless Black children in a white dominated classroom, taught from white-oriented textbooks, by a white, middle-class teacher have slight chance of developing strong, assertive, Black-oriented personalities." Moreover, McKissick found promise in Ben Holman, director of the Justice Department's Community Relations Service, but worried about how Holman's similar doubts about integration, though representative of "both Black and white folks," would "offend some middle-class, still Negroes." After acknowledging his inability to persuade middle-class "Negroes," McKissick asserted the voice of the masses: Holman "said if he had children, he would not want them put on some 'damn bus' and sent off to 'integrate' a hostile white community. The fact that his words reflect the prevailing opinion in our community is indisputably true. Black people never have wanted to go to white schools to be with or near white folks." The real goal of early integration efforts, said McKissick, was to ensure the equitable distribution of government resources, and "as the Black community has increased in political power, it has correctly perceived that a better route to our goal is to bring the money and resources to our own community."[17] McKissick's plan was in retrospect just as damning as integration, rendering black politics available for co-optation by Nixon's "Black Capitalism."[18] Whatever the case, McKissick closed by describing Holman as a "vanguard member" of "this cleansing and refreshing reformation" and by appealing to the same divisions in black identity preferred by Edwards and Malcolm X: "This is the kind of position that Black professionals and leaders need to take. The day of the house nigger who spends his life trying to get close to the white boss man is fast coming to a close."[19]

In *Revolt*, Edwards had offered the same critique of sport and made similarly foreboding claims about the shifting direction of black politics. Integration on campus had exposed college athletes to the indignities of institutional racism: "Perhaps the grimmest, most dehumanizing experiences for black athletes arise from the dismal and repressive social conditions they encounter on white campuses. Particularly relevant here are the restrictions—formal and informal—involving participation in fraternity and sorority life, school dances, parties, and decisions affecting utilization of fees and funds." In this view, black athletes on campus were simply invited into systematic alienation. In addition, Edwards dramatically rendered the dehumanizing circumstances of integration: "The black athlete on the white-dominated college campus, then, is typically exploited, abused, dehumanized, and cast aside in much the same manner as a worn basketball. His lot from that point on does not differ greatly from that of any other Afro-American. His life is riddled with insults, humiliations, and all other manner of degrading experiences."[20] Edwards's rendering offered in many ways a better context for understanding the experiences of Flood, who expressed resentment in *The Way It Is* (published about a year after Edwards's work) at having been treated like "a used bottle cap" or an "IBM card." The response of what Edwards saw as both the Negro and white establishment press was either Bob Broeg's offensive declaration that Flood was too rich to be insulted or to say that Flood might have a point and that baseball should therefore again be reformed. But Edwards removed the problem of dehumanization from the compromising temporality of press coverage and slowed the narrative down to a social fact structured into black experience.[21] "Worn basketball," "used car," "insult," "humiliation," "dehumanization": such, according to *Revolt*, were the masses' experiences with integration.

When Edwards pivoted from the sociology of amateur athletics to his analysis of professional sport, the dehumanization problem did not disappear; it intensified. "By and large, the same humiliations and degradations that plague the athletic careers of black amateurs also haunt black professionals," he said. Edwards then moved to a point that Flood had repeatedly tried to make: "All professional athletes—black and white—are officially and formally classified as property. They exist to make money for the club owners."[22] Flood persisted publicly with this idea, often to rolling eyes and patronizing pats on the shoulder, even from those who claimed to be on his side. Of course, Flood used this point—"all players, black and white"—to demonstrate the color blindness of his cause. In identifying the players as "official property," Edwards took a different turn. All players might exist in a dehumanizing relationship to owners as human capital, "but here the similarities between black and white professionals cease. Racism and discrimination are the exclusive lot of the black professional. And, unlike the amateur scene, practitioners of hate are seldom subtle."[23] Edwards continued with a list of indignities, the *practice of hate* precipitated by the integration of professional sport: Black athletes earned smaller salaries than whites despite superior or equal achievement; black athletes were excluded from the lucrative endorsement deals that white athletes found easily; and the accommodations of black athletes (both on the road and at home) were degrading in comparison to those available to whites. After the basic structural classification of professional sport as intrinsically dehumanizing, Edwards presented the social life of the black athlete as a piece of property. In other words, both white athletes and black athletes were property, but only black athletes were treated as such.

The *New York Times*, the *Sporting News*, and the black press (with rare exception) saw the slave as nothing more than a sensitive black man's way of putting things. But *Revolt* enacted a mode of address that referenced, by political necessity, the facts of lived experience. Blackness could not even be quarantined in the mind; Edwards's identification of the white "black sportswriter," had proven that much. Instead, blackness structured a field of experiences taken by Edwards and others—possibly even Flood—to be constitutive of one's social and political existence. The black press on the whole oriented itself rhetorically according to the supposition that the meaning of blackness was damaging and regrettable. Attempts to revise the meaning of blackness ran through the logic of inclusion, rendering the revised black public subject paradoxically both color-blind and hoping for the day when race would disappear. This is not to say that Flood would have been better off taking Edwards's turn toward racial expressivity. Indeed, Flood probably would never have received the symbolic and financial support of the Players' Association that came in Puerto Rico in December 1969. What if Flood, as he put it in *The Way It Is*, had instead "exhausted the point" about race in that meeting? Quotations from Robert Brown Elliott were not going to impress Tom Haller or any other baseball player who heard echoes of the Black Panthers. Legal bills needed to be paid, after all. The counterfactual may be academic, but the *Revolt* approach to the significance of blackness would have been self-marginalizing and self-defeating for Flood. Regardless of how well his case fit within the circulatory space imagined and projected by Edwards, participating in its circuit with a full commitment to its discursive resources was an efficient route only to personal bankruptcy, a fate that befell Flood nevertheless.

Put differently, Flood's public address bespoke a doomed attempt to defer choice in a political context increasingly characterized by the imperative to declare one's race loyalties. On the one hand, the interconnected fates of organized labor, antitrust law, the federal court system, and the modernization of sport's economic framework were crucial to his success. Here, no one would take seriously "slavery."[24] On the other hand, Edwards, who had called these phenomena "the establishment," already took very seriously "slavery" and its ability to describe the dehumanization of black athletes in integration. As imagined by Edwards, McKissick, and others, however, the "revolt of the black athlete" demanded a kind of loyalty to blackness that Flood could not offer without further imperiling himself. In *Revolt*, mere outspokenness was not enough. In contrast to the cobbled ethos of black athletic activism offered on countless occasions in black newspapers (and into which Flood was frequently inserted between 1970 and 1972), Edwards insisted that what one said mattered a great deal. The facts of one's speaking disclosed an obvious black intellect hidden by historically degrading stereotypes—a welcome development, according to Edwards, but insufficient: "Robert Kennedy with Rosey Grier and Rafer Johnson, Hubert H. Humphrey with Ralph Metcalf, Richard Nixon with Wilt Chamberlain, and Nelson Rockefeller with Jackie Robinson attest that the stupid, plow-jack stereotype of the black athlete is no more. Whether they made a truly significant contribution to black progress or merely prostituted their athletic ability for the sake of other aims is a matter of keen debate among politically conscious blacks."[25] As Edwards pantheon of speaking athletes developed, it seemed that the only way to be sure that blackness was operating in the service of black people was to be on the alert for sellouts; intellect alone did not make a political consciousness. These men would have to choose.

About a week before Flood attended the Puerto Rico meeting in December 1969, McKissick opined on the significance of black athletes to contemporaneous struggles for racial justice in an *Amsterdam News* column. Coming one week before he attacked the wisdom of integration in the same space and extending themes formalized in *Revolt*, McKissick announced that "a Black athlete is expected to play ball like a white man, but live like a Black man in a white world." McKissick painted a portrait of the black athletic revolt that, like Edwards's writing, identified the moment as a turning point:

> The white public has no problem loving the docile, semi-literate Black athlete who through his strength and coordination can outrun, out-hit, and outshine his white competitor. He can be fitted into the racial myth. Black folks are supposed to be able to run, jump, and throw balls. And, indeed we can! What we are not supposed to do, however, is stand toe-to-toe and eyeball-to-eyeball to a white racist and tell him to go to hell. Young, Black athletes who are doing just that are being faced with all kinds of threats, recriminations, and criticisms. The whites clearly ain't ready. They don't know how to deal with this kind of Black man.

"This kind of Black man" enacted the truth of black intellect in resisting the white establishment. Like Edwards, McKissick assailed the social ostracism that black athletes experienced on campus, recognized the symbolic significance of Carlos and Smith's protest in Mexico City, and argued that Muhammad Ali's refusal to be drafted into the Vietnam War "added several inches to the stature of the Black athlete in this country."[26] In *Revolt*, Edwards had called Ali "the saint of this revolution in sports" because he had "maintained and enhanced the most crucial factor in the minds of black people anywhere—black dignity."[27]

McKissick's language of "manhood and dignity," was characteristic of both Edwards's injunction to a revolutionary social consciousness and the notion of humanism that underpinned much of Flood's rhetorical performance in *The Way It Is*.[28] Despite the obvious extent of the thematic, tropological, and argumentative commonplaces between Edwards, Flood, and McKissick, the consequential and provocative dimension of McKissick's observation resided in its concomitant announcement of how revolutionary forces were aligning: "Frequently, the Black athlete is torn between two loyalties—to the team or to his Black sisters and brothers who sometimes demand that they participate in the white university's athletic program, or that he use his influence to change the school's racial policies and practices. The number who speak out against racism is increasing rapidly." Though he used the context of university athletics, McKissick explained that black athletes acting on their consciences must often do so at the expense of their teams. The conflict became especially acute, asserted McKissick, when collegiate athletes considered their prospects in professional sport:

> The white press is bemoaning the fact that these men are risking future professional careers, that they are causing white coaches to hire fewer Black players, and they are jeopardizing their own positions on the team. White America would undoubtedly be more comfortable with the inarticulate, humble Black athlete who would depend upon the good white man to look out for his interest. It is clear that the country is not ready for the independent, fearless, militant athlete ready to make whatever sacrifice necessary to protect his own manhood and to liberate and uphold the honor of his people.[29]

For McKissick, the choice was clear: Liberty and honor depended on the type of independent black militancy that both justified sacrifice morally and made sacrifice rewarding politically. In an idiom that evoked Flood's case (complete with all of the evocative rhetorical signatures—"dignity," "manhood," "independence," "sacrifice"), McKissick valorized the political ethos of the new black athlete not merely for the willingness to speak but for the willingness to settle inevitably torn loyalties on the side of racial justice.

In late 1969 and early 1970, several black newspapers published editorials alerting readers to the birth of the *Black Scholar*. The journal's first issue appeared in January 1970, and its introduction heralded the possibility of something members of the black press had found previously elusive: a unified definition of black identity. In December 1969, the *Chicago Defender* traced the journal's origin to the social fissures its reporters struggled to narrate on a weekly basis: "Out of the chimera of the ghetto convulsions and college campus tremors has come a scintillating, soul searching, edifying new journal, called The Black Scholar." For the *Defender*, the contemporary moment was one of transformation, and the *Black Scholar* thus appeared "at a propitious moment when the old social order which had tied the nation's feet to a virulent racist tradition, is undergoing drastic transformation." Having diagnosed the virus of racism as weakening, the *Defender* saw the hope of the *Black Scholar* as residing in its potential to effectuate "the conversion to the theology of racial equality." Whether the *Black Scholar* could produce a new "theology" was unclear, but the *Defender* was sure that "it remains the task of black intellectuals, unwavering in its dedication and pursuit of liberating aims, to convince doubting white America of the reality and substance of its black components. It is a process in which the black man himself will find a true definition of his own intrinsic values and place in the struggle for power."[30] With strident rhetoric, the *Defender*'s logic (which seemed to rehearse its constitutive self-understanding) amounted to the idea that the *Black Scholar* might produce performances of blackness that whites would take seriously and through those performances might reveal an empowering self-definition of black identity.

The *Los Angeles Sentinel* similarly hoped that the *Black Scholar* would "provide meaningful definitions of black existence" in "a crucial period of divisiveness in the American Community—divisiveness between and within groups." The *Sentinel* welcomed this recognition of divisiveness, however, only in the context of an aspiration that division might be overcome in the figure of the "black scholar," "defined as one who recognizes this divisiveness. He is a man of both thought and action, a whole man who thinks for his people and acts with them, one who honors the whole community, a man who sees the entire group all sharing the same experience of blackness, with its complexities and rewards." Charged with the responsibility of representing black experience by "thinking for" and "acting with" the "entire group," the black scholar in the *Black Scholar* might, in the *Sentinel*'s view, solve the crucial problem for the "'Black'-American Negro population," which "with or without design" "has historically lacked unity and definition."[31] Like the *Defender*, the *Sentinel* seemed to sense the movement from an old social order to a new one and to place the appearance of the *Black Scholar* at the fulcrum of the transformation. Furthermore, both the *Defender* and *Sentinel* hoped that the journal would produce politically efficacious bonds of black unity out of frustrating internal tumult. Such unity might have been desirable and might even have organized the *Black Scholar* teleologically, but for Edwards and other rhetors, many of whom used the *Black Scholar* as a forum in which to speak, the logic of performing politically effective forms of black unity for the benefit of whites was repugnant.

Perhaps more fairly stated, the black press' citational gestures toward the *Black Scholar* contained more instability relative to the formation of collective black identity than their editorializing had admitted or probably even intended. The meaning of blackness was in fact a matter of open debate in the *Black Scholar* in its early years (and beyond), but this debate existed only in and through speakers making demands for revised meanings. The black press attempted to assign itself agitation and delegate withdrawal and regroupment to the *Black Scholar*. But writers in the *Black Scholar* simply did not regard their discursive activities as purely academic or in any way self-sealed. While authors in black newspapers addressed black audiences with a self-consciousness of how blackness was being represented to whites, writers in the *Black Scholar* addressed black audiences with a self-consciousness of how blackness was being represented to itself. And although this process sounds in theory like Nancy Fraser's "withdrawal and regroupment," the placement of the political meaning of blackness onto a public agenda depended on a rhetoric that would separate truth from lies for the purpose of authenticating agitational activities. The *Black Scholar* may have been pleased to hear that the *Defender* and *Sentinel* were on its side, but especially for Edwards, unity was a knot of complicity to be diligently untangled before it was a hope to be rendered. False hope, after all, seemed his most formidable opponent. That is not to say that Edwards (and just about everyone else) failed to claim the voice of the masses, but the *Black Scholar*, like *Revolt of the Black Athlete*, freely addressed white audiences with hostility to perform revelations about liberalism, tokenism, and indignity. Revelation emerged only from internal division, and the kind of unity the *Black Scholar* held in its imagination bore little resemblance to the kind being both beckoned and asserted in black newspapers.[32]

Getting from the *Black Scholar* to *Revolt of the Black Athlete*, however, is not a self-evident move, and it presents a minor historiographic puzzle worth mentioning. Two years into its existence and after its mention in the *Defender* and *Sentinel*, the *Black Scholar's* November 1971 issue was devoted almost exclusively to an elaboration of the black athlete. Edwards contributed an essay on "The Sources of Black Athletic Superiority," which, along with founder Nathan Hare's piece on prizefighting and Charles Aikens's article on Flood, advanced an understanding of black athletes heavily informed by what came to be known as the "sociology of sport." The third article in the issue was "The Emergence of the Black Athlete in America," with the author listed as Michael Govan, "a teacher at Havenscourt Junior High School in Oakland, California," and a graduate of the black studies program at California State–Hayward. But nearly all of the essay was copied from the first three chapters of *Revolt*, with no meaningful paraphrasing. Nineteen of the article's twenty-nine footnotes cite *Revolt*, while the remaining ten are verbatim citations to *Revolt's* sources. It is likely (especially in light of the Bay-area connections) that Edwards gave permission for the *Black Scholar* to reprint the material under Govan's name, perhaps because the journal was trying to create the impression that Edwards's single voice was instead many. Govan's piece essentially seems to have been a partially masked attempt to directly insert *Revolt* into paired circulation with the *Black Scholar* by bypassing the cumbersome and unpredictable step of mere citation. *Revolt* represented precisely what the *Black Scholar* wanted participating in its "kind of scene."[33]

Perhaps, then, there should be little wonder that very few extended elaborations of Flood's case were expressed in the idiom of *Revolt*. Flood could offer only a diluted form of black loyalty, a generalized loyalty immanent in his blackness but purposefully perforated from the specifics of the cause, simultaneous facts that complicated his uptake everywhere. Such complications, however, did not mean that Flood completely lacked *Revolt*-oriented advocacy. The same issue of the *Black Scholar* in which Govan's reiteration of *Revolt* appeared also included "The Struggle of Curt Flood," by Charles Aikens, listed as a professional baseball player in the Baltimore Orioles organization in the early 1960s and a graduate student in journalism at the University of California–Berkeley. If there were any question that Flood's story, like in *The Way It Is*, could not be modulated by racialized affect (lest one stray from the "facts"), Aikens erased that pretense in the opening paragraphs of his essay, which recounted the author's reaction at learning of Flood's lawsuit: "I looked at the paper, angrily tossing it to the floor. I could not eat dinner that evening following work. Flood felt the same way I'd felt seven years earlier after finding out I was an indentured servant bound by the reserve clause."[34] Aikens offered his feelings of disgust as confirmation of Flood's, rendered from within a black player's experience in baseball under the reserve clause regime. Flood had "consulted a beer" when he woke up on the day he was traded, but Aikens had lost his appetite completely when he read about Flood's trade.

Tellingly, Aikens saw reform rhetoric as a fraud. Recalling Flood's last day in a Major League uniform, when Washington Senators manager Ted Williams had replaced Flood in centerfield in the middle of an inning, Aikens put the embarrassing episode in the pervasive context of baseball's structural condition of slavery: "The substitution also followed Judge Ben Cooper's August 12, 1970 ruling which said that the reserve clause Curt Flood was fighting should be modified by the players and owners. This was like telling the slavemasters that they should modify slavery. The slaves and any fool knew that couldn't happen." Aikens's deep suspicion of reformist reasoning accompanied his deployment of the slave as a tropological force in his representation of the power relations shaping Flood's experience. Williams's "benching of Flood put him in the position of the slave overseer who flogged the rebellious slave by the embarrassment of a benching as he ran toward the outfield for the next inning." And in the spirit of Edwards's instinct to demystify the sensationalism of the news, Aikens quoted a headline without citation, reading "Flood Hits Famine: Just One of Nats' Many Headaches." To be fair to the anonymous headline writer, Flood was playing very poorly (simply living up to his reputation for slow starts, insisted Aikens), and he was not Washington's only problem. The team was dreadful. Nonetheless, Aikens insisted, "This was a blatantly racist headline," adding, "This indicates how writers can place the blame for a team's failure on a particular ballplayer who isn't liked because he is a rebel."[35] Perhaps positioning himself as one of Edwards's "black sports reporters," Aikens enacted the kind of sports journalism Edwards had endorsed in *Revolt* and Govan had repeated in the *Revolt* excerpt in the same issue of the *Black Scholar*. For Aikens, telling the truth about black experience in sport entailed examining the functioning of race in those experiences. After establishing the fitness of the slave narrative for Flood's case, Aikens disclosed their shared experiences with a "black sports reporter's" inflection.

Flood "contended he was being sold as 'chattel' and being made to work as a 'slave,'" explained Aikens, using this observation to offer a comparison that Flood had also presented: "Flood's suit is mindful of the Dred Scott decision in 1857 (the same year organized baseball clubs started). Chief Justice Roger B. Taney ruled against Scott, a slave, saying that blacks could not be citizens of the United States because they formed no part of 'the people' referred to in the Declaration of Independence and the Constitution, and had 'no rights which white men were bound to respect.'" The narrative that followed from the fact of Flood's slavery had little to do with abstractions; it instead illuminated its principled ground by weaving the implications of slavery into a representation of Aikens's (and by extension, Flood's) lived experience as black. Claiming to have seen Flood play in front of scouts on Oakland's sandlots, Aikens noticed, "a gravel voiced man standing behind the backdrop, who said, 'Them scouts up there in the stands are watching that boy. He's going to be another Jackie Robinson.'" Once again casting Robinson's symbolic influence into doubt, Aikens recalled, "I looked across to the stands behind the first base side of the dugout and saw two well-tanned men who looked different from the usual pale-faced whites who lived in West Oakland or came there to work. They reminded me of plantation owners coming to buy slaves at a slave auction. I saw them jotting down information in the small notebooks they had, so I curiously went over to see what they were up to. One told the other, 'That kid Flood can do everything.'" As Aikens developed the scene, which was as vivid as a Hollywood film, he elaborated through this conversation with white scouts a form of interracial interaction that he would later critique as dehumanizing:

"Do you see anyone who might make some money?," I said.

"Yea," the cigar smoking one said, "that kid [Frank] Robinson might make some dough one day if he keeps his nose clean."

"You mean a baseball player has to keep his nose clean to play baseball?"

"Yea kid, if a player stays out of trouble with the law and is a nice boy and don't ask too many questions, he might be able to get a chance and go out and play for money."

"Flood is also a good-looking player along with that catcher. . . . But you can't tell what might happen to a youngster who grows up in this area."

"Whut you mean."

"I mean, if a player chases women all the time he might not be able to play ball like we want him to. He also has to stay in at night and keep out of night clubs at late hours."

"Um gonna be a ballplayer one day," I said.

"Ok—Ok kid, be anything you want to be but would you leave us alone so we can watch Flood hit."[36]

The accuracy of this exchange is unknown, but faithfulness to the facts was not Aikens's point in sharing it. Keeping one's mouth shut, keeping one's nose clean, and being a nice boy were the conditions of a young black player's entry into baseball. With the "nice boy" again alluding opaquely to Jackie Robinson, this story would have a much different ending.

Aikens returned to an account of his experiences in Oakland's black ghetto, including success on the sandlots and trouble in the streets. Remembering a brief stint in juvenile detention following an accusation of purse snatching, Aikens—like Flood in North Carolina—had begun to have revelations. "That horrible experience of being caged up like an animal and seeing a juvenile hall almost full of blacks had a lasting effect on me and my approach toward life and freedom." He hoped that baseball would provide a path out of squalor, as it had for Flood. But such a path, as the conversation with the scouts had hinted, was circumscribed by the way in which the expression of his black identity would have to be muted, limited, or abandoned. Remembering stories told by Oakland sandlot heroes returning from the Majors, Aikens continued, "They were bitter because they felt that the white people in control of professional baseball clubs eliminated any black who did not fit into the humble role of a dumb, stupid know-nothing ballplayer who would go out and break his neck, sweating like a slave in a cotton field, in order to get an advancement to the majors. I realized that I could not be my usual arrogant self if I ever got the opportunity to play professional baseball because scouts usually frowned when you talked to them like you had sense or knew the value you would be to the club."[36] With slavery analogizing not the abstract economic relation contained in the reserve clause but instead the experiential features of racialized life in baseball, painted here as a sporting plantation, Aikens figured the intelligence that he possessed and that Edwards revered would be criminalized through his blackness. The bitter pill of accommodation thrust in the face of black athletes (in Edwards's view) found expression here in Aikens's slave narrative as a refusal of blackness to one's sense of self, as a form of disembodied confinement damaging not only to one's abilities but also to one's confidence and voice.

Like Edwards, Aikens listed some of the economic inequities black baseball players faced, including those influencing salary negotiations and access to endorsement deals. He lamented that "when it came to negotiating, [black players] were all unprepared to deal with the racist white man who was in control of the dollar bills and could not bargain on an equal level as white players could." But economic analysis was not Aikens's point. As his story moved toward a conclusion, it acquired a rhetorical shape similar to Flood's *The Way It Is* in at least one other respect. Speaking in a voice seemingly positioned behind the veil of race, Aikens announced a final awakening occasioned by having observed years of racial inequality in integrated sport:

> I was awakened to the facts of life about the intelligent black athlete in professional baseball. Poor, racist, white baseball managers and scouts despised the intelligent black, and he was the first to be put on the release roster, no matter how good his ability. Other intelligent blacks from the Oakland area like Curt Motton and Tommy Harper were able to remain in uniform because they managed to act humble. Motten [*sic*] acted as if he didn't know A from Z when he was coming up in the minor leagues. Serious black guys like Alex Johnson always got labeled strange, distant, or as of late, rebellious.

Fully awakened to the racial realities of sport, Aikens saw how baseball punished black intelligence and rewarded black humility, life-denying circumstances that in the context of both the revolt of the black athlete and the *Revolt of the Black Athlete* were fated for reversal—provided the right voices spoke blackness into politics. In the end, then, it was time to place Flood back into the racialized social order: "Today, Curt Flood and other black athletes are hip to the white sports establishment's game. Black athletes are no longer willing to play by the racists' rules. Flood's suit is among many events in the black struggle that have heightened awareness of a brutal system where people are still treated as 'chattel,' although slavery was supposed to have ended over 100 years ago. The Curt Floods, the Alex Johnsons and Duane Thomases form the vanguard of the recent emergence of the militant black athlete who is striving to attain human rights and equal opportunities in the sports world."[37] With a final rhetorical gesture to Edwards and Govan, Aikens put Curt Flood at the center of the "emergence of the black athlete" (as Govan's piece was titled) destined to transform sport not just from an old economic order to a new one but also from a dehumanizing plantation into the space of freedom and opportunity that had often been promised. In Aikens's account of Flood, race was hardly "beside the point." Black experience had permitted a way of putting things that revealed not only the cold economic analogy to slavery to be found in the reserve system but also its consequences for black experience. From behind a racial veil, Aikens narrativized the master-slave relationship in dehumanizing detail and assigned Flood, the protagonist in this performance of *Revolt*'s idiom, to the revolutionary vanguard.

These features of Aikens's essay evince its rehearsal of Edwards's model of public address: Beginning with a racialized identification with Flood expressed in the loss of his appetite, Aikens suspected reform rhetoric of being disingenuous and described the experiential texture of the player-manager relationship: Both occurred through the figure of the slave—slave masters were liars, and Ted Williams was their cruel overseer. As Aikens disclosed the facts of black experience in baseball, he read race into dominant media representations like one of Edwards's "black sports reporters." For Aikens as for Flood), Dred Scott illuminated the official status of baseball players as slaves, a fact that led Aikens not toward economic analogues and consternation about baseball's legal troubles but instead toward a revised narration of black experience in integrated baseball. Revealing, like Flood, what racism sounded like through allegorical memories of conversations with snarling white authority figures, Aikens identified the master-slave relationship as grounded in the degradation of the slave. The likelihood that Aikens's dialogue was idealized purposefully and not a product of precise memory demonstrates the importance of black corporeality and affect to the truth of his insights. Operating as a point of articulation between Edwards and Flood, "The Struggle of Curt Flood" depended on what the experience of blackness meant and on how it felt to be black in integration's dehumanizing spaces.

About a week before the start of the 1970 baseball season, Flood's familiar nemesis in the *St. Louis Post-Dispatch*, Bob Broeg, wrote a feature on Cardinals owner Gussie Busch that also appeared in the *Sporting News*. Busch had given a series of melodramatic press conferences that spring, and the latest concerned star pitcher Steve Carlton's desire for a significant salary increase. Busch, frustrated with what must have seemed like widespread sedition, grouped the Carlton problem with annoyance at the salary demands of Richie Allen (one of the players for whom Flood was traded) and of course Flood's lawsuit. Announcing his ostensibly sacrificial commitment to resisting the assault on baseball, Busch said, "I can't understand Allen. I can not understand Flood. We have to take a stand for the good of baseball. I hate to be the sucker to do it, but I'm willing to do it." Busch was certainly not the only owner experiencing anxiety about the players' surging boldness in contract negotiations. Speaking for his colleagues, Busch expanded the scope of the problem and attempted to reverse the perception of exactly who was being treated like a fool: "The fans are going to resent this situation. I can't understand it. The player contracts are at their best, the pension plan is the finest, the fringe benefits are better, yet the players think that we (the owners) are stupid asses." His "disillusionment" was a matter of national pride that an unappreciative generation lacked: "I don't know what's happening among our young people—to our campuses and to our great country. We've taken a stand, anyway, and I just hope that some of the other clubs have the guts to do what I've done to get the situation back to normalcy."[39] Busch's harangue was simply the latest showy display of paternalism that comprised the owners' rhetoric of gratitude. From the players' perspective, Busch was failing to understand why the players refused to accept their salaries gratefully, as if they were undeserved. More important, Busch's comments presented a line of reasoning that was beginning to operate as common sense in public discourse: that the issues in sport reflected deeper patterns of social unrest. Busch quite explicitly sought to discipline expressions of unrest—for the benefit of the fans, for the good of the game, and for the love of country.

Arthur Daley extended this theme in the *New York Times*, advancing twin claims regarding sport's shifting present: Sport had become a microcosm of American life, and athletes had been consumed by a concurrent spirit of rebellion. Under the headline "Paging Sigmund Freud," which invoked the symbolism of mental disorder to diagnose sport's presumable disease, Daley worried about what changes in society would mean for the "sphere" of athletics: "The world of sports has always been a microcosm, a little world in itself. It faithfully reflected the outer world, of which it was a tiny part. When life was simple in the old days, the sporting life was also simple. But when it grew complicated, those complexities spilled over in tumbling fashion to engulf the entire sphere of athletics, professional and amateur, and that vast murky shadowland in between." After poking fun at professional hockey player Mike Walton, whom a psychiatrist had diagnosed as suffering from depression that could be cured only by a trade away from the Toronto Maple Leafs, Daley observed what he took to be a widening generational divide: "Perhaps it seems proper enough to the Now generation but even the more numerous 30-plus generation just can't get used to the way authority is challenged and eroded in sports just as it is to a greater extent everywhere else. The prime example, of course, is Curt Flood's lawsuit against the baseball reserve clause and that has to wind up as a legal milestone because it is now on the road to the Supreme Court."

Flood became the exemplar of the times, a symbolic crystallization of the way in which the challenges to tradition and authority were spilling over from "life" to "athletics." Shortly after the Supreme Court issued its decision against Flood in the summer of 1972, Daley did his best (as did others) to explain how and why the Court tortured logic. His support for Flood took the form of support for a new generation: "The mood of the players has changed with the times. The golden eggs have come cascading down from the geese in management and greed begets greed both on the field and in the front office. The players are more militant than ever before and are now making full-bodied demands that players of an earlier generation would not have dreamed of making."[40] Daley's characterization of ownership was not new, nor was his suggestion that everyone involved had succumbed to the worst of greed. But as the "necessary evil" confronted "full-bodied demands," what began to emerge was the clear recognition that the changing times, in addition to producing hippies and antiwar protesters, had also produced a new form of political identity through sport: the young, angry, activist-athlete.

Daley's pair of interrelated observations—that the troubles in sport reflected the troubles in society and that a new generation of athletes had emerged with new demands—combined to shape a political culture in sport that at the beginning of the 1970s was discussed with a combination of anxiety, confusion, and anticipation. Perhaps most significant, the national newspapers that gave sport its daily presence in cultural life increasingly regarded the activist-athlete as an agent of social volatility. As it became obvious that black athletes formed the cutting edge of sport's relationship to politics, the crucible conjured into existence by Jackie Robinson's noble experiment reinvested sport as the reference point for measuring national progress on race. This dynamic helps to explain some of the difficulty in accounting for the rhetorical consequences of the owners' argumentative tenor toward Flood. Gerald Early and David Leonard, for example, draw a racialized explanation from the owners' traditionalism, paternalism, and greed.[41] Though it may be fair to say that baseball owners as a group were probably no less racist than anyone else, the expressions that produced very reasonable accusations of reactionary paternalism fit better within the color-blind narrative of sport's loss of economic innocence. Flood's strategic identification with white players neutralized the possibility that the new economy of baseball was racially inflected, so in protecting baseball's economic traditions, the owners were characterized as no worse than nakedly greedy. Thus, arguments such as Daley's in the national papers produced volatility at exactly the point that owners were attempting to stabilize sport's public image. In other words, the activist-athlete emerging in the late 1960s became an idealized form of political subjectivity operating to move sport from the old to the new, away from the craggy sensibilities of ownership toward the economic modernization of sport. The inclination to describe Flood's challenge as antiracist arises from the unmistakable formal similarities between what the owners had to say and what racists often have to say: *This is ours, and you're lucky that we will even share it with you.* Be that as it may, the tale of Flood became a tale of "the economy," and the activist-athlete became the privileged ethos through which to issue critiques that might or might not have had anything to do with race.

Perhaps sensing the weight of these connections or perhaps arriving at them on their own, many of Flood's advocates in the black press placed him in specific relation to an emergent black athletic ethos made translucently visible by speakers such as Edwards and McKissick. In response to the owners' claim that abolition of the reserve clause would destroy baseball's financial structure, the *Baltimore Afro-American*'s Sam Lacy described baseball as a quaint anachronism, out of touch with a new way of seeing and doing things, both within sport and in the broader culture. Lacy said that the owners' argument in favor of the reserve clause "is good, sound argument—or was good, sound argument in the twenties and thirties. Today, young people of the prime age of professional athletes are throwing off the yoke of custom in every corner of the world. In every walk of life. . . . And in the world of professional sports, only baseball has been permitted to continue at the status quo."[42] Hardly a "sedentary member" of baseball's cast, as Flood saw most sportswriters, Lacy stressed baseball's active ignorance of disruptive new realities and positioned his critique as a disclosure of the owners' malignant traditionalism. Similarly, the *Chicago Defender*'s Doc Young urged the owners to give Flood's case an honest hearing in light of Young's recognition that professional baseball's institutional intransigence stacked the odds against Flood:

> Flood is in for a rough time. Baseball is a powerful, multi-million dollar entity with important connections. The baseball moguls might do well, however, to give the issues raised by Flood the full consideration they deserve. They should accept the facts that times have changed, their old ways aren't necessarily the best, and modern ball-players are neither dumb, helpless, nor likely to accept old rules which violate

their welfare, or their conception of it, merely because those rules are written down. . . . Baseball, over the years, has not been noted for its progressive thinking. It has been a sort of head-in-the-sands operation. It is time now for baseball to come up for air, and also to take a look around the new world.[43]

Like Lacy, Young characterized baseball as holding to a naive but stubborn orthodoxy that ignored the facts of social change. Implying cautiously that the owners' interests might best be served by embracing new player attitudes, Young both admitted that Flood posed a plausible threat to baseball's continued institutional existence and nervously affirmed the rising status and political legitimacy of the rebellious, socially conscious black athlete.

The turn to the new decade also occasioned reasons for the black press to pause on the meaning of the new athlete that seemed to have emerged from the 1960s. In January 1970, the *Philadelphia Tribune* promised that the 1970s would be "vintage years for the black athlete," in accordance with Claude Harrison's assertion that "during the 1960s, especially the last part of the decade, black athletes took steps toward gaining their full rights, on and off the playing field." Just like Cosell, Harrison recognized the newly visible relationship between sport and society, proclaiming that "sports, like education, labor, and every other venture, can no longer hide behind scholarships and salaries. It must face the issues and not try to escape the social changes that are upon this great nation." Presumably, then, the social changes "upon this great nation" were those that could be forestalled not by more scholarships and larger contracts but only by careful attention to the substance of dissent. "Demonstrations and dissensions of the 1960s clearly proved that in the seventies, college and pro club directors will have to deal honestly with black athletes or learn to live with boycotts and protests that can be costly in both money and spirit," Harrison insisted. Even as he acknowledged the unique role of the black athlete as the agent of change, Harrison was sure to tincture the substance of dissent with a color-blind imaginary. Regarding the increasing likelihood of a black manager in baseball, Harrison intoned, "Baseball knowledge and the ability to handle men doesn't come with the color of one's skin. You have it or you don't. It's that simple." Progress was inevitable, he persisted, especially since the "men who run the nation's collegiate and professional teams . . . will see the handwriting on the wall and make the 1970s a vintage decade for the black athlete."[44]

In late December 1969, the *Chicago Defender*, through the voice of a familiar activist luminary, took the decade's transition to mean something even stronger. Without quite as much optimism as the *Philadelphia Tri-bune*, the *Defender* presented a list of items that worked both descriptively (an account of what was happening) and prescriptively (an assertion of what would be required). The list included organized demands made by black players on the campuses of Brigham Young University and Indiana University, the successful campaign for an outsized contract by O. J. Simpson with the National Football League's Buffalo Bills, the hiring of Lenny Wilkens as the second black National Basketball Association head coach, retired Chicago Cub Ernie Banks's appointment to the board of the Chicago Transit Authority, and the outspokenness of tennis's Arthur Ashe, who characterized all of this activity as revelatory. The *Defender* said, "For many Negroes, what surfaced at the college level in 1969 certainly had its beginnings at an earlier age and one of the persons most cognizant of that fact is Negro tennis star Arthur Ashe, himself a victim many times of racial prejudice." Moreover, the *Defender* closed with a key injunction: "'Athletes have influence and charisma and we could do a lot to get these kids to believe in themselves and fulfill their potential,' Ashe said. 'The name of the game now for all of us on sports is: Get committed. Each one of us who has a name has an obligation to the blacks that need help.'"[45] From Busch's disillusionment to Ashe's call to conscience, the appearance of the "new black athlete" was in fact a reality with which any observer of sport would have to cope. For the establishment, the new athlete was a worrisome threat that resulted in paranoid harangues; for legendary renegades such as Ashe, the new athlete was simply the symptom of society moving forward. However athletes might have fit themselves into this position, the start of 1970 presented an image of volatility that made the imperative to act available, intelligent, and politically rewarding. The widespread announcements of instability (racially induced or otherwise) indexed fissures measured by some as a threat but measured by others as opportunity. The arrival of the new decade produced, in short, both worry and excitement, a combination indicative of a potential energy that might occasion social change.

In the *New York Times* at least, Red Smith (a consistent Flood defender) persisted with a line of reasoning that exercised the idiom Edwards assigned to the black sports reporter. Smith narrated Flood's case within a context characterized by a corporeal rendering of the slave metaphor. Smith emphasized not the abstract "economic" relation implied in the slavery metaphor but instead the dehumanizing relation and the sports establishment's role in imposing it. In the spring of 1972, Carlton again inspired widespread player movement and salary escalation, a situation Smith described as "the busiest flesh market in many years. More bodies were bought, sold, and bartered, and more players of distinction changed address than in any comparable period within memory." Amid worries that "the Curt Flood case might limit [the owners'] freedom to make such deals in the future," Smith opined that "not since the days of Nat Turner have escaped slaves wrought such destruction, especially at the expense of their former masters." He attended closely to the movement of bodies and the dehumanizing vocabulary that allowed slavery to work without calling attention to itself: "The employers aren't necessarily bad guys. If they are sometimes less than sensitive in their dealings with the help, it's probably because they have grown so accustomed to regarding the players as possessions that they forget they players are people. Their speech betrays this, 'The strongest arm in the league,' they say of this man, or a 'great pair of hands,' or 'I want his bat in the line-up.' Taking refuge in the vernacular they can forget that they are dealing with human lives."[46] Smith offered no such vernacular sanctuary. Indeed, he attempted to shift sport's vernacular to one in which corporeal expressivity became possible. In Smith's view of sports, bodies were real, and the owners, though perhaps even well-intentioned, concealed the objective conditions of bondage from public view with a rhetoric that reified dehumanization. A few months later, in June 1972, Flood lost his Supreme Court case. Explaining his feeling that the Court had "passed the buck" of illogic to Congress, Smith wrote, "It is a great disappointment because this Court appears to set greater store by property rights than by human rights."[47] Evoking Flood's analysis of the term *tampering* in *The Way It Is*, Smith presented slavery not as an analogy that shed light on an economic relation, not mere metaphor, but as a real, corporeally significant social relation cloaked in a dehumanizing mode of address. In contrast to reformers' assumptions, Smith saw property rights and human rights as in opposition, and the Supreme Court, perhaps itself committed ideologically to the same dehumanizing rhetoric, had discursively legitimated the facts of slavery.

The slave narrative's appearance in the national sports press, however, sometimes produced awkward results when its speakers attempted to expand its scope past the abstract economic relation in baseball. In *A Well-Paid Slave*, Brad Snyder points out that the *Los Angeles Times*'s Jim Murray, though speaking sarcastically, came to Flood's defense by writing, "If Curt Flood wants to remain in St. Louis, baseball (and society) should let him." The *Sporting News* printed Murray's column directly beneath Broeg's "principle or principal" article in as a kind of counterpoint, but Murray's piece showed only how the lampooning power of sarcasm easily became ignorant and acidic in the wrong context. In a bizarre attempt to represent the experience of baseball's slaves, Murray wrote, "The 'reserve clause,' to be sure, is just a fancy name for slavery. The only thing it doesn't let the owners do is flog their help. You can't flee over the ice, there's no underground railway. All you can do is pick up your glove and hum spirituals. You can wrap an old bandanna around your head and call the boss 'Marse,' if you like. Lift that bat, chop that ball, git a little drunk and you land in sale." The inanity contained in these stereotypes should be obvious, but their function became apparent as Murray wondered about the owners' handling of the reserve clause: "You would think . . . the slave owners would be more careful with it. I mean, you all know what happens to slavery when it gets out of hand and word of it leaks up to Washington. Recall how upset Mr. Lincoln got, and John Brown's body, and Harriet Beecher Stowe? 'Uncle Curt's Cabin' may hit the bookstalls any day now." In the end, Murray offered baseball officials some advice: "If I were Bowie Kuhn—or Gussie Busch—I would try to keep that Flood right between its banks. Otherwise, when baseball sends those doves out, they may come back with salmon in their teeth. And every baseball park in America may have a sign 'No Game Tonight—On Account Of Flood.'"[48] This brand of support was nearly worse for Flood than a naked rebuttal. Murray may have attempted to represent the experience of the players as slaves, but the cruel foolishness of his sarcasm neutralized its insight and led straight back to the owners' criminalizing dystopia.

Just as Smith's elaboration of the slave narrative in the *Times* illustrated the occasional entry of the Edwards idiom into the national sports press, Flood found advocates in the black press deliberately positioning themselves outside of the sports establishment. In January 1970, Dick Edwards (whom Harry Edwards had personally identified as a black sports reporter), offered his opinion of Flood in the *Amsterdam News*. "Sock it to 'em Curt!," he wrote under the headline, "The Principle." Like the *Defender*'s Bill Nunn, who had insisted that understanding the slave metaphor required understanding Flood "the man," Dick Edwards noted that "to really understand Curt's point in suing baseball for treating him like a rich peon—you must understand Flood-the-individual." But unlike Nunn, who tried to accommodate the owners, Edwards presented uncompromising choices: "There are howls that baseball is dead if Flood wins his suit. That's tough, because if making the Lords obey one of the basic tenets upon which a democracy is built will kill baseball, it's time it was dead anyway." Catastrophic consequences were utterly beside the point here: To affirm democracy, baseball might have to be destroyed. Edwards recommended that Flood hold a generalized antagonist to account for perversions in democracy: "We hope Curt Flood stays as cold-blooded as the Man—and the establishment. . . . So, Curt Flood, stay cold. Stick it to the Man, elbow deep—and twist it. If you kill baseball—it needs to die anyway."[49] Instead of urging improvement, modification, or anything else that might stabilize the volatility of revolt, Edwards welcomed the potential black divestiture of baseball rapaciously if it meant realizing the genuine meaning of democracy—by sticking it to the Man.

Smith's rendering of the slave narrative had found the rich tropological territory of slavery, which in addition to the rejection of baseball "reform" also found other entry points in the black press. The *Chicago Defender*'s William Lloyd Hogan wrote a pair of columns in late 1969 (around the time that Flood was meeting with the players in Puerto Rico) that racialized a slave narrative for baseball's black manager debate. Jackie Robinson also was campaigning openly for a black manager but would never have said the kinds of things Hogan said. Robinson surely saw the slow pace as regrettable but also personally understood and advocated the pragmatism of patience. Hogan, in stark contrast, pointedly inserted racism into the fabric of sport: "The racially bigoted powers that be in these two big businesses [baseball and football] should hang 'for white only' signs on the doors of their front offices. It's my strong conviction that something should be done about the brutal discrimination practices of these flesh-peddling exploiters of black athletes."[50] Harry Edwards had hailed speakers with "conviction," and Hogan freely advanced his. "Flesh-peddling" brought the body back to public debate in a manner that lent dramatic presence to dehumanizing exploitation.

Moreover, Hogan offered a form of political action modeled on the urgency of Harry Edwards's *Revolt*. Assessing the unfair advantages white baseball players enjoyed in the postathletic labor market, Hogan exposed flaws in the rhetorics of race neutrality and political patience, wondering how the black athlete's "problems [could] not be peculiar to the color of his skin?" Hogan saw the solution in direct political pressure: "To get some action from the fat cat racial bigots who sit atop their thrones on their wide behinds and lord over the destinies of professional athletics, the black athlete must have a separate player's association, a black pressure group with a singular goal!" As Flood figured out in his encounter with Haller, however, such talk about race would not get very far in public disputes with baseball's establishment. Unimpressed by the allure of color blindness, however,

Hogan suggested that black professional athletes take political cues from campus activists: "All the black athletes in pro sports should get a black association going to present their demands to the robber baron bigots. The black pro should take a page from the black college athletes' book, doing their thing against the bigotry and racial prejudice confronting them at every turn . . . make their commitment and go on strike."[51] Hogan's extension of the black athlete's "obligation" (as Ashe had put it), resisted the compulsion to interracial coalition demanded by integrationism, reflected Harry Edwards's strike and boycott approach, and ultimately attempted to capitalize on the potential energy produced by the new black athlete's volatility. About a month later, in a commentary on Muhammad Ali, Hogan made the implications for black politics explicit: "It takes more pride to obey your conscience, doing what you think is right in the face of detestable obnoxious majority who think you should bow down to it, bend to its will because it's the Great White Father." The division Hogan attempted to forge was expressed with clarity and passion: "The black mechanical robots who go off to fight in Vietnam are stupid fools beyond the comprehension of any black man who has an ounce of gray matter. . . . [T]he war is here, within the confines of this racist nation. The Black Revolution has begun. . . . [I]t is being fought against poverty degradation, and for the right to maintain our self-respecting human dignity!"[52] Like Edwards, Hogan was deliberate in his attempts to locate political differences within collective black identity. Furthermore, Hogan lent powerful salience to the expressivity of blackness in public address by placing the urgency of social change on the rhetorical registers of black self-respect and racial self-recognition. Not only was this approach an implied repudiation of nearly everything Jackie Robinson ever symbolized, but it also separated blacks "with an ounce of gray matter" from "mechanical black robots"—a choice of subject positions delimiting loyalties to correspondent and mutually exclusive modes of political speech.

The history of Robinson's public address is instructive here. In the weeks following Robinson's 1949 testimony before the House Un-American Activities Committee, the *New York Times* published a letter from the Civil Rights Congress's William L. Paterson, who in repudiating Robinson's guarantees of black loyalty to American anticommunism had forced a choice similar to Hogan's: "Today the Negro is faced with a monumental task. He must elect to go with or against his oppressors here at home."[53] In the Cold War context of 1949, which included the Un-American Activities Committee's notorious paranoia, the choice was between the freedom fight of communism and the frustration of unkept racial promises. Communism had by no means been completely written out of the revolt of the black athlete (though its 1950s iteration met with variable success in the 1970s). Domestic opposition to the war in Vietnam, especially as characterized in and through Muhammad Ali, had provided for the reintroduction of a protest genre in sport characterized by the explicit injunction to choose sides. Similarly comparing an authentic freedom fight to the abusive sham of a shared, interracial American identity, Hogan put matters as bluntly to black folks as Patterson had twenty years earlier: *You're with us, or you're against us.* And, once again, this line of reasoning found its way back toward the faulty symbolism of Jackie Robinson. Hogan's indictment of those "bending to the will of the Great White Father" similarly helped frame Harry Edwards's synecdochic indictment of Robinson:

> For Jackie Robinson to challenge a white pitcher who may have bean-balled him or to go after a white fan who may have spit on him or insulted him was unthinkable. Such behavior would have branded him an "uppity nigger" or at the very least with having a chip on his shoulder. White athletes could sling bats at heckling spectators or rough up a pitcher suspected of throwing a spit ball at them, but not Jackie Robinson, the infinitely patient Negro. For had he lost control of himself, he also would have lost his job and Mr. Rickey's experiment would have failed. Jackie Robinson took it—and then returned to the locker room to wonder if it had really been worth it.[54]

Edwards represented Robinson's experiences within a narrative that evoked Flood's account of life in the minors in North Carolina, where he would cry himself to sleep at night. According to Edwards, the patience Robinson practiced in choosing false loyalties entailed his daily self-degradation. Branch Rickey had famously asked Jackie Robinson if he had the "guts to not fight back." For Harry Edwards (and Dick Edwards and William Lloyd Hogan), choosing the right side and having guts meant doing the opposite of what Robinson had done and saying the opposite of what he had said.

For the rare few including Dick Edwards, Flood may have been part of the vanguard, but only revolutions need vanguards. Hardly revolutionaries, black journalists instead went looking for "voices," finding one in Flood that helped the press determine its role in the epochal shift. The "new black athlete" was a reality, to be sure. The new athlete's identity and the meaning of the shift would be defined very differently in the pages of black newspapers than in *Revolt*, which operated as not much more than a rhetorical shadow, a looming, murky figure that activated journalists' inclination to constitute themselves as the agents of black activism. Flood, the latest addition to the list of new athletes, was sure to get their support. Apart from a handful of rhetorical gestures, Flood symbolized a new age of sport's economic modernization, a development crucial to protecting its availability for a form of symbolic representation carefully hewed through integration and thus its position as a crucible of social progress. The new age would, the black press hoped, be color-blind, and Flood's protest showed how a man did not need his blackness to fight for a universal freedom. After all, it was poetic justice that baseball's Abraham Lincoln would set the white folks free, too. That, of course, is not what happened. The Supreme Court awarded owners an awkward victory, declaring baseball seemingly subject to antitrust laws but bound by Congress's "positive inaction" with regard to a nearly century-old loophole in federal law—baseball's antitrust exemption, which was partially repealed in 1997 with the passage of the Curt Flood Act. Baseball players achieved free agency in 1975, but the Abraham Lincolns in question offered no poesis at all. Dave McNally and Andy Messersmith were not "new black athletes."

During the spring of 1972, with Flood out of baseball and awaiting the Court's ruling, Marvin Miller and the Players Association engaged in their first labor strike. A number of factors drove the dispute, but by the time eighty-six April games had been canceled, the owners had agreed to add $500,000 to the existing $5.5 million player pension fund.[55] On December 31, 1972, the collective bargaining agreement between players and owners expired, and a new three-year labor agreement was negotiated. The Players Association's gains included salary arbitration for any player with two years of service, reduced maximum salary cuts from one year to the next, and perhaps most important, the adoption of the "ten and five rule," which allowed players who had ten years of service in the league, including the last five with one team, to veto any trade. For the first time in baseball history, some players had earned the right to determine their movement among baseball's clubs.[56] Flood would have been among them.

In March 1973, when the *Baltimore Afro-American* wondered about the value of Flood's martyrdom, the editors took stock of the "ten and five rule" and lamented what they believed players would soon forget: "For this latter concession by the owners, the players owe a debt of gratitude to a man who, after only two years, is virtually forgotten." Flood had sacrificed his career "in order to battle singlehandedly against the reserve clause restriction that impales a player to the whim of a club which holds his contract." The editorial emphasized the loneliness of Flood's fight, pilloried the Players Association's reluctance to take dramatic symbolic action, and identified Flood as a martyr who gained nothing personally.[57] Nevertheless, the consequence of his martyrdom was to empower the evolving labor organization and help to secure for it gains that otherwise could not have been achieved.

The *Pittsburgh Courier's* Ric Roberts had already grasped this theme in February 1970, only a few weeks after Flood had filed suit. Unlike most observers, however, Roberts understood Flood's problem in terms of those similar to other black baseball players. First, he asserted what Flood and his other advocates seemed to know well—that baseball owners were relentlessly conservative: "Curt Flood has burned all bridges behind himself. Baseball is a vicariously administered sport, in which the deck is never shuffled. Any man who dares rebel against his lot, or decides to challenge the status quo, unknowingly tugs at the rope which makes the bells toll, for himself." Then, Roberts compared Flood to Jackie Robinson and Larry Doby, who had integrated the American League eleven weeks after Robinson made his debut with the Dodgers: "We mention Jackie and Larry, of course, because they led the black parade—from top black administered baseball, into the majors. Baseball's punitive code struck down both men. Unless Flood is the seventh son of a seventh son, the obit index rests upon the ex–St. Louis Cardinals star." Roberts's brief narrative took an unexpected turn, however, in referring to Flood's costly error in the seventh game of the 1968 World Series: "Embittered, the ego-wounded Flood decided to make somebody pay for his personal mortification. Hence, the historic court suit. As a matter of fact, Curt may eventually be permanently rusticated from the majors." Roberts was right and thus cast Flood into the role that would define him for future generations: Flood "has chosen the role of martyr and, on the surface, will remain representative of that dubious legion of the suddenly doomed and/or damned, of major league baseball."[58] Roberts's argument prefigured the one that Stuart Weiss would feature in his biography; Roberts inferred that Flood was motivated in part by an embarrassing play that might have cost the Cardinals a championship title. In this context, Roberts predicted that Flood would be a tragic figure whose obituary was already written onto a lawsuit against baseball and whose role as a martyr, however self-inflicted, sealed an unfortunate fate.

Roberts's assessment of Flood vacillated between an appreciation for the structural limits that constrained black athletes and the suggestion that Flood might have brought his demise on himself. Relative to the recognition of Flood's status as a martyr, however, Sam Lacy's assessment was unequivocal. Like the *Courier*, which forecast Flood's tragic loss in February 1970, Lacy offered a prediction in the *Afro-American* about what would happen to Flood in the public's memory following the Supreme Court's decision: "By 1982, the average American, hearing the name mentioned, will want to know, 'Who was Curt Flood?' It is a harsh premonition, but such is the way of death for the martyr who fails in his self-appointed task."[59] As Lacy peered ten years into the future, he saw Flood's martyrdom as a failure, not just in terms of Flood's court loss but also relative to his influence on the public's understanding of baseball history. More to the point, Lacy expressed the worry that since Flood had lost in court, his attempt at martyrdom was futile: Flood was destined to be forgotten.

Black newspapers were hardly shy about trying to explain the ultimate meaning of Flood's ill-fated challenge, which seemed to contain two basic lessons: *Flood was right, but we told you this would happen* and *We will try to remember what he did for baseball but probably will forget*. Flood's martyrdom certainly was figurative, not literal: As Lacy pointed out in the aftermath of the Court ruling, "the former baseball star is alive and kicking, somewhere in the world."[60] Rather, Flood relinquished his baseball career, and as enthusiastic public defenders, the black press mourned that loss in a way that lent dramatic presence to the righteousness of the sacrifice. Here, the notion of Flood's principle returned to the rhetorical scene but once again was animate only through the political reckoning characteristic of black newspapers' self-understanding. If martyrs die in the name of a cause—and the black press named Flood as a martyr—then the definition of Flood's martyrdom was bound to express the cause that gave the black press its reflexive cultural, social, and political significance. With color-blind liberalism anchoring these descriptive habits, Flood was a *baseball* martyr, an unfortunate casualty in a preexisting war. Blackness, when there, as it appeared to murmur in Ric Roberts's 1970 worries about "Flood's big gamble," suffered mere collateral damage.

Along these lines, Lacy's June 1972 *Afro-American* column stands out as an early attempt to shape the meaning of Flood's significance through the figure of the martyr. Titled "Flood Delivers His Last Sacrifice," Lacy took the adverse Court decision as an opportunity to speak in a tenor proper to a eulogy:

> Since his distaste for baseball led him to defect from the then Washington Senators in the early summer of 1971, Flood has been reported

in the Netherlands, the Balkans and the Far East—stoic in his beliefs and firm in his desire to be away from it all.

But the whereabouts of Curt Flood is not the concern of A to Z in this piece. . . . The concern is that the young man "played the game" right up to the end. . . . He sacrificed himself in the hope that his team might score. . . . In his case, though, it was not in the form of the bunt which is normally employed—Curt's took the shape of a clout that frightened the whole ball park before it was caught and thrown out by the Supreme Court.[61]

Lacy's baseball metaphor, though awkward, portrayed Flood in a way that knotted his persona, his principle, and his sacrifice into the kind of tangle Harry Edwards would try to undo. Lacy characterized Flood as a potential threat to professional baseball, neutralized by the stabilizing force of the U.S. Supreme Court, perhaps a fair characterization by anyone's standards. The bunt metaphor helped Lacy link Flood to a team far different from the alliances Floyd McKissick had hoped black athletes would develop. A bunt is typically employed when a batter concedes an out to advance a runner to the next base, a play otherwise known as a sacrifice. Flood's sacrifice, according to Lacy, benefited not just the Cardinals or any particular group of players but all of them—anyone in a baseball uniform. And since the opposing defense was now the owners, expressed institutionally in the synecdochic figure of the "whole ball park," the bunt was a lyrical but insufficient term. Flood issued a clout—indeed, Flood *had* clout—until the Court rescued the whole ball park.

As Flood's reformulated collective identity took shape, Lacy offered an explicit interpretation of his martyrdom:

Flood's martyrdom is rooted in the fact that he had the strength to quit a well-paying job rather than surrender his principle. . . .

To prove the faith he had in his cause, Flood remained out of baseball through the 1970 season, and when he attempted a comeback with assurances that it would not prejudice his case, Curt found that the year's idleness had dulled his talents. . . . Dissatisfied with his own performance, he abandoned the playing field, broken by the realization that, had he remained in action, neither his experience nor his earnings would have ended so abruptly.

In the meantime, the "team" for which he delivered his final sacrifice continues to thrive, and strike, and reap more dividends . . . while he awaits that day in the not-too-distant future when America will be asking: "Who is Curt Flood?"[62]

This passage crystallized the rhetorical texture of the black press' coverage of Flood's case when it was at its impassioned best. The logic, however unassailable, came straight from the liberal narrative that had made Flood such an easy protagonist: His wealth and prestige were coincident, his professional stature was unimpeachable, his financial losses were unfair, and loyalty to conscience went unrewarded. Not a "black thing" by any means, but an experience nevertheless destined to result in sacrifice.

. . .

From a broad perspective, Curt Flood operated as a figure through whom the black athlete's dilemma, as envisioned by Floyd McKissick and others, could be reconciled with the black press's liberal imagination. McKissick had worried about the paternalistic and infantilizing social dynamics of integration. For him and for Harry Edwards, the political commitment to integration entailed the kind of racialized experience that forced black athletes to trade dignity for opportunity, manhood for education, and principle for inclusion. According to the poesis of *Revolt*, the proper political conscience of the black athlete demanded the kind of fearless sacrifice involved in telling white racists to go to hell, which is presumably what Edwards meant in announcing that America's "'colored boy' in athletics is rapidly becoming a man."[63] In practical terms, the willingness to alienate white teammates (with all due respect) and the courage to deny oneself the social and economic opportunities offered as liberal tokens helped to constitute the ethos of *Revolt*. Circumscribed by a principled assertion of black identity, self-sacrifice was construed as a politically conscientious disavowal of the social advantages obtained through a relationship with the white establishment. The racial politics of sport in 1970 cannot be reduced to McKissick's division of loyalties, but his December 1969 *Amsterdam News* column provides a heuristic counterpoint to black press coverage of Flood because of both its timeliness and its dramatization of the political choices available to black athletes in the context of the "revolt." Its insertion into the *Amsterdam News* evinced a public struggle to define the meaning of the new black athlete, but it would also be fair to say that McKissick's view of the "dilemma" was a rare exception to dominant sport narratives occupying the pages of black newspapers. Apart from a generically valorized sense of courageous speech that could collapse the differences between Jackie Robinson and Muhammad Ali, Harry Edwards might have believed, this approach seemed to make courage awfully cheap.

The difference between Flood and other civil rights martyrs goes beyond the fact that they lost their lives and Flood merely lost his baseball career. The socially unique dimension of his martyrdom is that the sacrifice he made for others was not for a racial cause but for every player in Major League Baseball, whites included. McKissick's dilemma highlighted conflicting loyalties: Should black athletes stand with their white teammates, or should they stand for racial justice? Furthermore, McKissick's dilemma critiqued the legitimacy of institutionalized sport for its requirement that black athletes rely on whites to protect their interests. On these points, the stakes were high—they posed a threat to the story of progress that sport (especially baseball) helped black newspapers tell. But coverage of Flood settled the question elegantly: Flood was a black man fighting for a universal principle whose enforcement would reform professional sports, hold baseball to account to the inclusive potential of American free market democracy, and illustrate the political merit of interracial coalition. Flood's martyrdom protected baseball as a field of progressive symbolic representation and provided a concrete exemplar of what might be accomplished when racial difference was left behind in favor of universal principles. In short, black press coverage of Flood revealed the errors of radicalism by placing him in relation to radicals—the "angry black athletes"—and then animating him with liberalism's proper persona. All things being equal, the reserve clause was an institutional arrangement that could easily be divorced conceptually from racism, but not all facts were equal. Some of Flood's advocates, as Aikens showed, could summon a racialized idiom with evocative results. Flood's case had nothing to do with race only in the sense that he told Haller so and that the press constantly promised the same. Thirty-five years later, why would one think of race except to deny it?

6

Race and Memory in Sport's Public Sphere

"Activism has helped the black athlete get where he is today. That's what sets him apart from the white athlete in this discussion. Activism by Curt Flood and John Mackey, pioneers in free agency, made baseball and football players rich." So says *Newsday*'s Shaun Powell in his recent book, *Souled Out?* an exegesis of the selfish amnesia of contemporary athletes. Never lacking in critical advice, Powell excoriates contemporary players for deferring obvious invitations to "activism," which is what makes his appreciation for the likes of Curt Flood significant to a story in which the new era has seemingly lost its soul. His nostalgic remembrances of Flood, however, produce troubling anxieties when Powell seeks an explanation for the disappearance of the black activist-athlete: "Highly paid black athletes are too busy hiding behind their precious public profiles and endorsement deals to lend a voice to activism, which means they've Souled Out in their worship of the almighty dollar."[1] Powell's puzzling chain of sentences arrives at the same point that Dayn Perry calls "ironic": Flood may have "heralded the sad demise of the activist athlete."[2] Powell and Perry, along with William Rhoden and even recently Harry Edwards, participate in a widespread contemporary narrative that announces the disappearance of the activist-athlete and holds the current generation of black players responsible for forgetting or refusing to acknowledge the fertile history of athletic protest that has made their success possible.

As easy as it is to judge the cultural performances of athletes these days and to infer their ignorance and amnesia, it is often difficult to come fully to terms with the political cultures in which black athletes, including Curt Flood, found themselves in the 1970s. Douglas Hartmann provides a reason to think that the demise of the activist-athlete is grounded not in the selfish and selective memories of contemporary athletes but instead in the convoluted politics of sport throughout the 1970s and 1980s. "Perhaps," he asserts, "the most significant factor hastening the decline and eventual collapse of the African American athletic protest: the reforms undertaken by the various agencies and authorities of the sporting establishment." In the end, Hartmann and most other well-reasoned observers agree that Edwards's "revolt" was a flop that in itself amounted to little more than an academic exercise. The 1970s and 1980s, according to Hartmann, were defined in sport by "the complexity and contradictions of the racial rearticulation process the world of sport was working through."[3] Perhaps dispensing with the nostalgia reserved for the ethos of lost heroes permits a new line of sight relative to broad historical movements and social structures, but the black activist-athlete, if we can believe this story—whether forgotten by the selfish or consumed by the predatory—is no less lost.

In all fairness, a cursory look around reveals little contrary evidence. ESPN's Stephen A. Smith, whose television persona is in many ways linked to a contemporary sense of public truth telling stylized through blackness, wrote in the summer of 2008, "In recent history we've seen Michael Jordan and Tiger Woods break records and break down stereotypes. But let's be real: When it comes to political activism, American sports has lacked a spokesperson for years. Muhammad Ali and Jim Brown are long gone from the spotlight, and [Arthur] Ashe left the stage far too soon. The closest thing we have to a truth-teller today is Charles Barkley, who's conveniently dismissed as 'Charles just bein' Charles' whenever folks want to ignore the legitimacy of his criticism."[4] Even this observation, which establishes the disappearance of the black activist-athlete through distinctions finer than those typically offered, places demands on public memory easily satisfied by nostalgia. The problem with nostalgia is not just that it permits us to expound unreflectively on "the evils and shortcomings of today's (read: black) athlete."[5] In addition, in assuming a disciplinary form, nostalgia requires the collapsing of difference into a voice, speaking not necessarily about anything in particular but speaking loudly nevertheless—in a certain kind of way—that often cannot be defined but through the allusive ethos of the sporting black speaker conjured out of a list: Muhammad Ali, Jim Brown, Arthur Ashe, and (what *has* it come to?) Charles Barkley.

What do such lists mean? It is fair to say that they reveal as much about the list makers as those appearing on the list, but that observation robs them of their influence about as ineffectively as it slows their proliferation. Other than being able to safely assert that they emerge at least in part from a compulsion to canonize sporting heroes (for example, in the various halls of fame), they present enough differences to urge a lucid consideration of the question. The call to conscience, especially when the comparison between past and present is so acute, seems perfectly suited for the times. Smith wonders, "Today's athletes show very little interest in standing up for something bigger than themselves—whether it's war, tyranny, economic deprivation, global warming. Who among them will have the conscience to embrace the challenges that lie ahead, no matter what the sponsors or, yes, the TV networks, think?"[6] This, on the face of things, is a fair and useful line of inquiry. Then again, "the times," whenever they are, probably will always produce this line of criticism. Relative to the activist-athlete, no less, this seems to be exactly Smith's point: "Think about it! The African-American stars of the 1930s through the 1960s, from Jesse Owens to Jackie Robinson to Bill Russell, met the obligations of their time."[9] Acuity is one thing, insight is another. Some historical precision and perhaps some follow-up questions are in order: Who defined the obligation of "their time?" And what is the obligation of ours?

From one angle—the one along which contemporary athletes are scolded for having "souled out"—black activists in the late 1960s (Ali, Brown, Ashe) shaped their times in a manner that athletes in the present refuse to imagine, let alone risk repeating. After having capitalized on the spirit of the 1960s to challenge established institutions with courage and conviction, individual athletes have become irresponsible with the power that wealth has conferred. From another angle—the one along which sport as an institution was hijacked by reform—the demands of a previous age produced compromises that leave us doubting whether it is even possible to summon sport to the service of social transformation. Amid widespread concerns that the black activist-athlete may be lost to history, one side problematizes the collective consciousness of individual black athletes in sanctimonious befuddlement, while the other problematizes the social and political structures into which athletes are inserted and with which they must cope.

This conclusion addresses the twofold significance of Flood's rhetorical history. First, if Flood can be fairly remembered as existing within the lineage of heroic black rebels, then his contribution to, influence on, or correspondence with the black freedom struggle must have mattered. This historical investigation is in part a story about Flood's ultimate fate, about how his argument for abolition of the reserve clause became ensnared in the vagaries of black political culture. Perhaps more than any other person in the twentieth-century narrative of the black athlete, Flood embodies the tensions in black public life. Jackie Robinson may have meant more, but his history fits easily into the national progress narrative: Some observers might still say that with respect to race, Robinson is proof positive of liberal integration's triumph. Flood, of course, fails at telling the same smooth story. A loser at virtually every level except as a historic symbol of sport's unjust traditionalism, he is now seen as an individual "ahead of his time"[8] as the righteousness of his cause is rehearsed in public memory. David Leonard's reclamation project asserts that Flood's legal challenge to the reserve clause "may have been the most effective and determined; his was certainly the most demonized, denounced, and surveilled, which reflects the historic moment of his challenge, his blackness, and the realities of American racism."[9] Flood was, in fact, ultimately run out of the country, but was it merely the realities of American racism that organized and led the chase? Quite literally, the answer depends on how we are encouraged to see him, and herein lies a tension worthy of exploration: Flood's case both was and was not "racial," and sometimes when it was, it was simply because it was said to be not. This project illuminates Flood as a historical figure, as a public rhetor seeking a concrete objective, as a hopeful agent— in no unambiguous terms—of his own destiny, coping with the treacherous ground of a thoroughly racialized social terrain.

Second, Flood reveals that the two angles of vision into the intersection of race and sport provide an insufficient account of the contemporary story of the activist-athlete's demise. With accusations of amnesia on one side and a concern for co-opting forces on the other, Flood's case is unique for what it discloses about the complicated, contradictory, and often self-defeating dynamics of black political culture in the early 1970s. The "obligations of their time," as Smith put it, for Jesse Owens, Jackie Robinson, and Bill Russell, were hardly self-evident at the time. Consequently, the contemporary call to conscience, especially as it takes the form of canonical inventories operating a fortiori, is hasty and unfair. Smith's list speaks wisely to forms of protest separated in time, but Owens was saying things in the late 1960s and early 1970s that might have made Russell bristle, and Russell was saying things at the same time that would have embarrassed Robinson. Black political culture mediated the obligations of the era by nurturing preferred forms of black athletic protest and disciplining others. Thus, the obligations of our era are hardly self-evident, and attempts to define them are fraught with peril.

· · ·

From the moment Flood filed suit, "the public" was at stake. Always on the agenda (and not only relative to the "public interest," as it was for baseball

owners), the public's constitution, the fallaciousness of its form, the distort-
ing potential of its influence, and its social agency were matters of pointed
contestation and detailed rhetorical elaboration, evincing basic anxieties
about the fact of public mediation. What occurred in black public life was
a contest over what mode of speech would be in charge of authentically
asserting black identity. Through a representational challenge to the political (in)significance of black experience, Harry Edwards insisted that the
expression of one's racial self-consciousness count in public debate; blackness was not just an unfortunate mark used to oppress but also the basis of
a social experience whose rendering mattered to politics if political action
were to be made meaningful. Black newspapers, in contrast, treated blackness as a presumed marker of marginality that could be erased in an assimi-
lationist movement into the American socioeconomic mainstream and thus
exercised a compulsion to minimize its importance. Flood knew how both
of these strategies worked and was doomed to be caught between them.

There were many ways of being on Flood's side, just as there were many
angles to Flood. In *The Way It Is*, Flood's sophisticated sense of humanism
and double-consciousness resulted in a public challenge to baseball's reserve
clause that was both abstract and concrete. Carefully retold details of his
own racialized experiences led him to be on alert for oppressive double-talk,
but once the condition of slavery had been established, racialized reckoning gave way to an assertion of abstract principle that seemed awfully difficult to define. As supporters such as the *New York Times*'s Leonard Koppett
made Flood's case, his experiences with race were privatized, inserted into
the uniqueness of his consciousness, and removed from substantive debate
about the reserve clause's restrictive properties. Black newspapers explicitly
denied the significance of race, and the "principle" became abstract and economic, safely confined to the labor practices of baseball. When blackness
made an appearance, it was privatized in ways that resembled those present
in the national sports press.[10] Moreover, Flood enabled the eradication of
internal difference in the representation of black labor; his principle was
said to matter because he might as well be a plumber or auto mechanic, both
of whom deserved the protections of the American way.

Operating in complementary ways, the national sports press and
the black press assembled what might be called Jackie Robinson's public sphere. I recognize the temptation to overdetermination in that label,
but at least relative to what was being said on sports pages, Robinson was
more than a stock example of black athletic accomplishment: He was the
embodiment of sport's contribution to the dominant national narrative of

racial progress. Being compared to or even mentioned in the same sentence as Robinson was nearly always a compliment. It was a multidimensional compliment as well, capable of condensing athletic achievement, racial comportment, a pioneering spirit, and civic courage. In Robinson's public sphere, speaking politically meant rhetorically attaching oneself to "militancy" and "outspokenness" but picking one's fights carefully, pushing the ideals of color blindness, and collapsing the internal differentiation of blackness into abstraction, often in the name of "unity." In Robinson's public sphere, mediation through Branch Rickey (whom Malcolm X called Robinson's "white boss")[11] was either left behind strategically or inserted back into a representational system in which interracial cooperation stood for progress and institutional reform. Furthermore, the Robinson abstraction was middle class, upwardly mobile, and deeply invested in the fate of the nation.

In sum, Robinson crystallized what Manning Marable calls "the logic of inclusionism," which "reinforced the logic and legitimacy of America's economic system and class structure, seeking to assimilate blacks within them."[12] Robinson ideally occupied the liminal zone of E. Franklin Frazier's "world of make-believe." Frazier had argued that the black bourgeoisie rejected identification with the black masses in the ill-fated hope of achieving identification with white society. Marable's description of inclusionism helps to explain Robinson as the black press's main bourgeois character. He gained access to the prerequisites of power and demonstrated the effectiveness of assimilating blackness into "the aesthetic norms and civil society" of whites by performing the cultural philosophy of integration tout court. Of course, an inclusionist orientation presumes one's exclusion, a calculation that came to Flood's aid as he entered the world of make-believe. Robinson may have peerlessly expressed integration's cultural philosophy, but perhaps no other black athlete has ever better expressed the first of Marable's inclusionist ideals, "the logic and legitimacy of America's economic system and class structure." In the black press and in the nationally circulating papers that supported him, Flood was above all a symbol of freedom as understood through that legitimacy.

The idiom of Edwards's *Revolt* not merely was anti-inclusionist but also demanded the expression of concrete experience to elaborate on the meaning and significance of racial particularity. But in the national sports press, experiential knowledge was damning, and disincorporated address helped explicitly to limit the meaning and significance of race. "Sweet reason," Leonard Koppett had called it, eliding the problem of Flood's blackness as he both explored the things that Flood could do for baseball and doubted the sincerity of its dystopian productions. Flood was, in the eyes of the national sports press, more evidence that sport was undergoing an economic transformation that the owners were too greedy and stodgy to accept. Koppett's reasoning, however committed in its support of Flood, accused everyone involved of dramatic rhetorical manipulations and made the impending changes in baseball's labor situation seem inevitable. On this score, Flood was right—race was irrelevant, and regardless of whether he won his federal lawsuit, baseball's economic modernization was on the way. Sam Lacy and his black press cohorts told basically the same story but added two elements: Black journalists put Flood in relation to the new black athlete, who also had to cope with the coming changes, and added depictions of Flood as a black man working to set white folks free. Most often observed as a historical irony, as in *Ebony*, this move translated slavery into a racially neutral description of a baseball player's labor status, a disincorporated trope for a universal injustice, with race irrelevant and class beside the point.

Today, Flood's narrators and biographers suggest that he and his case were caught up in the climate of the 1960s, a claim Flood also made in an interview with Ken Burns.[13] Though I have labored against the generality of this claim throughout this project, the reality is that there is something to it, but it is almost never presented with nearly enough nuance. Perhaps afflicted with the same woozy nostalgia that idealizes the internal differences out of the black activist-athlete, the placement of Flood into the spirit of the 1960s too often presumes a monolithic kind of protest activity that both makes it easy to romanticize identity politics as they once operated and makes it difficult to understand the uniqueness of Flood's circumstances. The "climate of the 1960s" explains more than Flood's private motive for challenging the constitutionality of baseball's reserve clause; it also captures a certain texture to public life, one made fleetingly visible by the crucial question from Tom Haller: *Are you doing this because you're black?* No and yes but not really, said Flood, a fine strategy for fitting himself partially within the public address of both the black press and of *Revolt*, but a poor strategy for fitting fully within either. Flood's attempt to split differences, in the end, made no difference for him at all.

Flood's case could certainly be made in terms of *Revolt*. Charles Aikens did so with passion and sophistication but not without awkwardness. In a narrative structure that mirrored Flood's in *The Way It Is*, Aikens likened his racialized experiences in baseball to those of Flood, explaining not just how it felt to be treated like a slave but also how the voices of white oppressors sounded. He made no mention of Flood's important connection to his white teammates and placed Flood not just in the tradition of the activist-athlete but at the vanguard of a revolutionary movement designed to reverse the complicity of the "happy Negro" and bring justice to sport. The problem here is that despite Flood's similarly detailed descriptions of racialized experience (especially in the minor leagues), and despite the loftiness of his appeal to principle, Flood never really saw himself as revolutionary—even *The Way It Is* retreated in the end: "Not abolition. Improvement." Not the full force of freedom measured on a revolutionary's scale, but a little bit of freedom to exercise one's profession. Some who enacted their black activist obligations, like Flood and his supporters, coped deliberately with political realities that made the languages of cooperation and compromise valuable, perhaps even indispensable. Others, such as Harry Edwards, saw cooperation and compromise as producing a political performance of black self-degradation. What is sometimes said of Malcolm X can also be said of Edwards: His disconnection from the realities of statist politics allowed him to say whatever he wanted. Indeed, Edwards sometimes seemed to act a little bit like Holden Caulfield, finding phonies everywhere while asserting a unity every bit as false as the one claimed by the black press. Be that as it may, in Aikens's *Black Scholar* piece, the idiom of *Revolt* recognized Flood as meeting an obligation far more demanding than the one defined in black newspapers.

Flood's hopes for success required an alliance—at least symbolically—with white players that, in *Revolt* and in Floyd McKissick's "dilemma," could be swallowed only as a poison pill. In fact, as a raw speculative hypothesis (for which there is little evidence), it is possible that Edwards and the editors of the *Black Scholar* understood Flood's case to be a slight problem. Just as they assembled in 1971 a coherent account of the meaning (or "obligation") of the black athlete in terms inflected by the principled assertion of black identity and experience, along came Flood to demonstrate the importance of interracial coalition politics to the pursuit of freedom in sports. In any case, Aikens's piece turned the provocative imagery of Flood's slave narrative back toward blackness. The risk, in other words, was that the "white sports reporter" and the "Negro sports reporter" would colonize the language of slavery in ways that reified establishment politics instead of critiquing them. In fact, in the 1970 reprint of *Revolt*, Edwards mentioned Flood in passing, suggesting that "if Flood is successful, he will have pulled off the greatest victory for justice in pro athletics since another black man turned a similar trick in the late 40s when Jackie Robinson entered professional baseball."[14] Though it is fair to call Edwards a Robinson apologist—perhaps by necessity, since no one ever won friends or influenced people by taking cheap shots at Robinson—Edwards was repelled by Robinson's symbolic effects. As such, the Robinson-Flood comparison in 1970 may not have been much of a compliment coming from Edwards, who saw Robinson as a representative of liberalism's foundational symbolic sham. "Infinitely patient Negroes" were unwelcome in the *Revolt*, but Flood, seeking a fairer share of what Malcolm X called the "boss's crumbs," needed their help as well as the help of his white colleagues.[15]

A slave narrative saturated with racial corporeality, in which blackness was a necessary feature of the slave, would have forced Flood into confrontation with the political discourse expressed in Haller. Flood's exchanges with Haller and Howard Cosell were the two most significant rhetorical events in Flood's public history. Cosell gave Flood the opportunity to announce that a well-paid slave was nevertheless a slave, and Haller allowed Flood to achieve the labor coalition he would need by erasing the slave's blackness. In essence, Haller asked Flood if he was trying to make race salient to consciousness, because if he was, Haller (and those for whom he stood) wanted no part of Flood's effort. The abstract, race-neutral, universalized, and disincorporated turns the slave narrative took in 1970 and beyond were already in motion by December 1969 in Puerto Rico. The explosive imagery of slavery surely showed that Flood meant business, but as it circulated in places such as the *New York Times*, the *Sporting News*, and the black press, it became mere metaphor; perhaps it was a fair analogue to the baseball laborer, but writers such as Leonard Koppett and Sam Lacy and Bill Nunn Jr. saw that Flood would ultimately push owners and players toward meaningful labor negotiations. In their account, Flood had said "slavery," the owners had said "chaos," and somewhere in between had lain the bare economic realities of baseball, which would sooner or later adjust themselves to the new age. Nevertheless, in *The Way It Is*, Flood invoked his racialized experiences in an effort to lend voice to dehumanization. Bob Broeg had scolded Flood for refusing color-blind politics, but that was hardly the point. Flood did not attempt to repudiate color blindness in *The Way It Is*; he instead attempted to identify the reserve clause, in and through race, as an intrinsically race-neutral dehumanizing structure.

The important point here involves observing the results of the different turns that followed the identification of baseball's dehumanizing architecture. Just as Flood had spoken from the position of an insider who could expose the truth—that is, "the way it is"—through a representation of his experiences, Edwards disclosed dehumanization by detailing the physical, psychological, and emotional experiences of the "black athlete," synecdoch-ically expressed. But whereas Edwards became more concrete in delivering racialized corporeality and affect to the experience of the slave, Flood, as "property," labored to keep his argument tethered to the principled, abstract ground of baseball's basic economic form lest his case come to be damn-ingly regarded as a "racial thing." The way in which Edwards described the experiences of professional black athletes in 1969 certainly seemed to prefigure, nearly trope for trope, what Flood would say about himself in *The Way It Is* the following year. Nevertheless, Flood moved away from race, detailing his experiences in vivid fashion but expressing quite self-consciously the effects of the reserve clause on "all players equally no mat-ter where." Edwards had made clear, however, that the reserve clause did not affect all players equally. Black players suffered acutely and uniquely in all of integration's spaces, even those that were intrinsically dehumanizing. Edwards gave public expression to the particularity of blackness as expe-rienced by black athletes, and Flood tilted the slave narrative toward the race-neutrality of the reserve clause's universal restraint. In short, Flood struggled to connect the racialized corporeality represented in sharing his experience to the self-abstracting territory of public discourse. He vacil-lated and parried, invoked Dred Scott and Frederick Douglass, enacted an ironic conceit worthy of Malcolm X, and told anyone who would listen that as much as his ill-fated lawsuit had everything to do with principle, it had little to do with race.

· · ·

As surely as the obligations of the age were perpetually under black review, the nostalgic figure of the activist-athlete and the meaning of that athlete's blackness as imagined today is no less up for grabs. Manning Marable offers some insightful observations on the sources of racialized affect and their consequences on the meaning of "racism" for black Americans:

> At its essential core, racism is most keenly felt in its smallest manifes-tations: the white merchant who drops change, rather than touch the hand of a black person; the white salesperson who follows you into the dressing room when you carry several items of clothing to try on, because he or she suspects that you are trying to steal; the white

teacher who deliberately avoids the upraised hand of a Latino student in class, giving white pupils an unspoken yet understood advantage; the white woman who wraps the strap of her purse several times tightly around her arm, just before walking past a black man; the white taxicab drivers who speed rapidly past African-Americans or Latinos, picking up whites on the next block. Each of these incidents, no matter how small, constructs the logic of the prism of race for the oppressed. We witness clear, unambiguous changes of behavior or language by whites toward us in public and private situations, and we code or interpret such changes as "racial." These minor actions reflect a structure of power, privilege and violence which most blacks can never forget.[16]

For Marable, racism at its "essential core" is neither a grand idea nor a conspiratorial project. Racism is affective and experiential, both felt and observed. Producing what sounds much like racialized double-consciousness, racism is not just a matter of white attitudes—though it is in part that—but is also a problem for black identity. Racism is, in other words, not just a pathology whites must eradicate from consciousness but also an experienced fact of daily life woven into the worldview of those constituted as racialized beings. Marable's detailed gestures to the quotidian lend expression to what experience with the markers of race mean to those who bear them, a "prism" that comes to structure one's understanding of the world.

In *The Way It Is*, Flood used baseball to express his experiences with blackness—his "prism," if you will—in an attempt to expose the dehumanization expressed in oppressive rhetorics. More than anything, perhaps, this history invites attention to the dangers of attempting to project "the logic of the prism of race for the oppressed" into public space. An ongoing question in this vein concerns the way that opposition to racism works in a political rhetoric. There is no question that both black newspapers and Harry Edwards imagined themselves to be antiracist; just as Edwards offered an ostensibly radical vision of black politics, the black press viewed itself as the distilled essence of the public fight for social justice. Both attempted to influence social, cultural, and institutional life through alternative modes of speech. Their attempts to craft antiracist agendas turned on the divergent manners in which they constituted public space in and through public address, not just as arguments with more or less persuasive effect but in competing rhetorical performances that represented differently the relationships among speech, black experience, and blackness itself. In the late 1960s and early 1970s, black newspapers played host to a contest[17] over the public form of antiracism but often decided its inclusionist form in advance. *Revolt* and the *Black Scholar* put the "prism" of race front and center, insisting that one was either an apolitical dupe or a prostitute for the establishment in leaving blackness behind.

In 1998, Edwards was interviewed in the online magazine *ColorLines* by David Leonard (author of a 2008 academic account of Flood). Asked about the purported demise of the activist-athlete on the thirtieth anniversary of the Mexico City protests, Edwards answered by referring to Michael Jordan's covering of the Reebok slogan on his Olympic apparel while on the medal stand in 1992: "Thirty years ago there would not have been any issue of them covering the Reebok slogan because they would not have had the Nike contract that was in conflict with it. That would have gone to a white athlete." This account, cited by Dayn Perry in an article appearing on the commercial Web site for Alex Belth's biography of Flood, not only announces a changing of the times but also alludes to changes in black athletic experience. Integration into the business matrix apparently has meant that black professional athletes have lost their incentive and impulse to activism. Ever the sociologist, Edwards offered a detailed account of the problematic implications of the shift: "One up-and-coming NBA star was asked about Oscar Robertson and he said, 'Don't know, don't care, and don't take me there.' ... The sad part about it is that when people forget how things came about, they are almost certainly doomed to see them go. And I think that is where this generation of black athletes may be headed in sports." And in an account of the activist-athlete's demise wrought in response to the resurgence of interest in Flood, Perry offers a similarly pessimistic diagnosis of black athletic amnesia: "Elite athletes of any color are paid beyond their wildest hopes, and it's no surprise that, like many of the exorbitantly well heeled, whatever rabble-rousing edge they once had is—to pilfer T. S. Eliot for a moment—lying etherized upon a table." And black athletes in particular? "Even the black athlete these days is so woefully removed from the hoi polloi that their laments are perhaps nothing more than nostalgic vacuities. . . . But today's athletes are so lavished in money that they no longer are in somber accord with the blighted classes in America."[18] With blackness forced out of articulation with the "blighted classes" in the business matrix, and with militant ignorance prevailing in the divorce from the hoi polloi, rich black athletes have lost any reason to care about anything but themselves. So goes the story of the demise of the activist-athlete:

Today's black athletes lack the proper racialized experiences to be activists; they have been etherized by wealth.

Perry implies that nostalgia for the activist-athlete is bound up with an anxiety in public memory. In the case of the activist-athlete, though, approved memories such as Shaun Powell's not only wish for a past that never was but also express nostalgia for something that the liberalism they express worked deliberately to erase: the appearance of racialized particularity and experience in public discourse. Edwards and Perry seem to lament the successful operation of symbolic representation in the universe of sport. Many black athletes have in fact struck it rich through the expansion of sport's social framework over the past forty years, these observers believe, resulting in the distortion of black athletes' experiential contacts with the "blighted classes." The obvious moral error here is that this in many ways amounts to a wish that contemporary athletes had endured the afflictions of the past, a paternalistic position not unlike wishing that your spoiled children had it as badly as you once did. Taken more charitably, nostalgia about the demise of the activist-athlete expresses anxiety over the meaning of racial struggle, about the disappearance of a distinctly racialized form of protest from the scene of American public life.

With respect to Flood, Perry calls this process an "irony," since Flood set the stage for the high salaries of contemporary athletes. But this is an irony only to the extent that the present is measured against the nostalgic image of a past in which black athletes were writing a revolution with an alternative and superior end in mind. As such, the black activist-athlete figures into a contemporary political rhetoric of sport that uses Muhammad Ali to castigate Tiger Woods or uses Arthur Ashe to shame Michael Jordan.[19] As Leonard says, "While today Flood can be viewed as courageous and willing to risk all for a cause, today's athlete can be easily spun as selfish and concerned only with money and material possessions."[20] This, unfortunately, is what passes for critical memory these days: blaming the athletes of today for having experienced race in ways that had been defined for decades by liberalism as progress. The critical point is essentially that nostalgia has come to colonize the critical memory of the black activist-athlete, as the active "substitution of allegory for history" has usurped the impulse to "judge severely" and "censure righteously."[21] It is not just that public memory of the activist-athlete is dominated by idealized allegories of who and what once was but more problematically that nostalgia and critical memory have collapsed onto each other, and idealized allegories have become the grounds from which judgment is rendered and censures are issued. Flood's contribution to the loss of the activist-athlete is no irony—it instead indexes liberalism's constitutive psychosis: the impossible universality of the righteous public advocate.

Taking stock of the memories of Flood that appeared following his death in 1997, Leonard worries that Flood's recent appearance as a "superhero" has "erased his place within a larger revolt of the black athlete." For Leonard, the discourse that emerged right after Flood's death "tended to minimize, if not discount, the importance of race and identity as it related to both his fight and the subsequent societal reaction." At the center of Leonard's concern is the fact that Flood's racialized experiences, both prior to his lawsuit and in the reactions that followed, shaped biographical details that are too easily omitted from the historical record. After 1997, although Flood "was linked to other so-deemed black troublemakers and agitators, his fight in their estimation was that of a baseball player. Although he received letters that began, 'Dear Nigger,' and used slave analogies within his fight, the vast majority of articles in an effort to reclaim Flood in a colorblind America celebrated him as a courageous man for who race means little now when it shouldn't have meant anything back then."[22] Although I cannot quarrel with Leonard's assertion that race has disappeared from contemporary memories of Flood, Leonard commits two crucial errors. First, he compares the current erasure of "the revolt of the black athlete" to his revisionist interpretation of Flood's near-uniform racist demonization in the early 1970s, which, as chapter 3 demonstrates, I find simply an untenable position. Second, Leonard unfairly places what he takes to be the racist facts of Flood's case as the contemporaneous truth. Leonard presumes an obvious, if not conscious, connection between Flood and Edwards's Olympic Project for Human Rights. Leonard is correct to say that Flood exists now as a symbol of color-blind justice and reform, but in virtually ignoring the support that Flood enjoyed in the early 1970s, from the *New York Times* to black newspapers, Leonard is at a loss to explain how the political discourses that imagined themselves as oppositional, agitational, and progressive abetted the mechanisms of color blindness that helped to disarticulate Flood from the "revolt." Indeed, the color-blind memories of Flood underwent formulation as early as the mid-1970s and virtually without exception claimed a rooting interest in Flood's achievements.

Flood may be the most remembered forgotten athlete in the history of professional American sport. This paradoxical circumstance seems to have begun in 1973, when the *Baltimore Afro-American* wondered about the value of martyrdom, or perhaps in 1972, when Sam Lacy predicted that folks would one day wonder, "Who was Curt Flood?" Most baseball fans cannot forget the 1994 strike that canceled the playoffs and World Series, causing Major League Baseball to fail to crown a champion for the first time since 1904. When the strike finally ended in federal court, the *New York Daily News*'s Bill Madden found a reason to remember Curt Flood: "It had to be the cruelest of ironies for the Lords of Baseball yesterday to have Judge Sonia Sotomayor drop the hammer on them in the very same courtroom where 24 years ago Curt Flood lost his case to have the reserve clause struck down. To the best of anyone's knowledge, that was the last time the owners beat the players in court. Since then the Lords have been on one of the longest legal losing streaks in modern history."[23] Putting aside the compulsion to figure Flood into historical irony one way or another, Madden's observation is an exemplar of the manner in which Flood is often cited—as a loser who inspired a winning streak for baseball players in their ongoing feud with ownership. But just as the *Afro* had imagined, public rhetors would in fact wonder what happened to Flood. A 1976 feature by the *New York Times*'s Murray Chass remembered Flood as a forgotten man only four years after the Supreme Court loss. "He challenged baseball's reserve rules that bound a player to his team for life, he lost and was forgotten," Chass asserted.[24]

Thirty-three years later, sportswriters still registered Flood's omission from baseball's self-defining spectacles. The 2009 Major League All-Star Game was played in St. Louis, and *Post-Dispatch* columnist Bryan Burwell conducted a passing analysis of the tribute to Cardinals history that played on Busch Stadium's giant screen during the game's festivities: "Even the best parties have a few surprising no-shows and disappointing omissions, and this video tribute only highlighted the fact that one of the most historic names in St. Louis baseball history was neither present nor accounted for. And no it wasn't the defrocked home run king Mark McGwire, who remains in self-imposed exile, far away from those inquiring investigative eyes. . . . No, the man whose presence was missing—and most surely needed—from the All-Star party was the late Curt Flood."[25]

Perhaps the reason that Flood is so frequently remembered as forgotten is that when the economic modernization of baseball is examined closely—at least on the abstract register that sees him as the "Abe Lincoln" *Ebony* once hoped he would be—Flood's vivid symbolism fades rapidly. The day after Flood's death, Chass, who in 1971 had worried that Flood's one-way trip to Europe betokened an "evil spirit" in baseball, wrote that "the players who came after him in the major leagues ... should count their blessings for having had a man of his stature and dignity precede them."[26] But in a 1979 *Times* analysis of baseball's antitrust exemption, Chass clarified the identities of those who really made a difference: "Peter Seitz is a name that will live in infamy as far as baseball owners are concerned. To the players, though, Peter Seitz was their Abe Lincoln, the man who freed the slaves."[27] In addition to assisting in the perforation of Flood's blackness from his slave metaphor, the comparison of Flood to Seitz, the labor arbitrator who released Andy Messersmith and Dave McNally from their contracts, helps to renarrate the labor negotiation story advanced by the nation's newspapers in the 1970s. In Cooperstown in 2006, Ed Edmonds presented a history of Flood that covered similar ground: "Nearly six years to the day after Flood signed and mailed his letter to Kuhn, arbitrator Peter Seitz forced Major League Baseball to acknowledge the free agent status of two white players, Andy Messersmith and Dave McNally." Flood, however, "paved the way for changes in baseball's labor history, and players today owe a great debt to this graceful player and man who struck a simple blow for human dignity."[28] The point about Flood having "paved the way" is repeated with such frequency that the story of Flood's influence operates as a mere recitation of the line of reasoning Koppett offered in the summer of 1972. Flood was courageous, Flood raised awareness, and Flood legitimized the Players Association, but Flood did not create free agency in baseball. As Koppett had stated right after Flood lost the Supreme Court case, Flood's influence was merely indirect: "It was Flood's case that *moved them into that position.*"[29]

Since at least the mid-1970s, the Flood story has assumed a clear trajectory—he should not be forgotten because he sacrificed so much to set his colleagues free, a process that took shape once Messersmith and McNally became free agents. In 1976, Chass insisted that, "the name—Curt Flood—should not be forgotten by anyone playing baseball today. . . . But seven years ago, Curt Flood, boldly and at great sacrifice to his own career and future, pioneered an effort to gain some freedom for himself and his fellow players, an effort that has now reached fruition."[30] In his Flood obituary, Chass acknowledged the importance of the Players Association to the case: "With the board's support, Flood took his challenge all the way to the United States Supreme Court. He lost, but his effort eventually emboldened the other players, Messersmith in particular. Unfortunately, besides losing the case, Flood saw his career die."[31] A 1997 *Houston Chronicle* obituary observed that "Flood's case led to sweeping change, with baseball's system ultimately crumbling, when in 1974 an arbitrator ruled that major leaguers

Dave McNally and Andy Messersmith should be granted free agency. In the years since Flood's case, every major league sport has opened doors for free agency. Hundreds upon hundreds of athletes have benefited because of Flood's courage to stand up."[32] In a 2005 essay on Flood, Jonathan Leshanski told a similar story: "Curt Flood, one of the finest centerfielders of his day, took baseball to court and sued them for unfair labor practices. He lost the case and at a huge price, it cost him his career and more. However it opened the door to the modern era of free agency, yet few people understand just what happened."[33] In late 2006, Bill Fletcher, described by the *Berkeley Daily Planet* as a "long-time labor and international activist," implored Hall of Fame voters to reconsider Flood by noting, "Flood was the person who threw himself on the barbed wire that encircled the baseball players, making it possible for others to jump over not only the restrictions imposed by the reserve clause, but to jump over him as well."[34] And Carl Bialik asserted in 2007 that "Flood's trial failed in a questionable Supreme Court decision, but opened the floodgates for free agency and today's economic structure that more-equitably splits the lucre between players and owners. Flood himself never benefited from his selfless struggle, and died in 1997."[35] The story is nearly always the same, even as the metaphors mix. After McNally, Andy Messersmith, and Catfish Hunter acquired the right to shop their baseball services, Flood was characterized variously as having "pioneered an effort to gain some freedom," "emboldened other players," "opened doors for free agency," "threw himself over barbed wire," or (with the cleverest pun of all) "opened the floodgates for free agency."

What purports to remove this mode of remembrance from incoherence is its displacement of amnesia onto contemporary athletes. Those who write the stories, of course, never forget—the athletes of today are the culprits. In 1979, similarly lamenting the shortness of memory regarding Messersmith, Chass again invoked the comparison: "Messersmith was the one who put his career on the line . . . , but players have shown as much appreciation for him as they have for Curt Flood, who prematurely killed his baseball career with an earlier freedom fight."[36] The gaps in player memories, it would seem, are not limited to Flood, as Chass reiterated in 1997: "Professional athletes, for the most part, live their time. They generally don't care what happened before them and, worse, they often don't know. Sadly, many baseball players wouldn't even be able to identify Flood, wouldn't even know he was the forerunner of Andy Messersmith, another name they wouldn't recognize for the impact he had on their lives."[37] Chass's reprimand of current players' failure to remember or acknowledge their forerunners evokes Harry Edwards's accusation of "militant ignorance" and Spike Lee's admonishing tone regarding the disappearance of the activist-athlete from the contemporary sports scene. However, according to Chass and others, the militant ignorance practiced by contemporary players has little to do with race, social justice, or political significance but instead revolves around the failure to appreciate what has made massive athlete wealth possible. In its elegy, the *Houston Chronicle* contrasted Flood with a dubious list of the craven and selfish who probably did not know that he had lived, let alone died: "Of all the millionaires Curt Flood helped make, when Flood succumbed to cancer last January, not a single contemporary player attended his funeral. Not Shaquille O'Neal, he of the $110 million free-agent contract with the Los Angeles Lakers. Not Chad Brown, of the $24 million free-agent contract with the Seattle Seahawks. Not Albert Belle of the more than $50 million free-agent contract with the Chicago White Sox. Not anyone. Sadly, Flood experienced in death the kind of neglect and solitude he once knew in life."[38] And little seems to have changed by the summer of 2009. As Burwell put it the day after the St. Louis All-Star game, "Mention Flood's name around All-Star clubhouses, and the reactions are mixed with touches of vague recognition."[39] "Neglect and solitude," says just about everyone, provided that the targets of disdain are overpaid professional athletes.

In a recent essay on the rehabilitated reputation enjoyed by former Boston Celtic basketball star Bill Russell, Murry Nelson argues that the shift in the Russell narrative is motivated less by racial atonement or revaluation than by a desire to discipline contemporary black athletic style. Russell at one time was detested by a media establishment that coded his surliness as "black anger," a lens that resulted in racially tinctured characterizations of his athletic ability. Since then, Russell has come to be regarded as one of the National Basketball Association's ideal ambassadors. Writes Nelson, "A man so reviled in youth has become in his senior years a spokesperson for comportment in a sporting milieu perceived by many to be overrun with antisocial misfits and hedonists motivated solely by self-promotion."[40] This line of reasoning echoes Leonard's concern that Flood has become a convenient figure against whom contemporary black athletes can be measured as selfish. But the reversal of the Russell narrative centers fundamentally on the shifting meaning of his blackness. With respect to Flood, one wonders exactly what his contemporaries are enjoined to remember: His courage? His sacrifice? The bare facts of his history? Maybe all of those. But almost never his racialized experiences. Burwell's 2009 All-Star Game lamentation offered the memories of two important baseball figures in the present as proxies for public memory. Dave Campbell was a Major League pitcher who has gained greater fame as a baseball analyst for ESPN. Said Campbell, "As a guy who gets a pension check every month, if [Flood] hadn't done what he did, I don't think I'd be getting that pension check. Or it certainly wouldn't be as large as it is now." Burwell also turned to Ozzie Smith, the Hall of Fame shortstop who played the bulk of his exemplary career with the Cardinals and who said, "Before there can be change, there's always someone who has to sacrifice. [Flood] was the guy who sacrificed it all so that we can experience what we're doing today." Presenting the memories of Campbell and Smith as superior to those of the current generation of players and, it would seem, to our own memories, Burwell concluded, "It's time for baseball to honor and remember just how significant that sacrifice was."[41] As the public memory of Flood is upgraded, the meaning, influence, and significance of his racial identity is no more visible than it was in the *New York Times*, the *Sporting News*, and most black newspapers in 1970.

As race creeps back into Flood's story in the popular imagination, it is rarely if ever understood in relation to the complex terrain on which Flood attempted to fashion a strategic public position. Apart from Stuart Weiss's *Curt Flood: Man behind the Myth*, which asserts an objectivity that simply does not hold, public memory leaves little with which to quibble. Brad Snyder's *A Well-Paid Slave* is in fact a lucid and insightful history of Flood's legal context. Accented by the relationship between the civil rights movement and the U.S. court system, Snyder's account offers informed biographies of federal judges, careful readings of legal opinion, and a complete historical explication of labor law in sport. But as he, Michael Lomax, Gerald Early, and Leonard burn energy toiling to find the argument that gives race meaning in Flood's case, they labor to find an agency that emerges from Flood's racialized reckoning. These observers rarely escape the dilemma that vexed Flood and that continues to trouble those in public life who strain to remember just how forgotten he is.

The best that most observers can do is to put Flood next to Jackie Robinson, assert the complementarity of their struggles, and recite the argument from extension. Bill Fletcher's piece from the *Berkeley Daily Planet*, which is perhaps the most pointedly racialized plea for Flood's entry into baseball's Hall of Fame (since he has been forgotten), makes an argument not much different from Snyder's. Set against a familiar context, Flood gains meaning: "Flood's actions took place in the context of the great battle to expand democracy that was represented by the social movements of the 1950s, 1960s, and early 1970s. Flood became a champion for the goals of those movements on the field of baseball." In Fletcher's view, Robinson again offers a useful counterpoint: "While Jackie Robinson, by his presence, broke the color line in baseball, Flood, by his actions, challenged the feudal-like system that restricted the ability of players to get out from under the thumb of team owners. In that sense, Flood was more than a symbol, but was as much an agent of change."[42] Fletcher underestimates the importance of Robinson "symbolism" but offers a distinction that makes the case for Flood's significance by comparing his "agency" to the mere symbolism of Robinson. Because Fletcher regards Flood as a representative of no less than two and a half decades of social movements, Flood could arguably be positioned as even more important to baseball's progress narrative than is Robinson. Though Fletcher's argument is not precisely the commonly repeated position that Flood extended what Robinson began, Fletcher surely demonstrates the requirement that any attempt to recover race from Flood's case must cope with Robinson.

Perhaps anticipating the strength that Flood can gather when his relationship to Robinson is examined in such a way, Snyder clarifies the argument from extension: "I don't want to equate Jackie Robinson's suffering or struggle with Curt Flood's impact or struggle, because Robinson's impact was much larger, and his struggle much harder. There's his symbolic importance, and the timing of it all: in 1947, eight years before the Montgomery Bus Boycott even began. Martin Luther King told Jackie Robinson there would have been no bus boycott without him. I think Robinson's impact was enormous and almost incalculable. Curt was taking the baton from Jackie Robinson in a lot of ways, and taking the next step. The reserve clause was the next step—it had to go."[43] As confidently as Fletcher's position vaults Flood into importance at the expense of Robinson, Snyder's argument insulates Robinson's symbolic hegemony from the effect of over-remembering Flood. Whether Flood was an "agent" in contrast to Robinson's symbolic effect or Robinson's "incalculable" symbolic effect dwarfed Flood's influence, the racialized dimensions of Flood's case are recovered through the Robinson connection, which explicitly and implicitly requires positioning Flood within the liberal progress narrative of the "civil rights movement" or the "social movements of the 1950s, 1960s, and early 1970s," a relay race in which Flood received the baton.

But in the early 1970s, Robinson was not a reference that racialized Flood but was instead one of the many means through which Flood came to represent the same color-blind political imaginary now desperately in search of the black activist-athlete's lost civic ethos. Robinson may help to make Flood's blackness visible but does so only to the extent that wherever race manifests in public memory, it can be abstracted into the same universal principles Robinson ostensibly represents, thus trumping the crass facts of a professional athlete's salary. A well-paid slave, as Flood famously announced, is nevertheless a slave. As Flood is continually remembered as the man that baseball forgot, the effort to fit race into public memory belies the near-universal systematic expulsion of race that characterized both Flood's public address and that of his supporters. Remembering Flood's courageous challenge in the context of racism, in the context of a white backlash, or in the context of Black Power, however those problems may have saturated the contemporaneous social or political atmosphere, produces instead an image of black athletic activism that works to index the failures of the present—the memory of Flood as forgotten imposes exactly the kind of amnesia that presses nostalgia into service.

. . .

Shaun Powell and Bill Rhoden have offered the two most elaborate and compelling recent public arguments on the disappearance of the black activist-athlete. Powell's *Souled Out?* (2007) and Rhoden's *Forty Million Dollar Slaves* (2008) express common cravings for an earlier age in which black athletes acted on the courage of their convictions. Moreover, the arguments in both books turn on a problem with which Harry Edwards did not have to cope in 1968: the social experiences of black athletes. Edwards had used the brutal facts of black experience in integration in 1968 to mount his critique; Powell and Rhoden argue that wealth and celebrity culture have deprived contemporary black athletes of both the experiences with race that produce an activist's consciousness and the willingness to risk lucrative financial opportunities by speaking politically. Without careful sociological investigation, it is difficult to know whether they are right. Their line of reasoning, which gestures incisively toward the limits of sport's progress narrative, attacks individual black athletes for essentially doing what was asked of them in liberalism's political imaginary. Powell and Rhoden, in short, accuse black athletes of abusing the progress that liberalism's narrative told them they were constituting through their color-blind performance of excellence.

To be clear, Powell's and Rhoden's arguments lack neither nuance nor an acumen for diagnosing the problems of lost black experience and consciousness. Across his case studies, Rhoden assesses the influence of what he calls "the belt": a process involving summer camps, campus athletic cloisters, and quasi-professional nonplaying performances (such as meeting with potential sponsors) into which those who will become professional athletes are inserted as if on conveyor belts. By the time athletes reach the pros, Rhoden says, any impulse they may have had to speak conscientiously through their blackness often becomes consumed by a deeply socialized sense of political neutrality. While noting the experiential shifts many black athletes incur and registering, like E. Franklin Frazier and W. E. B. Du Bois, these athletes' inherent gift for second sight as occupants of "two worlds," Rhoden still describes contemporary black athletes as no less than traitors:

> Occupants of two worlds—the world of the streets and the world of wealth—these athletes can speak from a perch of power and influence, while holding to the kind of "keep it real" pedigree that makes them relevant to the core black community. But now that they occupy a position where they can be more than mere symbols of black achievement, where they can actually serve their communities in vital and tangible ways, while also addressing the power imbalance within their own industry from a position of greater strength, they seem most at a loss, lacking purpose and drive. Given the journey that has led to this point, contemporary black athletes have abdicated their responsibility to the community with treasonous vigor.[44]

On the point about "keeping it real," Rhoden finds agreement with Powell, who asserts that "street cred" is "the most destructive force known to poor black kids."[45] In a comprehensive and craven swap of wealth for freedom, Rhoden insists that the racial imbalance of power in professional sport ought to be traced to a fundamental abdication of black athletes' personal responsibility to their communities.

What do their communities need? And who are "their communities" in a postintegration political environment? Flood showed that even the most seemingly just expression of athletic activism could turn on such questions. And there is no doubt that Rhoden remembers Flood, whose fight supposedly "transcended race." Throughout Rhoden's text, the answers to the complexities of coalitional politics are unclear, but the distortions that "the belt" builds into black (double-)consciousness are so widespread and possess such delusive force that the potential energy of collective black power goes tragically untapped: "The community of black athletes, like the black community at large, is wealthier and in some ways more powerful than ever before, but in many other ways it resembles that wandering lost tribe, a fragmented remnant unable to organize itself to project the collective power it embodies but is afraid to use." Instead of hanging with radicals, as their predecessors did, today's black athletes are "isolated in summer camps and prestigious universities and pampered as the budding millionaires that many of them will become." As a result, "today's big-time college and professional players are far less prepared to deal with the racial realities that exist in America than any previous generation of athletes."[46] As a "wandering lost tribe," a "fragmented remnant," Rhoden seems to say, black athletes have access to a common cause they refuse to claim lest they sacrifice their pampering in a way that puts them in touch with America's racial realities. To be fair to Rhoden, his solutions include an insightful understanding of sport's ownership structure that amounts to an urgent insistence that black athletes seek paths to ownership not just for the sake of disrupting the plantation dynamic of sport but also for the sake of exercising control over images of their blackness.

Powell's argument is similar but far more attentive to the ways in which professional experience causes black athletic amnesia. Consequently, his direct admonition to black athletes is even more pointed than Rhoden's. "A sizable group of young athletes today, because they were born later, have no concept of history or the athletes who paved the way for them to make millions and enjoy a better lifestyle," Powell asserts. This state of affairs suggests that "modern-day black society has lost some soul in the process of switching from one generation to the next."[47] Powell's position often claims to remember Flood, who presumably made everyone rich (even though he never won anything except a few Gold Gloves). But would a "concept of history" or the memory of the black athletes of the past be enough for today's athletes to reclaim their soul? As Powell searches the sporting landscape for individuals in whom we might believe, he sees some figures whose coherence with his conservative solutions is highly tenuous: "Any concerns about the plight of the black community and racism are being voiced almost exclusively by [Tommie] Smith, [John] Carlos, [Harry] Edwards, a few sports sociologists, a smattering of media people, and every once in a while, a lonely cry in the wilderness from the rare black athlete who chooses to speak out on issues. Otherwise, muffled by wealth and softened by a fawning society, black athletes today share a common role model and mentor. They'd rather not be like Tommie Smith or John Carlos. They'd rather be like Mike"—Jordan, of course.[48]

Rhoden and Powell seem to be in complete agreement, finding Jordan the easiest sellout to target. Criticism of Jordan reveals what Rhoden takes to be the consequence of the shifting experiential conditions of black athletes—that in public discourse, blackness is made to disappear: "Jordan became larger than black and white. You could look at him and really not see his color. Like O. J. Simpson, Jordan was racially and politically neutral." Rhoden's analysis of some well-known commentary from Jordan's agent, David Falk, narrates the expulsion of blackness entailed by the Michael Jordan model of success through transcendence: "The answer was to have blacks act neutral, but perform spectacularly. Like Mike."[49] Rhoden speaks insightfully to the thoroughly racialized political dynamic that undergirds dangerously shallow appropriations of Martin Luther King's oft-cited color-blind wish but leaves one to wonder where a better reading of King leads. For instance, Rhoden arrives at a provocative point in analyzing Jordan's refusal to join students at the University of North Carolina who pressured school administrators to construct an African American studies building on campus in the mid-1990s. "Jordan, the world's megastar, could have helped ignite a sea change in the role of the black athlete in America," Rhoden laments, noting that Jordan instead "favored the building of a library for family life that had his name on it. He wanted something for all students, of all races. This was his signature: the universal man."[50] As Rhoden buries contemporary black athletes in naked scorn, he demonstrates that the insights delivered through his critical instincts about color blindness are paradoxically confounded by his abiding liberalism.

Michael Jordan is not the first "universal man" for whom vast swaths of public space have been carved in sport. Neither was Jackie Robinson, who, unlike Jordan, often appears on those proliferate lists of activist-athletes. But the history of Robinson's symbolic significance certainly shows that sport's universal man has a long and complex history. Beyond having "made everyone rich," Flood illustrates this history with compelling difficulty. The history of sport's universal man shows tangled junctures and perilous traps for those speaking truth to power. In exhorting athletes to address the public in transformative ways, Rhoden becomes hostile in his nostalgia for a mode of black political speech that possessed the courage of conviction but misplaces the very careful and deliberate ways in which black public life turned universal men into its most useful symbolic resources in sport.

Rhoden wondered when Hall of Fame voters would "embrace" Flood, just as Robinson did.[51]

Reading Rhoden charitably, one might say that he simply wishes that black athletes would make their blackness matter—a kind of nostalgia for what was lost in the dilution of Edwards's *Revolt*, a hope for the return of the "particular man" to do battle with Jordan. If the arguments from Rhoden and Powell are understood as comprehensively evaluating the state of the black athlete, then this is where their arguments take oddly divergent turns. Rhoden's argument, especially with its attention to the institutional realities of "the belt" and their consequences for black athletes' understanding of their blackness, seems to be well suited to recirculating the kinds of injunctions to rebellion that presume the racialized character of sport's "plantation" and put the realities of black experience back into political speech. But, Rhoden says, those realities do not produce activists—they produce traitors. Nostalgia in this sense operates as a way to deliver an experience that cannot be had today, so he pleads: *Remember*. And in *Forty Million Dollar Slaves*, a text that both covers roughly one hundred years of black athletic participation and claims authoritative recognition of the activist's role in that history, Rhoden fails to mention Edwards, the "egocrat"[52] of athletic protest. As usual, inferences are difficult to draw from omissions, but Powell, whose berating of contemporary athletes exceeds even the vitriol of Rhoden, delivers the goods on Edwards, placing him in direct contradistinction to Jordan.

But Powell has trouble telling athletes to speak without first telling them to sit down and shut up. Powell essentially uses the spirit of protest embodied in Edwards (and Carlos and Smith and those few others) to defend a model of racial comportment that can be described only as Cosbyism. Citing Edwards's assertion that sport is filled with athletes "focused on themselves, who draw tremendous attention not necessarily to a greater cause, but to themselves," Powell takes nearly prudish exception to contemporary forms of resistance to authority. In many ways echoing the acidic mockery of Lin Hilburn, who in 1970 gave readers of the *Los Angeles Sentinel* a reading of the "rhetoric of the ghetto," Powell delivers insight only at the expense of problematic black speaking styles: "A touch of danger, a healthy dose of defiance, and anything else that frightens authority is exactly what strikes a nerve among those young black kids who reject any thoughts of joining the mainstream, along with those wanna-be-def white kids from the suburbs. And who better to deliver those goods than a rebellious black athlete with nothing constructive to say or do except, you know, keep it real?"[53]

Who shall lead when the "nonthreatening, noncontroversial, and nonpolitical"[54] Jordan is just as insufficient as a "touch of danger?" Powell's best answer is Bill Cosby—not just the actor but more precisely his character from television's *The Cosby Show*, Heathcliff Huxtable.[55] According to Powell, Cosby's well-known criticisms of black culture represented the views of a "silent majority in the black community that took notice and lent support. Cosby became a refreshing voice, especially when compared to the dreadful collection of self-appointed black leaders who are fearful of criticizing the people they claim to represent."[56] Moreover, Cosby (or, rather, Huxtable) represents a model of black fatherhood that Powell takes to be in need of obvious rehabilitation: "Any examination of the state of blacks in sports, or blacks in general, starts with the father. Many of the problems currently faced by black athletes, along with solutions to those problems, can be attached to him. When he is involved in the lives of his children, the result is mostly negative. We can list all the evils of black society until our vocal chords snap. But the most critical issue by far is the health of the black family, which depends heavily on the father and whether he handles his business."[57] *Would that they were Cliff Huxtable!* Powell cries. Perhaps Powell is right about the "silent majority," and perhaps his broad understanding of black families is accurate, but it seems that Cosbyism offers a solution to the dilemma produced by the choice between spoiled, foolish sporting children and the malignant political deferrals of Jordan, whose only notable off-court achievement was to make "a movie with Bugs Bunny."[58] But if the history of black public address is any guide, a Cosbyist commitment to mainstream racial comportment seems to be an awfully unconvincing formula for producing radicals like Harry Edwards.

Several such tensions appear in *Souled Out?* "Given a choice," writes Powell, "I'd rather have the eye of America trained on the legions of blacks from all walks who nourish children, elevate their communities, and show a willingness to mesh comfortably into the mainstream while staying true to their heritage."[59] Maybe this is what Harry Edwards was after, or maybe not, but Powell seems committed to a notion of the "mainstream" that Edwards might not have welcomed in his "kind of scene." My point here is not to measure Powell's verdicts on contemporary activism against the truth of the *Revolt* model of black activism but to reveal where the story of the activist-athlete's demise finds its own limits. If those troublingly incoherent canons of black athletes ought to be modeled in civic spirit, then surely they took us somewhere we are supposed to measure as progress. But if progress's cash value is mere cash, the liberal politics of representation retains only the power to blame the victims of progress for treachery and abandonment. The black athlete who appeared in vivid synecdoche on campus and in pro locker rooms in 1969 has transformed in public memory into a hesitant hoarder of cash, especially when images of Mexico City arise: "Smith and Carlos were black athletes of a different era, cut from a different mold, because money is most certainly on the mind of a typical professional black athlete today. He has a comfortable standard of living, a fair degree of fame, a healthy amount of respect from the public, and because he doesn't want to jeopardize any of that, he also has a severe case of laryngitis."[60] In its simplest terms, symbolic representation is a matter of who gets to stand for black identity. But when liberal integrationism shattered the activist mold over an anvil of economic opportunity—a process said to have originated with Curtis Charles Flood—the critics were left with nothing else to do but wag their fingers at spoiled children. They seem to want someone to voice the spirit of our age. But perhaps Jordan and Woods, as our craven sellouts, do in fact voice the spirit of our age just as succinctly as Robinson once did. Flood's history as a subject of public address demonstrates that the past that never was, in which our lost luminaries revolutionized sport's political vocabulary, really never was. Nevertheless, accusations of etherization, selfishness, triviality, and malign neglect abound. And the radicals are no more upon us than before.

· · ·

Curt Flood demonstrates the absurdity in the relationship between public memory and commentary about race in sport's public sphere. As the dominant story seems to go, he acted on the courage of his convictions at great personal risk to free white slaves who couldn't even recognize the facts of their own bondage. *Remember Curt Flood*, contemporary athletes are ordered, *for he represents what it means to be a principled black athlete.* At the same time that today's black athletes face the criticism that they do not behave politically in ways that would have satisfied their activist predecessors, they are asked to represent an experience that they cannot, on the full admission of the critics, advance with any sincerity. *Curt Flood made you rich,* these critics say, *so now you should stand up for something, however risky, just like Curt Flood would have.* But the complexities of a black athlete's public subjectivity proved perhaps nothing more painfully to Flood than the idea that the mere fact of speaking truth to power, even when those who will circulate your argument are many, provides few guarantees; what you say and how you say it matters a great deal. I do not mean to dismiss the powerful social insights that emerge from these contemporary concerns regarding the disappearance of the activist-athlete, because I see the productive outcomes incipient in holding athletes to the models of protest embodied in figures such as Carlos and Smith. I therefore have difficulty arguing with Stephen A. Smith when he wonders if any "modern day star will use his or her platform to speak up about terrorism, sweatshops in third world countries or other unspeakable human rights violations."[61] The insistence that black athletes speak for something may be the only place left to turn in sport, but the tendency to allow nostalgia to claim critical memory's resources, which requires that we ignore the politics of racial representation in its publicly mediated forms or at least that we take those publicly mediated forms for granted, can urge nothing but to speak for precisely the racialized experiences liberalism attempted to mute under the sign of progress. After all, in the face of a supportive black public sphere at odds with itself over how blackness would be expressed, Flood and his advocates centered on the universal choice, the race-neutral choice, the disincorporated choice, the color-blind choice. It was the more promising choice for Curt Flood.

Marable's critique of liberal integrationism includes his insightful list of symbolic representatives. Wary of a century of black politics organized around "a commitment to the eradication of racial barriers," Marable defines symbolic representation as "the conviction that the individual accomplishments of a Bill Cosby, Michael Jordan, Douglas Wilder, or Oprah Winfrey trickles down to empower millions of less fortunate African-Americans."[62] In remembrances such as Powell's, Cosby and Jordan surely do not belong next to each other in the directory of civic piety; they belong on different lists—the former on the list of ideal fathers and the latter on the list of those who have "souled out." Marable, however, sees something that Powell, Rhoden, and others not only overlook but conceal actively as they reproach athletes for being militantly ignorant: There is not and has never been a convenient or self-evident mode of representing blackness in public life. According to Marable, "The fundamental contradiction inherent in the notion of integrationist 'symbolic representation' is that it presumes that a degree of structural accountability and racial solidarity binds the black public figure with the larger masses of African-Americans."[63] Curt Flood knew this well. The pretense involved in the reported demise of the activist-athlete consists in the assumption that entry into public mediation is transparent, that a well-intentioned speaker can move politics in ways that will matter simply through the force of speech, as if blackness will simply speak for itself when a black athlete says something with a measure of social value. Flood knew that this idea was false as soon as he listened to Haller's question. *Are you doing this because you're black?* Flood knew that he would not be the only one measuring the weight of his blackness.

In a 1976 interview, Flood spoke openly and graciously about the emerging opinion that his failed Supreme Court challenge might have created new opportunities from which he never did and never would benefit. As smooth and self-effacing as he ever was in the early 1970s, Flood opined,

> But what I did then is relative today only because it happens that other people have benefited by it and that's cool. These guys are making more money and deservedly so. They're the show. They're it. They're making money because they work hard. Don't you tell me one minute that Catfish Hunter doesn't work his butt off. I know he does and he's the show. People come out and see the Bird, Mark Fidrych of Detroit. Every time this guy goes on he draws 50,000 people. Well, why not get paid for it? You could put World War II in that damn stadium right there and you couldn't draw 30,000 people.
>
> So what happened five years ago is significant in only one respect, that it gave the ballplayer a chance to think what am I worth, what is my talent worth? Do I have to spend the rest of my life in servitude to this one person? Can he juggle my life any way he wants to? Now these guys are getting what they're worth and that's cool.[64]

In the end, Flood claimed that what he did, he did for himself. Perhaps if the purveyors of public memory who pine feverishly for the lost ethos of the black activist-athlete would take him at his word, they would find ways out of the cycle of blame and accusation that results in labels of malicious cowardice and instead would come to grips with the racialized political culture that leaves us grasping for heroes. That probably would have been cool with Curt Flood.

NOTES

CHAPTER 1

1. Halberstam, *Playing for Keeps*, 359. This story may be apocryphal.

2. LaFeber, *Michael Jordan*. LaFeber presents a useful (but admittedly aging) account of Jordan's risk-averse corporate brand identity and attendant globalization scripts.

3. "America's All-Male Golfing Society."

4. See, e.g., Dorr, "Tiger Woods."

5. Longman and Brown, "Debate on Women."

6. Badenhausen, "Sport's First Billion-Dollar Man." One would expect that Woods's fortunes have changed since he began drawing media attention to his sex life.

7. The most prominent example of this announcement is Rhoden's *Forty Million Dollar Slaves*.

8. Harry Edwards, *Revolt*, xvi.

9. Harry Edwards, "Decline."

10. Ibid. This view is also a dominant theme in Boyd, *Young, Black, Rich and Famous*.

11. Baker, "Critical Memory," 4, 5.

12. Woods famously described himself this way on the *Oprah Winfrey Show*. *Cablinasian* is a neologism derived from the terms *Caucasian*, *black*, *Indian*, and *Asian*.

13. Harry Edwards, "Decline."

14. Lee, introduction, 10–11.

15. Harry Edwards, *Revolt*, xvi.

16. Ibid., xvii.

17. Baker, "Critical Memory," 4.

18. Marable, *Beyond Black and White*, 55, 56.

19. Marable, "History and Black Consciousness," 74.

20. Marable, *Beyond Black and White*, 56.

21. Harry Edwards, "Decline."

22. Perry, "Demise."

23. Ibid.

24. Hall writes, "Once it is fixed, we are tempted to use 'black' as sufficient in itself to guarantee the progressive character of the politics we fight under the banner—as if we don't have any other politics to argue about except whether something is black or not. We are tempted to display that signifier as a device that can purify the impure, bring the straying brothers and sisters who don't know what they ought to be doing into line, and police the boundaries that are of course political, symbolic, and positional boundaries—as if they were genetic. For which, I'm sorry to say, read 'jungle fever'—as if we can translate from nature to politics using a racial category to warrant the politics of a cultural text and as a line against

which to measure deviation" ("What Is This 'Black'?"). I critique this view of black athletes throughout this book.

25. Leggett, "Not Just a Flood." The label "Best Center Fielder in Baseball" appeared on the cover of the issue of *Sports Illustrated* containing Leggett's article.

26. Flood's career statistics can be found at http://www.baseball-reference.com/players/f/floodcu01.shtml.

27. See, for example, the relationship between Robinson and Dodgers manager Burt Shotton, discussed in Moss, "Burt Shotton."

28. Flynn, *Baseball's Reserve System.*

29. Weiss issues the most damning indictment of Flood's moral choices in *Curt Flood Story.*

30. Snyder, *Well-Paid Slave*, 384 n. 76.

31. Flood and Carter, *Way It Is*, 17.

32. Snyder, *Well-Paid Slave*, 76.

33. Marable, "History and Black Consciousness," 74.

34. Metzler, "Barack Obama's Faustian Bargain," 406.

35. Flood and Carter, *Way It Is*, 120.

36. Appiah, *Ethics*, x–xi.

37. Ibid., xi.

38. Warner, *Publics and Counterpublics*, 114–15.

39. Baker, "Critical Memory," 6.

40. Warner, *Publics and Counterpublics*, 115.

41. Ibid.

42. Baker, "Critical Memory," 9.

43. Marable, "History and Black Consciousness," 74.

44. Warner, *Publics and Counterpublics*, 165–66.

45. Snyder, *Well-Paid Slave*, 113.

46. Korr, *End*, 97.

47. Gene Roberts and Klibanoff, *Race Beat*, 20.

48. Harry Edwards, *Revolt*, xv.

49. Harry Edwards, "Decline."

50. Marable, *Beyond Black and White*, 83–84.

51. Harry Edwards, *Revolt*, xvii.

52. Gray, *Culture Moves*, x.

53. Baker, "Critical Memory," 10.

54. Ibid.

55. Leonard, "Curt Flood."

56. Snyder, *Well-Paid Slave*, 352.

CHAPTER 2

1. Flood and Carter, *Way It Is*, 187, 15.

2. Snyder, *Well-Paid Slave*, 132.

3. Baker, *Betrayal*, 191–92.

4. Flood and Carter, *Way It Is*, 206.

5. Ibid., 16.

6. Ibid., 14.

7. Ibid., 197–98.

8. Ibid., 53–54.

9. From this perspective, Flood's book helped create a genre of truth-telling books about sport. Bouton's *Ball Four*, also released in 1970, may be the most recognizable example of the genre; it is often credited with undoing the owners' monopoly on baseball's public image. In the twentieth-anniversary edition of the book, Bouton argued that "*Ball Four* changed sports reporting at least to the extent that, after the book, it was no longer possible to sell the milk and cookies image again" (xi). Indeed, according to one influential publisher of sports books, *Ball Four* "created a very different appetite among the fans for inside stories, and especially for inside dirt. It was the first book to pierce the veil of the locker room" and "was one of the watershed events in the series of changes that has left us where we are" (Neyer, "Ball Four").

10. Haiman, *Talk Is Cheap*, 20–21.

11. Flood and Carter, *Way It Is*, 50.

12. Ibid., 48–49.

13. Ibid., 18.

14. Ibid.

15. Ibid., 16.

16. Haiman, *Talk Is Cheap*, 20.

17. Lomax, "Curt Flood," 61, 63.

18. Snyder, *Well-Paid Slave*, 77.

19. Belth, *Stepping Up*, 154.

20. Snyder, *Well-Paid Slave*, 76–77.

21. Wilson, "Towards a Discursive Theory," 195, 211.

22. Du Bois, *Souls*, 9.

23. Ibid., 171.

24. Ibid., 208.

25. Flood and Carter, *Way It Is*, 12, 13–14.

26. Ibid., 19, 25.

27. Ibid., 25.

28. Ibid., 26, 31.

29. Ibid., 34, 35.

30. Ibid., 39–40.

31. Ibid., 32, 39.

32. Du Bois, *Souls*, 166.

33. Fussman, *After Jackie*, 185, 186.

34. Quoted in ibid., 192.

35. Flood and Carter, *Way It Is*, 24.

36. Snyder, *Well-Paid Slave*, 104; emphasis added.

37. Flood and Carter, *Way It Is*, 90, 74.

38. Ibid., 188, 172, 138–39.

39. Ibid., 199–200.

40. Ibid., 188, 190.

41. *Baltimore Afro-American*, February 20, 1971.

42. Flood and Carter, *Way It Is*, 143.

43. Snyder, *Well-Paid Slave*, 104.

44. Flood and Carter, *Way It Is*, 143–44.

45. Ibid., 15. The allusion to Rembrandt was a comment on Flood's supposed ability to paint well enough to earn a living. Its gratuitous insertion by Flood dramatizes the smugness with which the owners leveraged the players against their livelihood.

46. Ibid., 190.

47. Ibid., 173.

48. Ibid., 15.

49. Ibid., 51.

50. Ibid., 139.

51. In 1966, Koufax and Drysdale hired a lawyer and asked for multiyear contracts worth more than a million dollars. Though Koufax and Drysdale, both of whom were among the best pitchers of their generation, never threatened to sue the owners, their public prominence made their contract demands one of the first plausible threats to the owners' total control of baseball's labor market. In the end, Koufax and Drysdale settled on standard contracts (including the reserve clause) worth $125,000 and $115,000, respectively. Koufax later noted that their professionalized negotiating strategy was adopted not just toward the end of securing more favorable contracts but "to convince [the owners] that they would have to approach us not as indentured servants but as coequal parties to a contract, with as much dignity and bargaining power as themselves" (Lowenfish, *Imperfect Diamond*, 198). For a tidy history of the Koufax/Drysdale contract issue, see Korr, *End*, 61–64. Important thematic commonalities exist between Koufax's comments and Flood's argument in *The Way It Is*; Flood's claim that baseball was "slavery," "peonage," or "indentured servitude" could hardly have taken the owners by surprise.

52. Flood and Carter, *Way It Is*, 29–30.

53. Malcolm X, "Message," 10, 11.

54. Malcolm X, *Autobiography*, 219.

55. Flood and Carter, *Way It Is*, 155.

56. Just as Early, "Curt Flood," is careful to qualify *Black Power* by noting its ability to mean different things to different users of the term, *black consciousness* is a flexible notion. The "consciousness" of black individuals is certainly subject to wide degrees of variance. Thus, the central task for making sense of Flood's use of the term is not to define black consciousness abstractly and then measure Flood's discourse against a predetermined meaning but rather to discern exactly what Flood meant by *black consciousness* through his rhetorical performance in *The Way It Is*.

57. Warner, *Publics and Counterpublics*, 114.

CHAPTER 3

1. Flood and Carter, *Way It Is*, 214.

2. Snyder, *Well-Paid Slave*, 111.

3. Gene Roberts and Klibanoff, *Race Beat*, 20.

4. Holloway, *Confronting the Veil*, 202.

5. Frazier, *Black Bourgeoisie*, 166, 174.

6. Vogel, *Black Press*, 7.

7. Fraser, "Rethinking the Public Sphere," 123; Asen, "Imagining," 351.

8. Jacobs, "Race, Media, and Civil Society," 357.

9. Fraser, "Rethinking the Public Sphere," 124.

10. This organization still exists, known as PROMAX, and describes itself as "the world's premier body for promotion and marketing professionals working in electronic and broadcast media" (http://www.promaxbda.org/about.asp?n=promaxbda).

11. "Negro Press Closest to Black Community."

12. Ibid.

13. "Role of Black Press."

14. Rangel, "Publishers Salute AFRO."

15. "Four Score Years."

16. Myrdal, *American Dilemma*, 48.

17. Jacobs, "Race, Media, and Civil Society," 366.

18. Wolesley, *Black Press*, 393. Wolesley cautions that the black press was a "moral press."

19. "Role of Black Press."

20. Alexander, *Civil Sphere*, 277.

21. "Four Score Years."

22. Sengstacke, "Publishers Salute AFRO."

23. Asen, "Seeking the 'Counter,'" 442.

24. "Four Score Years."

25. "Role of Black Press."

26. Whitney Young, "Unity, Coalition, Negotiation." Marable includes the National Urban League among those "inclusionist" organizations representative of "traditional leadership" and "the majority of the older and more influential black middle class, professionals and managerial elites" ("History and Black Consciousness," 219).

27. Whitney Young, "Unity, Coalition, Negotiation."

28. Frazier, *Black Bourgeoisie*, 24.

29. Ibid., 165.

30. Frazier, *Black Bourgeoisie*, 189. I am not creating a straw argument that reads black newspapers through Frazier's critique of *Ebony*. In fact, in the early pages of his chapter on "The Negro Press and Wish-Fulfillment," Frazier indicates that in addition to *Ebony* and *Jet*, he is concerned with the *Pittsburgh Courier*, the *Afro-American* newspaper chain, the *Chicago Defender*, and the *Norfolk Journal and Guide*, the first three of which I cite extensively in this volume.

31. "Vida? No Guts."

32. "Blacks Saved Majors."

33. Andrews, "H. Aaron's $200,000."

34. "Color of Sports."

35. Tygiel, *Baseball's Great Experiment*, 37, 3; emphasis added.

36. Wendell Smith, "Sports Beat," quoted in Rusinack and Lamb, "'Sickening Red Tinge.'"

37. Anderson, "New Plaque."

38. Robinson, *I Never Had It Made*, 79.

39. Ibid.

40. Robinson, *I Never Had It Made*, 81, 83, 85. See also "Jackie Robinson Disputes Robeson"; Robinson, "Text."

41. "Jackie Robinson Disputes Robeson."

42. Trussell, "Red Failures."

43. Trussell, "Jackie Robinson."

44. Robinson, "Text."
45. Ibid.
46. "Robinson Text Praised."
47. Daley, "Valuable Jackie Robinson."
48. Lamb and Bleske, "Democracy," 51.
49. Kelley, "Jackie Robinson," 640.
50. Myrdal, *American Dilemma*, 734.
51. Anderson, "New Plaque."
52. Tygiel, *Baseball's Great Experiment*, 9.
53. "Pollard, Robinson."
54. Ibid.
55. "In Three Years."
56. Doc Young, "Rickey and Roe."
57. Doc Young, "Jackie's Strange Way."
58. Frazier, *Black Bourgeoisie*, 213.
59. Wilkins, "There's a Smarter Way."
60. Whitney Young, "Which Way for Blacks?"
61. Wilkins, "Warning."
62. Hilburn, "In Lieu."
63. Early, "Curt Flood."
64. Snyder, *Well-Paid Slave*, 116.
65. Flood and Carter, *Way It Is*, 18.
66. Warner, *Publics and Counterpublics*, 120.
67. Wilson, *Reconstruction Desegregation Debate*, 102.
68. Koppett was awarded the J. G. Taylor Spink Award, the highest honor conferred by the Baseball Writers Association of America, in 1992.
69. Koppett, "What, If Anything."
70. Koppett, "Equal Time."
71. Warner, *Publics and Counterpublics*, 122.
72. Lacy, "Cheers."
73. Rustin, "In Support."
74. Lacy, "Cheers."
75. Lacy, "AFRO Foresees."
76. Peters, "Jess' Sports Chest."
77. Lacy, "AFRO Foresees."
78. Peters, "Jess' Sports Chest."
79. Warner, *Publics and Counterpublics*, 118.
80. Ibid.
81. Frazier, *Black Bourgeoisie*, 213. The book was published originally in France and in French.

CHAPTER 4

1. Lomax, "Curt Flood," 61, 62. Lomax's essay is an exceptionally loyal retelling of Flood's *The Way It Is* and thus offers little nuance relative to the notion of sensitivity as it would be elaborated in both black newspapers and the national sports press.

2. Early, "Curt Flood."

3. Leonard, "Curt Flood," 44.

4. Ibid., 33, 43.

5. Ibid., 40.

6. Flood and Carter, *Way It Is*, 15.

7. Broeg, "Just What Prompted Flood's Lawsuit?"; Broeg, "Does 'Principal'"; Leonard, "Curt Flood"; Broeg, "Cynical Flood."

8. This point anchored the "gratitude" rhetoric that many observers, including Lomax, Leonard, and Early, take to be the rhetorical signature of a racist discourse.

9. Koppett, "Flood's Suit"; Koppett, "Baseball Chiefs." The full text of the Cronin-Feeney statement was also published via the United Press International by a number of black newspapers, including the *Chicago Defender* ("Cronin, Feeney"). The congressional committee in question was assembled by U.S. Representative Emmanuel Celler in 1951, about twenty years before Flood's "attack."

10. Koppett, "Flood's Suit."

11. Koppett, "Reserve Clause."

12. Durso, "Color."

13. Spink, "We Believe . . ."

14. Newhan, "Baseball."

15. Ibid.

16. Ibid.

17. Vecsey, "$90,000-a-Year Rebel."

18. Ibid.

19. Flood, "Why I Am Challenging"; "Curt Flood's Complaint."

20. Nunn, "Change of Pace."

21. Ibid.

22. Ibid.

23. Flood had identified "What do you people want?" as a racist expression in Flood and Carter, *Way It Is*, 74.

24. Doc Young, "More About."

25. Flood and Carter, *Way It Is*, 188

26. "Found—An 'Abe Lincoln' of Baseball," 110.

27. Lacy, "Flood Delivers."

27. "Vida, Curt May Change Baseball Reserve Clause."

28. Perhaps these advocates took their metaphor from Flood, who made this comparison in *The Way It Is* (15). It is also possible that Flood borrowed this metaphor from his coverage in the press. In either case, the effect is the same: to resolve the tension between compensation and oppression through a comparison to baseball players and working-class forms of labor.

29. Peters, "Jess' Sports Chest."

30. Rustin, "In Support."

31. Lacy, "Cheers."

32. Nunn, "Change of Pace."

33. "On a Collision Course."

34. "Genuine Bargaining Only Solution."

35. Lawson, "Will Barry Case?"

36. Koppett, "Camps."

37. "Batter Up in Court."
38. Koppett, "Baseball Will Survive."
39. Koppett, "Baseball's Next Inning."
40. Koppett, "Hot Issue."
41. "Flood Might Sue"; "Players to Back Curt Flood."
42. "Flood Will Stick to His Guns."
43. "Brooks Robinson Backs Curt Flood."
44. "Killebrew Hits Flood Court Suit."
45. "Vida, Curt May Change Baseball Reserve Clause."
46. Doc Young, "More About."
47. Rustin, "In Support."
48. For an insightful discussion of Ward, as well as a brief history of the attempted Players' League, which had dissolved by 1890, see Zimbalist, *Baseball and Billions*, 4–6. Ward's challenge to an early version of the National League's reserve clause proved successful in the New York Supreme Court, but by the time his legal victory was achieved, the Players' League had dissolved due to insolvency. See also Di Salvatore, *Clever Base-Ballist*.
49. This agreement to arbitration led to Peter Seitz, the owners' appointed arbitrator, releasing Messersmith and McNally from their contracts in 1975. See Miller, *Whole Different Ballgame*, chap. 13, 238–53. As far as the owners were concerned, the damage had been done; nevertheless, Seitz was promptly fired. For an account of Seitz's firing, see Miller, *Whole Different Ballgame*, 250–51.
50. "Curt Flood Pointed Way."

CHAPTER 5

1. "Found—An 'Abe Lincoln' of Baseball," 110.
2. Lacy had made this point when he sarcastically wondered if his definition of reason was "all fouled up" (see chapter 3).
3. Warner, *Publics and Counterpublics*, 120.
4. Hilburn, "In Lieu."
5. Cosell, "Sports."
6. Harry Edwards, *Revolt*, 31.
7. Ibid., 31, 32
8. Ibid., 32, 34–35.
9. Ibid., 35.
10. Ibid., 35–36.
11. Ibid., 36.
12. Ibid.
13. Ibid., 58, 59. According to Edwards, the OPHR also had attempted to contact H. Rap Brown but could not do so.
14. Hartmann, *Race, Culture, and the Revolt*, 251–70, 124–26.
15. Harry Edwards, *Revolt*, xv.
16. Ibid., 7. For subsequent criticism of sports' allure as a path to success, see Hoberman, *Darwin's Athletes*; Harry Edwards, "Crisis."
17. McKissick, "Is Integration Necessary?" The article was part of a series, "From a Black Point of View."

18. Marable, *Beyond Black and White*, 83–84.

19. McKissick, "Is Integration Necessary?"

20. Harry Edwards, *Revolt*, 11, 20.

21. For a detailed discussion of the way in which publics are organized by temporality, see Warner, *Publics and Counterpublics*, 96–114.

22. Harry Edwards, *Revolt*, 22.

23. Ibid.

24. Flood's original lawsuit included a Thirteenth Amendment claim that was ultimately abandoned on appeal to the U.S. Supreme Court (Flynn, *Baseball's Reserve System*, 291).

25. Harry Edwards, *Revolt*, xvii.

26. McKissick, "Dilemma."

27. Harry Edwards, *Revolt*, 89.

28. McKissick, "Dilemma." Such language is also characteristic of what Scott and Brockriede call the "rhetoric of black power" (*Rhetoric*).

29. McKissick, "Dilemma."

30. Sengstacke, "Black Scholar."

31. "Black Scholar."

32. Mission statement, *Black Scholar* 1 (1969), inside cover. Here, the new journal attended to the problem of black unity: "We cannot afford division any longer if our struggle is to bear fruit, whether those divisions be between class, caste or function. Nothing black is alien to us." But this unity first entailed divisions: "We recognize that we must redefine our lives. We must shape a culture, a politics, an economics, a sense of our past and future history. We must recognize what we have been and what we shall be, retaining that which has been good and discarding that which has been worthless." The meaning of blackness to politics was explicitly on the agenda: "THE BLACK SCHOLAR shall be the journal for that definition. In its pages, black ideologies will be examined, debated, disputed and evaluated by the black intellectual community. Articles which research, document and analyze the black experience will be published, so that theory is balanced with fact, and ideology with substantial information."

33. Warner, *Publics and Counterpublics*, 120. Warner uses "this kind of scene" to describe counterpublic activity. I do not intend to suggest that the rhetorical texture of the *Black Scholar* was determined by or determinative of Edwards's *Revolt*. Rather, in the *Black Scholar*, *Revolt* found a public proxy, or what Lauren Berlant (Warner, *Publics and Counterpublics*, 164) might call a "prosthetic," an "identification with a disembodied public subject," giving Edwards the "negativity of debate" necessary to contest prevailing definitions of black identity.

34. Aikens, "Struggle," 10.

35. Ibid., 10–11. By contemporaneous (and contemporary) baseball standards, Flood's benching was a tremendous insult. Defensive players are rarely replaced by managers while the defense is on the field; such a move is an embarrassment and in Flood's case was uniquely hurtful. Flood had literally made a living in baseball through his reputation as the best defensive centerfielder of his era. As Aikens wrote, Flood "functioned on pride and desire, and Williams must have destroyed all of it on that particular day." Indeed, perhaps he did: Flood played for about another week and then never again. This is not to say that Flood did not deserve the benching; after all, managers do not typically factor the self-esteem of the players into their management decisions. But Flood must have found the incident humiliating. Washington finished the season with a record of 63–96. In Flood's thirteen games with the Senators, he batted only .200, with no extra-base hits.

36. Ibid., 11, 12, 13. Aikens's reference to Dred Scott is "mindful" of Flood's comparison of himself to Scott (see chapter 2) and George Will's well-known eulogy to Flood, "Dred Scott in Spikes."

36. Aikens, "Struggle," 13, 14.

37. Ibid., 14, 15.

38. After posting the National League's second-best earned run average for the 1970 season (2.17), Carlton asked for a raise from $24,000 to $50,000. The Cardinals had countered with an offer of $30,000, and by March 17, 1970, the two sides had agreed to a two-year deal worth $40,000 per year. Carlton was eventually voted into the Hall of Fame on the strength of a distinguished pitching career with the Philadelphia Phillies; he retired as arguably the best left-handed pitcher of his generation.

39. Gussie Busch quoted in Broeg, "Redbirds Owner."

40 Daley, "Paging"; Daley, "Sad Story."

41. Early, "Curt Flood"; Leonard, "Curt Flood."

42. Lacy, "Cheers."

43. Doc Young, "More About."

44. Harrison, "1970's."

45. "Black Athletes 'Get Involved' in 1970."

46. Red Smith, "Lively Times."

47. Red Smith, "Buck Passes."

48. Murray, "Uncle Curt's Cabin."

49. Dick Edwards, "Principle."

50. Hogan, "Now's The Time!"

51. Hogan, He's Got Guts!"

52. Ibid.

53. Patterson, "To Secure Civil Rights."

54. Harry Edwards, *Revolt*, 27.

55. Miller, *Whole Different Ball Game*, 221.

56. Jennings, *Swings and Misses*, 3; Zimbalist, *Baseball and Billions*, 20.

57. "Curt Flood Pointed Way."

58. Ric Roberts, "Flood's Big Gamble."

59. Lacy, "Flood Delivers."

60. Ibid. At the time, Flood was in Spain.

61. Ibid.

62. Ibid.

63. Harry Edwards, *Revolt*, 120.

CHAPTER 6

1. Powell, *Souled Out?* 28, xix.

2. Perry, "Demise."

3. Hartmann, *Race, Culture, and the Revolt*, 244, 240.

4. Stephen A. Smith, "Remember." 6. Smith raises racial issues seemingly without hesitation, especially through historical references. His catchphrase when approaching

touchy subjects such as race is "That's right, I said it . . . ," an expression that presumes, refuses, and exposes unstated facts and opinions.

5. Leonard, "Curt Flood," 44.

6. Stephen A. Smith, "Remember."

7. Ibid.

8. Steffy, "Free Agency"; Will, "Dred Scott in Spikes."

9. Leonard, "Curt Flood," 31–32.

10. One way to describe this idea is to compare what black newspapers did to Flood's racial identity with the classic arcade game Whack-a-Mole. Every time blackness popped up in Flood's case, black newspapers hit it with a rhetorical mallet, which sometimes took the form of explicit assertions of objective reason, sometimes stretched the slave metaphor to white ballplayers, and other times took the form of making Flood's blackness simply about Flood "the man."

11. Malcolm X, "Open Letter."

12. Marable, *Beyond Black and White*, 218.

13. Flood, "Deaf Ears."

14. Edwards quoted in Snyder, *Well-Paid Slave*, 115.

15. Malcolm X, *Autobiography*, 219.

16. Marable, *Beyond Black and White*, 7.

17. I think specifically of Hilburn, who gave readers of the *Los Angeles Sentinel* a taste of "the rhetoric of the ghetto" ("In Lieu").

18. Harry Edwards, "Decline"; Perry, "Demise."

19. Along very similar lines, Daniel Grano argues that such figures—specifically, Ali—operate as ghosts that express a longing for "voice" in contemporary culture. These ghosts are "haunting, monitory presences," summoned for strategic purposes, "that return to correct history by disrupting fantasies of justice and progress, ghosts that reinforce the very fantasies of equality that undermine the need for change, and ghosts that do both at the same time—reflect how the virtues of archetypal heroes are cut and recombined around forms of address and response unique to particular communities" ("Muhammad Ali vs. the 'Modern Athlete,'" 209).

20. Leonard, "Curt Flood," 45.

21. Baker, "Critical Memory."

22. Leonard, "Curt Flood," 43, 44.

23. Madden, "Judgment Day." Writing in 1995, Madden could not have imagined the further irony that Sotomayor would become the first Latina U.S. Supreme Court justice, having been nominated by President Barack Obama, the nation's first black president.

24. Chass, "Curt Flood."

25. Burwell, "Curt Flood."

26. Chass, "Flood Was a Man."

27. Chass, "Baseball's Abraham Lincoln."

28. Edmonds, "Enduring Legacy."

29. Koppett, "Hot Issue."

30. Chass, "Curt Flood."

31. Chass, "Flood Was a Man."

32. Lopez, "Flood's Willingness."

33. Lehanski, "What Every Baseball Fan Should Know."
34. Fletcher, "Curt Flood."
35. Bialik, "Curt Flood's Tragic Fight."
36. Chass, "Baseball's Abraham Lincoln."
37. Chass, "Flood Was a Man."
38. Lopez, "Flood's Willingness."
39. Burwell, "Curt Flood."
40. Nelson, "Bill Russell," 100.
41. Burwell, "Curt Flood."
42. Fletcher, "Curt Flood."
43. Snyder quoted in Bialik, "Curt Flood's Tragic Fight."
44. Rhoden, *Forty Million Dollar Slaves*, 8. Rhoden gets the conveyor belt metaphor from a conversation with former University of Michigan and National Basketball Association star Chris Webber, whose attempts to discuss the political economy of American athletics are often drowned out publicly by the fact that as an amateur, Webber took gifts from a supporter.
45. Powell, *Souled Out?* 6.
46. Rhoden, *Forty Million Dollar Slaves*, xiii.
47. Powell, *Souled Out?* xviii.
48. Ibid., 48.
49. Rhoden, *Forty Million Dollar Slaves*, 204.
50. Ibid., 213.
51. Rhoden, "Flood Lost the Battle."
52. Warner cites Claude Lefort on this point (*Publics and Counterpublics*, 172) but later offers an even better description of what I am suggesting: "There is a logic of appeal to which [Ronald] Reagan and Jesse Jackson equally submit. Publicity puts us in a relation to these figures that is also a relation to an unrealizable public subject, whose omnipotence and subjectivity can then be figured both on and against the images of such men" (175).
53. Powell, *Souled Out?* xvii.
54. Ibid., 35.
55. This is not much of an overstatement. Throughout Powell's text, Earl Woods (father of Tiger Woods) and Richard Williams (father of Venus and Serena Williams) operate as representative exemplars of the importance of attentive fathers to prevent young black athletes from selling out. Despite the oxymoronic logic of his argument, he clarifies what Earl Woods and Richard Williams have in common: a resemblance to Cliff Huxtable (Powell, *Souled Out?* 271).
56. Ibid., 10.
57. Ibid., 272.
58. Ibid., 35.
59. Ibid., 11.
60. Ibid., 26–27.
61. Stephen A. Smith, "Remember."
62. Marable, *Beyond Black and White*, 101.
63. Ibid., 101.
64. Chass, "Curt Flood."

BIBLIOGRAPHY

Aikens, Charles. "The Struggle of Curt Flood." *Black Scholar* 3 (November 1971): 10–15.

Alexander, Jeffrey. *The Civil Sphere*. New York: Oxford University Press, 2006.

"America's All-Male Golfing Society." *New York Times*, November 18, 2002.

Anderson, Dave. "New Plaque, Same Giant of a Man." *New York Times*, June 26, 2008.

Andrews, Chuck. "H. Aaron's $200,000 More Than Nixon Gets." *New York Amsterdam News*, March 4, 1972.

Appiah, Kwame Anthony. *The Ethics of Identity*. Princeton: Princeton University Press, 2005.

Asen, Robert. "Imagining in the Public Sphere." *Philosophy and Rhetoric* 35 (2002): 345–67.

———. "Seeking the 'Counter' in Counterpublics." *Communication Theory* 10 (November 2000): 424–46.

Badenhausen, Kurt. "Sport's First Billion-Dollar Man." *Forbes*, September 29, 2009. http://www.forbes.com/2009/09/29/tiger-woods-billion-business-sports-tiger.html.

Baker, Houston. *Betrayal: How Black Intellectuals Have Abandoned the Ideals of the Civil Rights Era*. New York: Columbia University Press, 2008.

———. "Critical Memory and the Black Public Sphere." In *The Black Public Sphere*, edited by the Black Public Sphere Collective, 5–38. Chicago: University of Chicago Press, 1995.

"Batter Up in Court." *New York Times*, May 28, 1970.

Belden, John T. "Publishers Salute AFRO on its 80th Birthday." *Baltimore Afro-American*, August 12, 1972.

Belth, Alex. *Stepping Up: The Story of Curt Flood and His Fight for Baseball Players' Rights*. New York: Persea, 2006.

Bialik, Carl. "Curt Flood's Tragic Fight." *Gelf Magazine*, December 4, 2006. http://www.gelfmagazine.com/archives/curt_floods_tragic_fight.php.

"Black Athletes 'Get Involved' in 1970." *Chicago Defender*, December 23, 1969.

"The Black Newspaper." *St. Louis Argus*, April 27, 1972.

"The Black Scholar." *Los Angeles Sentinel*, January 22, 1970.

"Blacks Saved Majors from 'Skids,' Six Whites Made Grade Then Faded." *Pittsburgh Courier*, March 7, 1970.

Bouton, Jim. *Ball Four*. 1970; New York: Wiley, 1990.

Boyd, Todd. *Young, Black, Rich, and Famous: The Rise of the NBA, the Hip-Hop Invasion, and the Transformation of American Culture*. New York: Doubleday, 2003.

Boyd, Todd, and Kenneth Shropshire, eds. *Basketball Jones: America above the Rim*. New York: New York University Press, 2000.

"Broadcasters Are Responsible for Damage Done Black People by Negative Images Projected." *Pittsburgh Courier*, May 30, 1970.

Broeg, Bob. *Bob Broeg: Memories of a Hall of Fame Sportswriter*. Champaign, Ill.: Sports Publishing, 1995.

———. "Cynical Flood Bathes Prose in Acid." *Sporting News*, March 27, 1971.

———. "Does 'Principal' or 'Principle' Motivate Flood?" *St. Louis Post-Dispatch*, January 25, 1970.

———. "Just What Prompted Flood's Lawsuit?" *Sporting News*, January 7, 1970.

———. "Redbirds Owner Busch Admits 'I'm Disillusioned.'" *Sporting News*, March 28, 1970.

"Brooks Robinson Backs Curt Flood." *Baltimore Afro-American*, January 24, 1970.

Burwell, Bryan. "Curt Flood Should Have Been Recognized in All-Star Festivities." *St. Louis Post-Dispatch*, July 15, 2009.

Butterworth, Michael L. "Ritual in the 'Church of Baseball': Suppressing the Discourse of Democracy after 9/11." *Communication and Critical/Cultural Studies* 2 (June 2005): 107–29.

Carroll, Brian. "Early Twentieth-Century Heroes: Coverage of Negro League Baseball in the *Pittsburgh Courier* and *Chicago Defender*." *Journalism History* 32 (Spring 2006): 34–42.

Chass, Murray. "Baseball's Abraham Lincoln." *New York Times*, September 25, 1979.

———. "Curt Flood, Forgotten Man in Baseball Freedom Fight, Lives in Self-Imposed Exile." *New York Times*, September 9, 1976.

———. "Flood Was a Man for Every Season." *New York Times*, January 21, 1997.

———. "The Next Step: A Couch in Every Dugout." *New York Times*, July 17, 1971.

"Color of Sports: Black Blends Well with Green," *Afro-American Magazine*, April 1970, 4 (*Baltimore Afro-American* insert, April 28, 1970).

"Communist Shut-Out." *New York Times*, July 20, 1949.

Cosell, Howard. "Sports and Goodbye to All That." *New York Times*, July 5, 1971.

"Cronin, Feeney: Curt Flood Suit a Sports Threat." *Chicago Defender*, January 19, 1970.

"Curt Flood Pointed Way," *Baltimore Afro-American*, March 3, 1973.

"Curt Flood's Complaint." *Newsweek*, June 1, 1970, 85.

Daley, Arthur. "Paging Sigmund Freud." *New York Times*, February 3, 1971.

———. "The Sad Story of the Leaky Umbrella." *New York Times*, June 22, 1972.

———. "The Valuable Jackie Robinson." *New York Times*, November 23, 1949.

Daughton, Suzanne M. "The Fine Texture of Enactment: Iconicity as Empowerment in Angelina Grimké's Pennsylvania Hall Address." *Women's Studies in Communication* 18 (Spring 1995): 19–43.

Delgado, Richard, and Jean Stefancic. Introduction to *Critical Race Theory: The Cutting Edge*. 2nd ed. Philadelphia: Temple University Press, 2000.

Di Salvatore, Bryan. *A Clever Base-Ballist: The Life and Times of John Montgomery Ward*. Baltimore: Johns Hopkins University Press, 2001.

Dorr, Dave. "Tiger Woods Inspires a Generation of Minority Golfers." *St. Louis Post-Dispatch*, April 6, 1997.

Du Bois, W. E. B. *The Souls of Black Folk*. 1903; New York: Barnes and Noble, 2003.

Durso, Joseph. "Color the Next Decade a Lush Green." *New York Times*, January 4, 1970.

Early, Gerald. "Curt Flood, Gratitude, and the Image of Baseball." 2006. http://www .alexbelth.com/article_early.php.

Edmonds, Ed. "The Enduring Legacy of Curtis Charles Flood: His Courageous Legal Struggle for Personal Dignity." Paper presented at the Eighteenth Annual Cooperstown Symposium on Baseball and American Culture, Cooperstown, New York, June 8, 2006.

Edwards, Dick. "Double Standard Blacks to Play-Only." *New York Amsterdam News*, December 20, 1969.

———. "The Principle: Sock It to 'Em Curt!" *New York Amsterdam News*, January 24, 1970.

Edwards, Harry. "Crisis of Black Athletes on the Eve of the Twenty-first Century." In *Sport and the Color Line: Black Athletes and Race Relations in Twentieth-Century America*, edited by Patrick B. Miller and David K. Wiggins, 345–50. New York: Routledge, 2004.

———. "The Decline of the Black Athlete: An Online Exclusive: Extended Interview with Harry Edwards." *ColorLines*, Spring 2000. http://www.colorlines.com/article .php?ID=340.

———. *Revolt of the Black Athlete*. New York: Free Press, 1969.

———. "The Sources of Black Athletic Superiority." *Black Scholar* 3 (November 1971): 32–41.

Entine, John. *Taboo: Why Black Athletes Dominate Sports and Why We're Afraid to Talk about It*. New York: Public Affairs, 2000.

Fleming, G. James. "No Political Gains without Black Press." *Baltimore Afro-American*, August 19, 1972.

Fletcher, Bill. "Curt Flood: 10 Years Later and No Closer to the Hall of Fame." *Berkeley Daily Planet*, December 19, 2006.

Flood, Curt. "Deaf Ears." Chapter 4 in *Baseball*, DVD 9. Directed by Ken Burns. 1994; PBS Home Video, 2000.

———. Why I am Challenging Baseball." *Sport*, March 1970, 10.

Flood, Curt, and Richard Carter. *The Way It Is*. New York: Trident, 1970.

"Flood Might Sue Baseball Clause." *Chicago Defender*, December 31, 1969.

"Flood Will Stick to His Guns in Suit to Have Option Clause Revised." *Philadelphia Tribune*, January 6, 1970.

Flynn, Neil F. *Baseball's Reserve System: The Case and Trial of Curt Flood v. Major League Baseball*. Springfield, Ill.: Walnut Park, 2005.

"Found—An 'Abe Lincoln' of Baseball." *Ebony*, March 1970, 110.

"Four Score Years." *Baltimore Afro-American*, August 21, 1972.

Fraser, Nancy. "Rethinking the Public Sphere: A Contribution to the Critique of Actually Existing Democracy." In *Habermas and the Public Sphere*, edited by Craig Calhoun, 109–42. Cambridge: MIT Press.

Frazier, E. Franklin. *Black Bourgeoisie*. New York: Free Press, 1957.

Fussman, Cal. *After Jackie: Pride, Prejudice, and Baseball's Forgotten Heroes: An Oral History*. New York: ESPN Books, 2007.

"Genuine Bargaining Only Solution." *Sporting News*, January 24, 1970.

Goldberg, David Theo. *Racist Culture: Philosophy and the Politics of Meaning*. Oxford: Blackwell, 1993.

Govan, Michael. "The Emergence of the Black Athlete in America." *Black Scholar* 3 (November 1971): 16–28.

Grano, Daniel A. "Muhammad Ali vs. the 'Modern Athlete': On Voice in Mediated Sports Culture." *Critical Studies in Media Communication* 26 (2009): 191–211.

Gray, Herman. *Culture Moves: African Americans and the Politics of Representation*. Berkeley: University of California Press, 2005.

Haiman, John. *Talk Is Cheap: Sarcasm, Alienation, and the Evolution of Language*. New York: Oxford University Press, 1998.

Halberstam, David. *Playing for Keeps: Michael Jordan and the World He Made*. New York: Broadway, 2000.

Hall, Stuart. "What Is This 'Black' in Black Popular Culture?" *Social Justice* 20 (Spring–Summer 1993): 104–14.

Harrison, Claude E. "1970's: Vintage Years for the Black Athlete." *Philadelphia Tribune*, January 13, 1970.

Hartmann, Douglas. *Race, Culture, and the Revolt of the Black Athlete: The 1968 Olympic Protests and Their Aftermath*. Chicago: University of Chicago Press, 2003.

Hilburn, Lin. "In Lieu of the Black Power Pimp—The Black Nationalist." *Los Angeles Sentinel*, January 29, 1970.

Hoberman, John. *Darwin's Athletes: How Sport Has Damaged Black America and Preserved the Myth of Race*. New York: Houghton Mifflin, 1997.

Hogan, William Lloyd. "He's Got Guts!" *Chicago Defender*, December 6, 1969.

———. "Now's the Time!" *Chicago Defender*, November 18, 1969.

Hollaway, Jonathan Scott. *Confronting the Veil: Abram Harris Jr., E. Franklin Frazier, and Ralph Bunche, 1919–1941*. Chapel Hill: University of North Carolina Press, 2002.

"In Three Years Majors to Get First Black Manager." *Los Angeles Sentinel*, August 13, 1970.

"Jackie Robinson Disputes Robeson; Baseball Star Offers to Tell House Group He Would Fight against Russia." *New York Times*, July 9, 1949.

Jacobs, Ronald N. "Race, Media, and Civil Society." *International Sociology* 14 (September 1999): 355–72.

Jennings, Kenneth M. *Swings and Misses: Moribund Labor Relations in Professional Baseball*. Westport, Conn.: Praeger, 1997.

Kelley, William. "Jackie Robinson and the Press." *Journalism Quarterly* 53 (Winter 1981): 640–44.

"Killebrew Hits Flood Court Suit." *Chicago Defender*, January 29, 1970.

Koppett, Leonard. "Baseball Chiefs Attack Flood Suit." *New York Times*, January 31, 1970.

———. "Baseball Will Survive Lawsuit." *New York Times*, June 14, 1970.

———. "Baseball's Next Inning." *New York Times*, October 20, 1971.

———. "Camps Expected to Open Calmly." *New York Times*, February 1, 1970.

———. "Equal Time for Other Opinions." *Sporting News*, February 21, 1970.

———. "Flood Backed by Players." *New York Times*, December 30, 1969.

———. "Flood's Suit Could Cost Baseball $3 Million." *Sporting News*, January 31, 1970.

———. "Hot Issue Now on Bargaining Table." *Sporting News*, July 8, 1972.

———. "Reserve Clause Breeds Bitterness." *New York Times*, January 25, 1970.

———. *The Thinking Fan's Guide to Baseball*. Toronto: SportClassic, 2004.

———. "What, If Anything, Has Flood Violated?" *Sporting News*, January 31, 1970.

Korr, Charles. *The End of Baseball as We Knew It*. Champaign: University of Illinois Press, 2005.

Lacy, Sam. "AFRO Foresees Tumbling of the Reserve Clause." *Baltimore Afro-American*, February 29, 1972.

———. "Cheers for Flood and His Compatriots." *Baltimore Afro-American*, January 6, 1970.

———. "Flood Delivers Last Sacrifice." *Baltimore Afro-American*, June 27, 1972.

LaFeber, Walter. *Michael Jordan and the New Global Capitalism*. New York: Norton, 1999.

Lamb, Chris, and Glen Bleske. "Democracy on the Field." *Journalism History* 24 (Summer 1998): 51–59.

Lawson, Earl. "Will Barry Case Set a Precedent for Flood's Suit?" *Sporting News*, January 31, 1970.

Lee, Spike. Introduction to *Baseball Has Done It*, by Jackie Robinson, 9–12. Brooklyn, N.Y.: Ig, 2005.

Leggett, William. "Not Just a Flood, but a Deluge." *Sports Illustrated*, August 19, 1968, 18–21.

Lehanski, Jonathan. "What Every Baseball Fan Should Know: The Curt Flood Case." *At Home Plate*, May 28, 2005. http://www.athomeplate.com/regular-articles/what-every -baseball-fan-should-know-the-curt-flood-case.html.

Leonard, David J. "Curt Flood: 'Death Is a Slave's Freedom': His Fight against Baseball, History, and White Supremacy." In *Reconstructing Fame: Sport, Race, and Evolving Reputations*, edited by David C. Ogden and Joel Nathan Rosen, 31–47. Jackson: University Press of Mississippi, 2008.

Lieberman, Leonard, and Larry Reynolds. "Race: The Deconstruction of a Scientific Concept." In *Race and Other Misadventures: Essays in Honor of Ashley Montagu in His Ninetieth Year*, edited by Larry Reynolds and Larry Lieberman, 142–73. Dix Hills, N.Y.: General Hall, 1996.

Lipsyte, Robert. "Expert Witness." *New York Times*, June 11, 1970.

———. "Revolt of the Gladiators." *New York Times*, January 5, 1970.

Lomax, Michael. "Curt Flood Stood Up for Us: The Quest to Break Down Racial Barriers and Structural Inequality in Major League Baseball." *Culture, Sport, and Society* 6 (2003): 44–70.

Longman, Jere, and Clifton Brown. "Debate on Women at Augusta Catches Woods Off Balance." *New York Times*, October 20, 2002.

Lopez, John. "Flood's Willingness to Battle System Helped Players Strike It Rich." *Houston Chronicle*, April 13, 1997.

Lowenfish, Lee. *The Imperfect Diamond: A History of Baseball's Labor Wars*. New York: Da Capo, 1991.

Madden, Bill. "Judgment Day Creates Chaos, Lords of Baseball Strike Out Again." *New York Daily News*, April 1, 1995.

Marable, Manning. *Beyond Black and White*. New York: Verso, 1995.

———. "History and Black Consciousness: The Political Culture of Black America." *Monthly Review* 47 (July–August 1995): 74–89.

McKissick, Floyd. "Dilemma of the Black Athlete." *New York Amsterdam News*, December 6, 1969.

———. "Is Integration Necessary?" *New York Amsterdam News*, December 20, 1969.

Metzler, Christopher. "Barack Obama's Faustian Bargain and the Search for America's Racial Soul." *Journal of Black Studies* 40 (January 2010): 395–410.

Miller, Marvin. *A Whole Different Ballgame*. Chicago: Dee, 2004.

Moss, Robert A. "Burt Shotton: The Crucible of 1947." In *Jackie Robinson: Race, Sports, and the American Dream*, edited by Joseph Dorinson and Joram Warmund, 121–31. New York: Sharpe, 1998.

Murray, Jim. "Uncle Curt's Cabin." *Sporting News*, February 7, 1970.

Myrdal, Gunnar. *An American Dilemma*. Vol. 1, *The Negro Problem and Modern Democracy*. 1944; New Brunswick, N.J.: Transaction, 1996.

"Negro Press Closest to Black Community, Broadcasters Are Told." *Philadelphia Tribune*, November 15, 1969.

Nelson, Murry. "Bill Russell: From Revulsion to Resurrection." In *Reconstructing Fame: Sport, Race, and Evolving Reputations*, edited David C. Ogden and Joel Nathan Rosen, 87–101. Jackson: University Press of Mississippi, 2008.

"Newark Pickets Robeson." *New York Times*, July 21, 1949.

Newhan, Ross. "Baseball Needs Era of Good Will—O'Malley." *Los Angeles Times*, February 15, 1970.

Neyer, Rob. "Ball Four Changed Sports and Books," ESPN.com, June 15, 2000. http://static .espn.go.com/mlb/ballfour/neyer.html.

Nunn, Bill. "Change of Pace." *Pittsburgh Courier*, May 30, 1970.

"On a Collision Course." *Sporting News*, January 17, 1970.

Patterson, William L. "To Secure Civil Rights" (letter to the editor). *New York Times*, July 25, 1949.

Perry, Dayn. "The Demise of the Activist Athlete." 2006. http://www.alexbelth.com/article_ perry.php.

Peters, Jess. "Jess' Sports Chest." *Pittsburgh Courier*, April 22, 1972.

"Players to Back Curt Flood in Test of Reserve Clause." *Baltimore Afro-American*, January 3, 1970.

"Pollard, Robinson Decry Lack of Black Sports Execs." *New York Amsterdam News*, December 20, 1969.

Powell, Shaun. *Souled Out? How Blacks are Winning and Losing in Sports*. Champaign, Ill.: Human Kinetics, 2008.

Rangel, Charles. "Publishers Salute AFRO on its 80th Birthday." *Baltimore Afro-American*, August 12, 1972.

Rhoden, William C. "Flood Lost the Battle but Won the Free-Agent War." *New York Times*, April 18, 2008.

———. *Forty Million Dollar Slaves: The Rise, Fall, and Redemption of the Black Athlete*. New York: Crown, 2006.

Roberts, Gene, and Hank Klibanoff. *The Race Beat: The Press, the Civil Rights Struggle, and the Awakening of a Nation*. New York: Vintage, 2007.

Roberts, Ric. "Flood's Big Gamble." *Pittsburgh Courier*, February 28, 1970.

Robinson, Jackie. *Baseball Has Done It*. Brooklyn, N.Y.: 1964; Ig, 2005.

———. *I Never Had It Made: An Autobiography*. 1972; New York: HarperCollins, 1995.

———. "Text of Jackie Robinson's Statement to House Unit." *New York Times*, July 19, 1949.

"Robinson Text Praised: Representative Klein Asks that 500,000 Copies Be Printed." *New York Times*, July 31, 1949.

"Role of Black Press Told as 145th Anniversary Commences." *St. Louis Argus*, April 27, 1972.

Rusinack, Kelly, and Chris Lamb. "'A Sickening Red Tinge': The *Daily Worker*'s Fight against White Baseball." *Cultural Logic: An Electronic Journal of Marxist Theory and Politics* 3 (Fall 1999). http://clogic.eserver.org/3-1%262/rusinack%26lamb.html.

Rustin, Bayard. "In Support of Curt Flood's Anti-Trust Suit against Baseball." *Philadelphia Tribune*, February 17, 1970.

Schwartz, Alan U. "And Now, Sports Fans, the F.S.C." *New York Times*, September 30, 1971.

Scott, Robert L., and Wayne Brockriede. *The Rhetoric of Black Power*. New York: Harper and Row, 1969.

Sengstacke, John. "The Black Scholar." *Chicago Defender*, November 19, 1969.

———. "Publishers Salute AFRO on its 80th Birthday." *Baltimore Afro-American*, August 12, 1972.

Smith, Red. "The Buck Passes." *New York Times*, June 21, 1972.

———. "Lively Times in the Slave Trade." *New York Times*, April 21, 1972.

Smith, Stephen A. "Remember When Athletes Had the Guts to Stand Up for Their Beliefs?" *ESPN.com*, July 15, 2008. http://sports.espn.go.com/espn/print?id= 3487980&type=story.

Smith, Wendell. "Sports Beat." *Pittsburgh Courier*, August 23, 1947.

Snyder, Brad. *A Well-Paid Slave: Curt Flood's Fight for Free Agency in Professional Sports.* New York: Penguin, 2006.

Spink, C. C. Johnson. "We Believe . . ." *Sporting News*, March 14, 1970.

Steffy, Loren. "Free Agency Has Become a Way of Life." *Houston Chronicle*, October 25, 2005.

Stewart, Alan, and Peter Gammons. *The Numbers Game: Baseball's Lifelong Fascination with Statistics.* New York: St. Martin's, 2004.

Terrill, Robert. "Irony, Silence, and Time: Frederick Douglass on the Fifth of July." *Quarterly Journal of Speech* 89 (August 2003): 216–34.

Trussell, C. P. "Jackie Robinson Terms Stand of Robeson on Negroes False." *New York Times*, July 19, 1949.

———. "Red Failures Here Told by Minorities." *New York Times*, July 14, 1949.

Tygiel, Jules. *Baseball's Great Experiment: Jackie Robinson and His Legacy.* 25th anniversary ed. New York: Oxford University Press, 2008.

Vecsey, George. "$90,000-a-Year Rebel: Curt Flood." *New York Times*, January 17, 1970.

"Vida, Curt May Change Baseball Reserve Clause." *New York Amsterdam News*, March 25, 1972.

"Vida? No Guts." *New York Amsterdam News*, March 11, 1972.

Vogel, Todd, ed. *The Black Press: New Literary and Historical Essays.* New Brunswick, N.J.: Rutgers University Press, 2001.

Warner, Michael. *Publics and Counterpublics.* New York: Zone, 2002.

Weiss, Stuart. *The Curt Flood Story: The Man behind the Myth.* Columbia: University of Missouri Press, 2007.

"Who Speaks for Blacks? Today's Answer Is, Many Do." *Atlanta Daily World*, November 27, 1969.

Wiggins, David K. "Wendell Smith, the *Pittsburgh Courier-Journal*, and the Campaign to Include Blacks in Organized Baseball, 1933–1945." *Journal of Sport History* 10 (Summer 1983): 5–30.

Wilkins, Roy. "There's a Smarter Way." *Washington Afro-American*, September 23, 1969.

———. "A Warning on Black Slogans." *Baltimore Afro-American*, January 12, 1971.

Will, George. "Dred Scott in Spikes." In *Bunts: Curt Flood, Camden Yards, Pete Rose, and Other Reflections on Baseball*, 276–79. New York: Touchstone, 1998.

Wilson, Kirt H. *The Reconstruction Desegregation Debate: The Politics of Equality and the Rhetoric of Place.* East Lansing: Michigan State University Press, 2002.

———. "Towards a Discursive Theory of Racial Identity: The Souls of Black Folk as a Response to Nineteenth Century Biological Determinism." *Western Journal of Communication* 63 (Spring 1999): 193–215.

Wolesley, Ronald. *The Black Press, U.S.A.* 1971; Ames: Iowa State University Press, 1990.

X, Malcolm. *The Autobiography of Malcolm X.* New York: Ballantine, 1966.

———. "Message to the Grass Roots." In *Malcolm X Speaks*, edited by George Breitman, 3–17. 1966; New York: Grove Weidenfeld, 1990.

———. "An Open Letter to Jackie Robinson." *New York Amsterdam News*, February 29, 1964.

Young, Doc. "Big Job for Bowie Kuhn." *Chicago Defender*, December 12, 1969.

———. "Jackie's Strange Way." *Chicago Defender*, February 14, 1972.

———. "More About: Flood's Suit." *Chicago Defender*, January 27, 1970.

———. "Rickey and Roe." *Chicago Defender*, November 2, 1969.

Young, Whitney. "Unity, Coalition, Negotiation Are Sound Strategy for 70s." *Baltimore Afro-American*, August 4, 1970.

———. "Which Way for Blacks?" *New York Amsterdam News*, August 29, 1970.

Zimbalist, Andrew. *Baseball and Billions.* New York: Basic Books, 1992.

INDEX

Aaron, Hank, 64
activist-athlete: canonical lists of, 16–17, 23, 117, 157, 178; demise of, 4–9, 156–59, 176–82; nostalgic image of, 157
Aikens, Charles, on Curt Flood, 134–39. *See also* slave narrative: in racialized idiom
Ali, Muhammad, 4, 8, 21, 47, 117
Allen, Richie, 139
American Dilemma, An. See Myrdal, Gunnar
Appiah, Kwame Anthony, 14
Ashe, Arthur, 16, 117, 144, 148, 157, 158, 168

Baker, Houston, 5, 24, 27
Banks, Ernie, 73, 144
Barkley, Charles, 157
Black Bourgeoisie. See Frazier, E. Franklin
black nationalism, 12–13
black power, 33, 77, 87, 176, 188n56
black press: aspiring ephemerality of, 19, 60–61; on baseball as labor, 101–6; on black manager debate, 72–74; on black unity, 61–63, 132–33; as counterpublic, 57–65, 85; disciplinary rhetoric of, 77–78; disincorporated rhetoric of, 17–18, 75–78, 81–85; Harry Edwards criticism of, 21, 121–23; on Curt Flood, 19, 82, 99–106, 150–54, 161–62; middle-class orientation of, 63–64; on new black athlete, 142–44; as public sphere, 117; relationship with Communist Party, 64–66; on reserve clause modification, 109–13; on slavery, 112–13
black public sphere, 16–18, 21, 24, 54, 57, 86, 88, 116, 183
Black Scholar, The: black press on, 132–33; and *Revolt of the Black Athlete*, 134; self-definition of, 193n32

Blue, Vida, 64
Bouton, Jim, 109, 110, 120, 187n9
Broeg, Bob, 89, 91, 139
Brown, H. Rap, 192n13
Brown, Jim, 4, 6, 7, 9, 16, 117, 157, 158
Busch, August A., 146; on Curt Flood, 43–44; on labor unrest, 139–40

Campbell, Dave, 174
Carlos, John, 4, 7, 8, 21, 179
Carlton, Steve, 139, 144, 194n38
Communist Party, 64–66
Cosby, Bill, 181
Cosell, Howard, 90; criticism of sports establishment, 120, 124, 143; with Curt Flood, 11–12, 97, 99, 111, 164
counterpublic(s): black press as, 57–65, 85; as discursive context for Curt Flood, 80; poetic racial expressions of, 117–18; Michael Warner on, 80–81, 85. *See also* public sphere
Cronin, Joe, 92

Daily Worker, The, 64, 66, 68
Dale, Francis, 107
disincorporation: black press use of, 75–78, 81–85; mainstream press use of, 80; rhetoric of, 17–18, 19–20
Doby, Larry, 151
double-consciousness: and demise of activist-athlete, 177; W. E. B. Du Bois on, 28–29, 34–36; as Curt Flood rhetorical strategy, 18, 25, 36, 40–48, 160; and racism, 166
Douglass, Frederick, 27, 165
Drysdale, Don, 51, 188n51
Du Bois, W. E. B., 28, 34–40. *See also* double-consciousness

Edwards, Harry, 4, 20, 137; on black athletic protest, 7, 129–30; on black youth, 22; on civil rights organizations, 124–25; criticism of racial integration, 125–27; criticism of sportswriting, 120–24; criticism of symbolic representation, 24; on dehumanization in sport, 126–28; on demise of activist-athlete, 4–5, 9, 167; racialized rhetoric of, 117–18, 124; as revolutionary, 163; on Jackie Robinson, 149; style of, 124. *See also* Olympic Project for Human Rights

Elliott, Robert Brown, 79–80

Feeney, Chub, 92

Finley, Charles, 64

Flood, Curt: baseball achievements of, 10, 186n26; and black political speech, 15, 28, 159–65; compared to Abraham Lincoln, 116; criticism of reserve clause, 49–50; on dehumanization, 40–52; and demise of activist-athlete, 9, 22–25, 156, 159, 166–76; double consciousness of, 33–44; and free agency, 156, 171–72; on good of the game, 18, 31, 44; as laborer, 104–5, 191n28; as martyr, 42, 114, 150–54; and meeting with MLBPA, 12; minor league experiences of, 34–38; motivation for suing MLB, 15, 48; as non-racial symbol, 170–74; and progress narrative, 23, 115; public memory of, 168–76; race politics of, 42–43; racial motivations of, 34, 78, 87–92, 159, 162, 169; racialized support for, 134–39, 162–64, 174–76; reaction to *Brown v. Board of Education*, 37; as revolutionary, 163; rhetorical strategies of, 26–33, 44–47, 79–80; sensitivity of, 97–101; and slave narrative, 12–14, 50–54, 90; trade to Philadelphia Phillies, 10–11, 29, 41, 45, 102, 110; use of enactment, 79–80; use of sarcasm, 29–33

Frazier, E. Franklin, criticism of Negro press, 56, 63, 85–86, 189n30

Gardella, Danny, 51

Gibson, Bob, 52, 64

Goldberg, Arthur, 13

good of the game, 18, 33; Curt Flood on, 29, 31, 41, 44, 49–51, 140

Gray, Herman, 24

Habermas, Jurgen, 15–17

Hall, Stuart, 9, 185n24

Haller, Tom, 12, 21, 27, 79, 89, 162

Helms, Jesse, 3

Hilburn, Lin, 77–78, 119, 180

Hoberman, John, 22

Johnson, Alex, 138

Jordan, Michael: comparison to Jackie Robinson, 179–80; and demise of activist-athlete, 3, 4, 5, 22, 25, 157, 179

Killebrew, Harmon, 111

King, Martin Luther, 72, 97, 124

Klein, Arthur G., 70

Koppett, Leonard: advocacy of Curt Flood, 80–88, 106, 108–9, 113–14, 160, 162; analysis of Curt Flood case, 171; criticism of baseball, 93–97; disincorporated rhetoric of, 80–81, 83, 161

Koufax, Sandy, 51, 188n51

Kuhn, Bowie, 11, 26

Lacy, Sam, 162, 164; criticism of baseball establishment, 142–43; and desegregation of baseball, 65; disincorporated rhetoric of, 82–84; on Curt Flood lawsuit, 103, 105, 114; on Curt Flood martyrdom, 152–53, 169

Lee, Spike, 6, 173

liberalism, 9; and activist-athlete, 22, 155, 176, 179; of black press, 110; and progress narrative, 115, 182; and race politics, 21, 25; rhetoric of, 14

Lomax, Louis, 124

mainstream press. *See* national sports press

Major League Baseball Players Association, 11

Marable, Manning, 17; on black political culture, 12; on inclusionism, 161;

on racism, 165–66; on symbolic representation, 8, 183; on Clarence Thomas, 8

Mays, Willie, 64, 73, 122

McClain, Denny, 46

McKissick, Floyd, 119, 124, 154; view of black athletes, 130–32; view of racial integration, 127

McNally, Dave, 150, 171

Meggysey, Dave, 120

Messersmith, Andy, 150, 171, 172

Miller, Marvin, 29, 48, 96, 107, 109–10, 114, 150

Murray, Jim, 145–46

Musial, Stan, 70

Myrdal, Gunnar, 55, 59

NAACP, 75

national sports press: coverage of Curt Flood, 19–20, 95–99; disincorporated rhetoric of, 80–81; on new black athlete, 139–42, 144; reformist rhetoric of, 94, 106–9

National Urban League, 62, 124, 189n26

Negro press. See black press

Nixon, Richard, 64, 76, 130; and black capitalism, 127

nostalgia, 73, 97; in black modernity, 5; effects on Curt Flood, 168; in public memory, 157, 176

Of the Coming of John. See Du Bois, W. E. B.

Olympic Project for Human Rights (OPHR), 125

Owens, Jesse, 4

Parks, Rosa, 72

Perry, Dayn: on demise of activist-athlete, 9, 156; on Curt Flood, 9, 22, 167–68

Pollard, Fritz, 72

Powell, Shaun: on demise of activist-athlete, 6, 156, 176–82; disciplinary rhetoric of, 180–81

public memory, 25; of Curt Flood, 168–76

public sphere, 15–18, 117; Curt Flood in, 159–60; racial aspects of, 166–67; Jackie Robinson's influence on, 160–61

Quinn, John, 29

Race Relations Information Center (RRIC), 73

Rangel, Charles, 59

reserve clause: antitrust violations of, 10, 83–84, 116; Curt Flood's view of, 47, 49–50; MLB's defense of, 92–95; racial dimensions of, 78; as slavery, 10, 112

Revolt of the Black Athlete, 7, 14, 20–21, 119–29; and The Black Scholar, 134. See also Edwards, Harry

rhetorical criticism, 14–15

Rhoden, William C.: on demise of activist-athlete, 5–6, 176–82; on Michael Jordan, 179; view of sports plantation, 180

Rickey, Branch, 55, 64–65, 67, 73–74, 123, 149, 161

Robeson, Paul, 65, 67–68

Robinson, Brooks, 110

Robinson, Frank, 64, 73

Robinson, Jackie, 4, 6, 8, 11, 16, 19, 88, 117, 137, 151; and black manager debate, 72–74; and communism, 64–66; comparison to Curt Flood, 25, 174–76; comparison to Martin Luther King, 72; courage of, 66; Harry Edwards on, 149; as model for race relations, 67–71; Most Valuable Player award, 71; in progress narrative, 158; as symbolic representative, 23, 70, 74; testimony to HUAC, 67–70, 148–49

Rockefeller, Nelson, 24

Russell, Bill, 4, 6, 117, 158–59, 173

Rustin, Bayard, 83, 105, 112–13

sarcasm, 28; Curt Flood's use of, 40; as form of irony, 30, 32–33

Seitz, Peter, 17, 192n49

Short, Bob, 46

Slaughter, Enos, 70

slave narrative: black press use of, 112–13, 146–48, 164; Curt Flood's use of, 11–12,

18, 20, 24, 28, 41, 50–54, 164; mainstream
  press use of, 145–46, 164; Malcolm X's
  use of, 52–53, 164; public mediation of,
  118; in racialized idiom, 129, 134–39,
  164; as racially neutral, 90; strategic
  complications of, 27, 90, 163–65
Smith, Ozzie, 174
Smith, Stephen A., 157–58, 183, 194n4
Smith, Tommie, 4, 7, 8, 21, 179
Snyder, Brad: on black press, 19; on civil
  rights organizations, 78; on Curt Flood
  motivations, 33–34; on mainstream
  press, 55, 145; on Jackie Robinson, 25,
  174–75; on slave narrative, 42, 47
symbolic representation, 8, 23–24; baseball's
  role in, 150; and demise of the activist-
  athlete, 168; Harry Edwards critique of,
  23; and liberalism, 182–83

Thomas, Duane, 138
Torre, Joe, 109

Walker, Chet, 111
Ward, John Montgomery, 112, 192n48
Warner, Michael: on counterpublics, 80; on
  public address, 54; on public sphere, 15–
  17, 75–76; and symbolic representation,
  23
Webber, Chris, 196n44
Weiss, Stuart, 151, 174
well-paid slave. *See* slave narrative
Wilkins, Roy, 75, 77
Williams, James D., 60
Williams, Ted, 135, 139, 193n35
Wills, Maury, 73
Wood, John S., 68
Woods, Tiger, and demise of activist-
  athlete, 3, 4, 5, 22, 25, 157, 185n6

X, Malcolm, 33, 52–53, 126–27, 161, 164, 165

Young, Whitney, 76